CHURCH AND STATE IN ENGLAND

By the same author

PHYSICIAN, HEAL THYSELF

THE CLAIMS OF THE CHURCH OF ENGLAND

CHURCH AND STATE IN ENGLAND

By

CYRIL GARBETT

ARCHBISHOP OF YORK

LONDON

HODDER & STOUGHTON

FIRST PRINTED FEBRUARY, 1950

Maae and Printed in Great Britain for Hodder & Stoughton, Limited, London, by Wyman & Sons Limited, London, Reading and Fakenham

PREFACE

THIS book is an argument for some readjustment in the existing relationship between Church and State. It attempts to show that, except possibly in early days, the Church of England never has had complete freedom. In the Middle Ages it was controlled by the Pope and the Crown; later by the Crown; and eventually by Parliament. To-day in actual practice the Church has great freedom, but by law and custom its bishops are nominated by the Prime Minister, its Prayer Book cannot be altered without the sanction of Parliament; its Convocations cannot meet or make canons without the licence of the Crown, and its doctrine in the event of an appeal from the Ecclesiastical Courts is interpreted by a committee appointed by the State and consisting of State Judges.

When the citizen was always a Churchman this position was tolerable, for it could then be argued that the King, Parliament, and the Judges represented the laity of the Church. But to-day the position is very different. Neither the Prime Minister, the Members of the Houses of Parliament, nor the Judges on the Judicial Committee are necessarily members of the Church of England. And however loosely the State may now hold the reins which connect it with the Church, there is the possibility that in the future a Totalitarian State might wish to control the Church for its own purposes.

There are some who would sever the connection between Church and State by disestablishment. It is, however, uncertain if this would result in complete freedom; and it would undoubtedly mean the loss of opportunities for influence now possessed by an Established Church; an even more serious result of disestablishment at this time, when many Christian Churches are exposed to the attacks of an aggressive communism, would be the interpretation of it as the national repudiation of religion. It is possible that it may prove to be the only way to complete spiritual freedom; but reverence for tradition and practical reasons should make both the Church and the State hesitate before their close and honourable association from the earliest days of our nation is brought to an end.

The alternative to disestablishment would be a change in the present relationships between Church and State so as to give the Church a larger amount of freedom than it has at present. In asking for this the Church should approach the State not as a hostile body, but with confidence that it will be ready to help the Church if it can be shown that the proposed reforms will strengthen true religion. When, some years ago, the State was asked to facilitate ecclesiastical legislation by giving Enabling Powers to the Church Assembly, it granted this request with ready sympathy. Before, however, the State can be expected to agree to changes in its present connection with the Church, Churchmen must make up their minds and reach practical unanimity on the constitutional reforms they require. There is no possibility of the State granting them unless there is first agreement in the Church. It would be unreasonable to expect the State to approve of proposals to which any considerable body of Churchmen objected. In this book an attempt is made to set forth the reforms which seem most necessary for spiritual freedom, but which are not inconsistent with the continuation of Establishment. If, after the Church has decided on the reforms which it regards as essential for spiritual freedom, the State deliberately and repeatedly refuses to grant them, then the Church will have to ask for disestablishment.

While this book was still unfinished the Church Assembly passed an important resolution on the relationship between Church and State : " the Assembly while valuing the Establishment of the Church of England as an expression of the nation's recognition of religion, nevertheless is of the opinion that the present form of it impedes the fulfilment of the responsibilities of the Church as a spiritual society, and therefore instructs the Standing Committee to appoint a small Commission to draw up resolutions on changes desirable in the relationship between Church and State and to present them to the Assembly for consideration at an early date." This resolution might well serve as a text for this book. The Commission is now sitting, and it is impossible to forecast the results of its deliberations, but there is a general hope that it may give the Assembly clear advice as to the priorities which should be given to the various reforms which are required, and the manner in which they should best be presented both to the Church and State. The debate and the voting of the Assembly made it plain that its members regard the problem as one of urgency.

The book, read by itself, would give a wrong impression, for of necessity it isolates one aspect of Church life—the constitutional relationship with the State; it is thus unavoidably full of controversial matters, of disputes between the officers of the Church and of the State, of the encroachments of the State, and of the resistance or subservience of the Church. This is not what is most important in the life of the Church. The background must never be forgotten; namely, the steady, faithful, quiet pastoral work in thousands of parishes in century after century. The true history of the Church of England is to be found in the parishes where its spiritual work has continued only rarely interrupted by political and constitutional disputes. This pastoral work, which has built up millions in the knowledge and love of God, and through which they have received inspiration and help in their daily lives, is the great and abiding contribution which the Church has made to the nation.

My approach to the problem has been historical. This is, to me, the most natural way in which to discuss the question of Church reform. The nature and purpose of institutions and customs cannot be understood unless something is known of their historical origin. The professional historian will not, however, find anything original in these chapters. I have neither the time nor the ability for original research. I hope in footnotes I have duly acknowledged my debt to the many whose writings I have used; here and there I may have borrowed what I remembered from reading many years ago, though the name of the author has been forgotten. I have also ventured to draw upon personal reminiscences when they seem to illustrate or lighten the argument, but I have done my best to keep these reminiscences within bounds, and I hope I have not strayed too often into irrelevance.

I am very grateful to the Bishop of Durham for his great kindness in reading through all the typescript and making a number of valuable suggestions and criticisms; to the Rev. P. Cowley, the diocesan missioner of York, for the thoroughness with which he corrected the galley proofs; and to Mr. Leonard Cutts, the head of the publisher's religious department, for undertaking during my absence in America to correct the page proofs and to provide the Index. I need hardly say that I am alone responsible for the statements and views expressed in the book. I must add a line of gratitude also to my secretary, Miss Steele, who had to decipher handwriting never very clear and to type and retype the manuscript.

CONTENTS

I

INTRODUCTION: CHURCH AND STATE IN EUROPE

THE right relationship between Church and State throughout the Christian era has been a subject of debate and often of bitter controversy. At first sight it might appear that their respective spheres of influence are so distinct that conflict between the two is improbable; the primary purpose of the Church is to make man a true citizen of the Kingdom of God, of the State to make him a useful member of an earthly kingdom; the Church trains him for life both here and hereafter, the State is concerned chiefly with this world; the Church uses persuasion, the State in the last resort coercion; the Church offers man spiritual and supernatural help, the State with the sword of justice protects him from injury, and gives him personal security.

In practice, however, it is impossible to draw a clear line of division between the respective provinces of Church and State, of necessity they deal with the same persons, for the citizen is often a Churchman and the Churchman always a citizen. The Church is not an invisible society in the sky, but a visible organisation of which the State must take account. The commands of Church and State may conflict, and then the Churchman must decide which has the greater claim upon him. The Church often has had to condemn the actions of the State as contrary to the law of God, and the State has retaliated by denouncing the Church as subversive to good order. The State may propose legislation which the Church must oppose as harmful to morals and religion. The Church always aims at securing that the children of the nation are brought up in the fear and love of God, but the State sometimes regards religious teaching as superfluous, dangerous, or untrue. The Church may accumulate great property, which the State may protect or confiscate according to the views it holds as to the social advantage or harmfulness of a richly endowed Church. Frequently the Church has regarded the State as an enemy to its faith, and the

State has treated the Church as a dangerous and insidious rival to its authority. The opportunities of conflict between Church and State are many, and the stronger each becomes the greater is the danger of a clash which may easily bring disaster to both.

Church and State in the First Centuries

In the earliest days there was no conflict between Church and State. The little Christian community stood apart from the nationalism of the Jews who taught the duty of revolt against the power of Rome. It obeyed the teaching of its Master. "Render unto Cæsar the things which are Cæsar's, and unto God the things that are God's." The Christians were taught to obey those in authority, and to honour and pray for the Emperor, even though the Imperial throne was occupied by Nero. On the other hand, the State protected the Church from the violence of its enemies. The *Acts of the Apostles* shows how the Imperial authorities treated with fairness and impartiality the first Christians, and relates how St. Paul appealed with confidence to the judgement seat of Cæsar. But there is no complete theory of the State in the New Testament; the first Christians had no need to define their attitude towards it, for they were convinced that the world and all its glory would soon pass away. It was right that they should submit to it during the short time which remained before the world came to an end, when the State and all its pomp would be burnt up as by fire. The State at first seems to have looked upon the Christian Church as a troublesome sect of the Jews, whose eccentricity and obstinacy must be tolerated. Not the most far-seeing of its statesmen ever dreamt that this small oriental sect would become a rival to the Empire; still less did any Christian imagine that within a few centuries the Empire would pay homage to his Crucified Lord. "No one in New Testament times envisaged or anticipated a situation in which the State, the Roman Empire, would consist of Christians, would be governed by Christians, or would be run on Christian lines."[1]

Various causes disturbed this peaceful relationship. The Jews stirred up hatred against those they regarded as apostates from the religion of their fathers. The masses of the people were exasperated by the exclusiveness and puritanism of neigh-

[1] Alec R. Vidler, "The Orb and the Cross," p. 7.

bours who neither worshipped in the temple, nor attended the public games; the magistrates and officials were irritated by what they regarded as unreasonable obstinacy. The unpopularity of the Christians gave Nero the opportunity of diverting from himself the anger of the people to a disliked and misunderstood sect. Spasmodic attacks and mob violence gave way to a policy of persecution as the Empire gradually became aware of a large association existing in its midst, with its own rules and morals, and separating itself from contemporary religious and social customs. In a day when all secret organisations were suspect, and when the worship of the Emperor was a test of loyalty, fear and suspicion were aroused by a society whose beliefs were not understood, whose worship was conducted in private, and whose members refused to pay the customary homage to the images of the reigning Emperor. Christianity was no longer tolerated; it was persecuted as dangerous to the State. The hostility of the Empire was certain as soon as it realised that the Church claimed to be an independent society, subject to laws greater and more binding than those imposed by an earthly Emperor. The Church, henceforth, was treated as a menace to the safety of the State, and at any time its members were liable to arrest and condemnation for high treason on the charge that they were Christians. The "whole principles and constitution of the sect were condemned as hostile to the established order, and mere membership of the sect, if persisted in, was reckoned as treasonable."[1]

The persecutions varied greatly in their severity, and there were long intervals of peace. At their worst many suffered martyrdom, especially those who held office; at their best, even during the so-called truces of the Church, there was a sense of insecurity and fear. There were some who were unable to withstand the terrors of exile, torture, or death, and lapsed from the faith; and at the end of each persecution the Church emerged smaller in numbers, but stronger in resolution and loyalty.

With the so-called Edict of Milan[2] the persecutions came to an end. "For the first time in history, the principle of universal toleration was officially laid down—that every man has a right to choose his religion and to practise it in his own way without

[1] W. M. Ramsay, "The Church in the Roman Empire," p. 356.

[2] See "The Cambridge Ancient History," Vol. XII, p. 686. "Technically it may be true that there was no Edict of Milan" (W. H. Baynes).

any discouragement from the State."[1] There has been much debate as to the causes which led to the Emperor Constantine making this startling departure from the policy of his predecessors for over two hundred years. A modern illustration may throw some light on the problem. Shortly after Stalin had allowed the re-establishment of the Russian Patriarchate I visited Moscow; on my journey there through the Middle East I met a foreign diplomat and a journalist, both of whom had spent many years in Russia. The diplomat said, "Stalin has had to take much from the people—their land, their food, their sons; he wanted to give them something, so he gave them back their religion." The journalist said, "Stalin above all wants unity in Russia; he has found he could never attain it as long as he persecuted for their religion a considerable section of its people." Motives like these may have led Constantine to tolerate Christianity; he had learnt to respect its adherents, and he wished to enlist the strength and vitality of the Church in the service of an Empire which was becoming weak. Reasons of State thus reinforced what was probably also a genuine religious conversion. His conversion and the edict made Christianity popular. At once the Church gained thousands of new members; and there was a rush on the part of many to receive Holy Orders. But it was not until sixty-two years later that Christianity became the established religion of the Empire, when Theodosius issued an edict declaring that all nations under his rule should "adhere to the religion taught by St. Peter to the Romans"; this was followed later by edicts against all heretics, depriving them of their churches. Though it was long before paganism entirely died out, Christianity was now the established religion of the Empire and closely associated with the Emperor, who presided at its councils and took an active part in all its affairs.

The Papacy and the Empire

With the conversion of the Empire the relationship between Church and State entered on a new phase. Previously the Church had been independent of the State; it had been a self-governing society which the State either ignored, tolerated or persecuted. The Church and the State had been distinct. No confusion between them had been possible. In the future, for

[1] "The Cambridge Mediæval History," Vol. I, p. 5.

many centuries, the Church and State were so closely associated that often they appeared to be identical. Patronage took the place of persecution, and the ruler protected the Church instead of harrowing it with fire and sword. The Church set an example of loyalty to the State instead of denouncing it as anti-Christ. Church and State were now allies; the Church showed the State the way to eternal life, the State protected the Church from its enemies and supported it by rich benefactions. When disputes arose they were not so much between Church and State as between their respective officials, for all accepted the ideal that the Church and Empire together should promote the Kingdom of God; and that the two sets of officials—the clergy under the Pope, and the State officials under the Emperor—should work in harmony for the good of the souls and bodies under their care. A famous mosaic in Rome shows on one side Our Lord giving to a Pope the keys of heaven and to the Emperor Constantine a banner with a cross; and on the other side St. Peter holds the key and gives the pallium to the Pope and the banner to the Emperor. "The Pope, as God's vicar in matters spiritual, is to lead men to eternal life; the Emperor, as vicar in matters temporal, must so control them in their dealings with one another that they may be able to pursue undisturbed the spiritual life, and thereby attain the same supreme and common end of everlasting happiness."[1] Dante in his great political treatise "De Monarchia", while denying that the temporal power of the papacy was given either by natural law or by divine command, argues that both the Pope and the Emperor are equally ordained by God, the one to lead man to eternal happiness, the other to preserve peace throughout the world to the end that man may have happiness in this life. Reverence must be shown to the Pope by the Emperor "so that he may the more excellently shine forth upon the whole world, to the rule of which he has been appointed by Him alone who is of all things, both spiritual and temporal, the King and Governor."

But the ideal of Emperor and Pope divinely commissioned, and each working in his special sphere for the temporal and spiritual welfare of mankind, was too great to be realised. Before long the laity attempted to control the Church, and the Emperor or national sovereigns appointed the bishops to their sees; and the nobles, the clergy to their benefices. The danger

[1] Bryce, "The Holy Roman Empire," p. 105.

that the Church might lose all sense of spiritual vocation was great. A succession of reforming Popes feared this and fought successfully for the freedom of the clergy from lay control. They saw it was necessary that they should be separate from the world and free from its entanglements, if the Church as the Body of Christ was to fufil its supernatural mission. They secured a number of reforms of vital importance. In the past Popes had been nominated by the Emperor and elected by the Roman nobles—in the future they were to be elected by the cardinals, though the Emperor was left with the right to veto an appointment. No longer were the kings to invest the bishop with staff and ring; this was to be the prerogative of the Pope. From the Pope the newly-appointed archbishops received the pallium, and at regular intervals bishops had to make the long journey to Rome to report to him. Celibacy was to be compulsory for the clergy, so as to separate them more effectively from worldly ties. Reforms such as these strengthened the Church and secured its spiritual independence of temporal rulers. But the Popes were not content with this. They claimed authority over all rulers, asserting that as they had been set on high by God over all kings, therefore they could excommunicate and depose them at will, putting down the mighty from their seat and exalting the humble and meek. Supported by forged documents the Popes declared that the city of Rome had been given to them by Constantine when he had made Byzantium the new capital of the Roman Empire, and they fought and schemed to increase this donation by the annexation of neighbouring territories. The Popes claimed not only to be the vicars of Christ with supremacy over the souls of men, with power to loose and to bind, but also to be sovereigns over sovereigns. Their temporal claims were fatal to their spiritual authority. They were carried to almost incredible lengths. Hildebrand demanded implicit obedience to his commands from emperors and kings as well as from ecclesiastics. For three days he made the Emperor Henry, with bare feet and clad in wool as a penitent, wait for absolution in the courtyard of the papal palace at Canossa, though the delay may have been partly due to the Pope's uncertainty how to deal most wisely with this unexpected and formidable penitent. Innocent III claimed to be the supreme judge in Christendom of spiritual and temporal causes. So as to secure and extend their possessions the Popes used indiscriminately spiritual and material weapons, excommunicating their foes in language of unbridled violence, and making unnatural alliances to obtain the help of armed forces. In 1300 the Pope Boniface, detested by Dante, declared to the crowds which had come to Rome for the Papal Jubilee, "I am Cæsar, I am Emperor." It was this combination of worldly power with spiritual claims that made Dante condemn so sternly the Papacy of his day:

> "Rome, that made the good world, was wont to have two suns, which made plain to sight the one road and the other; that of the world, and that of God.
>
> "One hath quenched the other; and the sword is joined to the crook; and the one together with the other must perforce go ill;
>
> "because, being joined, one feareth not the other."[1]

The extreme Papal claims led to reaction. With the growing sense of nationality the authority both of the Pope and the Emperor was weakened. The armies of the French king entered Rome, and the Pope was captured and insulted by his foes. A few years later the Popes left Rome for Avignon, where they were overshadowed by the French king. The spiritual authority of the Pope was still recognised, but his temporal authority had received a fatal wound; not even the later recovery of the Papal States made him more than a petty sovereign amidst rulers of far greater power; he intrigued with them to maintain his position, and they threatened him with invasion when he incurred their hostility. With the Reformation a series of fresh blows were dealt at both the spiritual and temporal claims of the Pope; and he retaliated by attempting to destroy the States which rejected his authority, using against them both spiritual and material weapons. Henry VIII and Elizabeth were excommunicated; and those who plotted the murder of the Queen were promised absolution if they were successful in their attempt. The King of Spain was urged to exterminate the Protestants in the Lowlands, and to invade England with the Armada. But by the middle of the seventeenth century the political power of the Papacy had greatly declined, and Bunyan was not far wrong when he described the Pope of his time "though he be yet alive, he is by reason of age, and also of the many shrewd knocks that he met with in his younger days, grown so crazy, and stiff in his joints, that he can do little more

[1] Dante, "Purgatorio," C. xvi. (Temple Edition.)

than sit in his cave's mouth, grinning at pilgrims as they go by, and biting his nails, because he cannot come at them."

The failure of the ideal must not allow us either to forget its splendour, or the greatness of the contribution which the Papacy made to civilisation in the Middle Ages. A spiritual head above all nations, judging and administering according to the law of God, blessing the good and condemning the evil, was a noble and inspiring ideal. If it had been successful Europe to-day would have been in reality a Western Union. It failed because of the sinfulness of human nature. No Pope was great enough to use his position disinterestedly and wisely. The aggrandisement of the Papacy became the goal, instead of the establishment of the Kingdom of God; to attain it the temporal instruments of unscrupulous propaganda, financial exaction, and even of war with all its horrors were used by one who claimed to be the Vicar of the Prince of Peace. At the end of the long struggle first with the Empire and then later with the national kingdoms, the Papacy emerged weakened and discredited. Many centuries had to pass before it regained, as it has in our own time, some of its ancient spiritual and political influence among the nations.

Church and State in the Countries of the Reformation

The Reformation made no immediate change in the theory that all the citizens of a nation should be of the same religion. This was accepted by the Reformers as strongly as by their opponents. The weapon of persecution which had been used by the medieval Church was taken up by the reformed Churches. There were no wholesale massacres on the scale perpetrated in the Netherlands or on St. Bartholomew's Day in France, nor atrocities such as took place in Spain, where *auto-da-fés* were frequent and torture was often used by the Inquisition; but imprisonment, exile, and death were sometimes the fate of those who refused to accept the worship and teaching of the reformed Churches. Quakers and Roman Catholics in England suffered alike as dangerous dissidents from the State and its religion. One State, one religion, was the principle almost universally accepted. But in reformed nations the authority of the sovereign was substituted for that of the Pope. The ruler was the Christian Prince divinely commissioned, and given the sword for the purpose of protecting his subjects in the true faith. In central Europe the religion of the Prince was to be the religion of the people, and dissent from the religion he professed would be no more tolerated by him than would rebellion against his laws.

Various attempts were made to define the relations between Church and State. The most remarkable of these was the Augsburg Confession of 1530, in which the German Evangelical Church declared that the Church and the State are both from God; but while the Church is concerned with the administration of the Word and the Sacraments, the State uses the sword for the defence of justice and peace. The Church must not interfere with civil or political matters; these must be left exclusively to the State. Lutheranism was concerned with the interior life of the Christian, and treated politics as beyond the sphere of its responsibility; the Christian must obey the ruler whoever he might be. If the ruler is bad, the good Christian must nevertheless submit until the evil day has passed. This doctrine explains the slowness of German Protestants in protesting against the Hitler regime compared with the instant vigour of the Roman Catholic opposition. The passivity of Lutheranism encourages the habit of submitting to the authority which happens at any time to be dominant in the State. When it was suggested that this attitude left Christians at the mercy of every rogue and brutal tyrant, Luther replied that the Government ought to see that this did not happen, and that if it failed to prevent it, then certainly the Christian must suffer for it. "Thus everywhere Lutheranism came under the influence of the dominant authority. The yielding spirit of its wholly interior spirituality adapted itself to the dominant authority of the day."[1]

In Calvinism the relation between Church and State was very different. To Calvin the sovereignty of God was everything. He was the "dominant authority" over the whole State. The laws of the State must be in accordance with the laws of God. The Church as God's chosen instrument was to enforce His Will upon the State and its citizens, while the State could claim no authority over the Church. The Church must possess absolute independence and must resist to the last any infringement on the sovereign rights of its Lord. It was this teaching which is the source of the sturdy independence of the Presbyterian

[1] Troeltsch, "The Social Teaching of the Christian Churches," Vol. II, p. 574.

Churches. Calvin saw the State as a theocracy in which the Church regulated the beliefs and morals of all its citizens. No interference with the Church was to be tolerated ; its spiritual freedom must be maintained at all costs. But the liberty of the individual was sacrificed to the control the Church exercised through its consistories of which both ordained ministers and the laity were members ; they became in Geneva a tyranny almost as burdensome as that exercised by the Roman Church in Spain.

Calvinism is thus in complete contrast to Erastianism, which takes its name from Erastus, a prominent layman at Heidelberg in the sixteenth century. Erastus appears to have taught (though an essay by J. N. Figgis on his teaching opens with the sentence " Was Erastus an Erastian ? "), that only the State had coercive power, and alone could punish offenders, so the Church must confine itself to warnings and censures. Erastus repudiated the theory that within a nation there can be independent Governments—the Church and the State—for the Christian magistrate alone has the right to punish. Erastianism is the term used to describe the subordination of the Church to the State. It existed long before the days of Erastus ; it was seen in the East in the supremacy of the Byzantine Emperors over the Orthodox Church. Later it was repeated in the control the Tsars exercised over the Russian Church; this was thorough and detailed ; shortly after the Revolution I met the lay procurator of that Church who was then an exile in Paris, in the course of conversation I asked him if he had known the Tsar, he replied that usually he had seen him every day to discuss with him the affairs of the Church.

The Papacy had saved the Western Church from the Erastianism or Cæsaro-Papism of the East, but with the growth of national sentiment and their rejection of the Papacy the reformed Churches found themselves in a position in which their independence was threatened both by the Pope and by an aggressive nationalism. The only protector to whom they could appeal was the king. In looking to him for protection the Church was not turning to a stranger, but to one of its own members. It relied increasingly on the good will of the Christian Prince, who in the time of danger steadily extended his authority over the Church. He appropriated powers which had in the past belonged to the Pope, and in return gave the Church the protection it needed. The price paid by the Church was heavy, unless, as with the Calvinist Churches, there was the determination to preserve at all costs spiritual freedom against the State. The king appointed the Church officers, exercised ecclesiastical discipline, and in various ways controlled the Church. But Erastianism in its most extreme form never claimed that the Sovereign had the right to consecrate or to ordain the ministers of the Church, to preach the Word, to administer the Sacraments, or to give absolution.

The Church of England, as we shall see, has not been free from Erastianism. There have been periods when the control of the State over it was very great, and it came to be treated and regarded as a department of the Government. The Church often gladly accepted this position, provided it retained its privileges and possessions. In the States into which Germany was divided, the rule of the reigning Prince over the Church was almost absolute. The temptation for the Church to accept State control, and the State to use it, is great. The Church abandons its spiritual freedom for a peaceful life and a position of privilege; while the State uses the Church for its own purposes, denying it any autonomy and resenting any criticism from it as impertinence or rebellion.

Church and State in modern days

There was one great assumption beneath the quarrels and negotiations between Church and State in the Middle Ages and in the century immediately after the Reformation. It was taken for granted that the citizens of the same nation all belonged to the same Church; if there were obstinate dissidents, for the sake of the State and the good of their souls they must either be converted or liquidated. The Churchman and the statesman of the sixteenth century would have been amazed to find nations of the twentieth century in which different Churches were all equally tolerated, and still more to find that usually their practising members were in a minority compared with the rest of the nation. These two changes have profoundly affected the relations between Church and State. In England until the seventeenth century it was assumed that there would be only one Church for the nation. Anglicans, Presbyterians, and Puritans attempted to fashion the Church into their special pattern. Cromwell was prepared to go a considerable way towards toleration, and under the Commonwealth Presbyterians, Baptists and Independents had their place within the State Church; but Anglicans and Roman Catholics were excluded from all toleration. At the Restoration Charles II provided that "no man shall be disquieted or called in question for differences of opinion in religion which do not disturb the peace of the kingdom," but this promise was shamefully broken and it was not until the Toleration Act of 1689 that Churches which were not Anglican were recognised as legal. Within Great Britain and in the United States all Churches and sects are now equally tolerated by the State. But even more revolutionary is the fact that within most of the nations which once formed part of Christendom the majority of the citizens remain outside the Churches, and many of them are ignorant of the simplest elements of the Christian faith. While in the past ecclesiastics, statesmen and people all belonged to the same Church, now in a nation there are several Churches, and its Government may consist of those who have no connection with organised religion. This makes a great difference in the relations between Church and State.

The new position has been met by the Roman Catholic Church making a series of concordats or treaties with the different States in which it has members. An authoritative explanation of the meaning and purpose of a concordat is given in the French Dictionary of Catholic Theology: "The Church and the State are the perfect societies. Their authority, however, is exercised on the same subjects, on matters often connected; and there arises the necessity of a law to determine their mutual connections. There is no difficulty when the State accepts purely and simply the application on its territory of the principles of ecclesiastical law, touching the relations of spiritual power and of temporal power. But this is not frequently the case. Usually to the Catholic theory the State opposes a national theory. To maintain the connection it is therefore necessary to make some arrangement, if not on the principles, at any rate on the practical results which follow from them. The concordat is the solemn act which expresses this transaction."[1] There was nothing new about the policy of concordats; they had been made with the medieval Emperor, and later with the rulers of different nations which had asserted their independence. But in modern days they have been made with much greater

[1] Dictionnaire de Theologie Catholique, "Concordats."

frequency, and the Vatican at the present time has a large number of concordats with States which are not Roman Catholic. They are of value, for through them the Papacy is enabled to give support to a local Church which unaided would not be able to sustain the pressure of a hostile State. The Papacy can rely on Roman Catholic opinion throughout the world to condemn the breach of these concordats, and can mobilise political influence in their support. The Roman Catholic vote is thus often used with great effect to advance the policy of the Vatican. It is difficult to over-estimate the weight of the moral and political influence which the Pope can exercise in defence of Churches in communion with him. It becomes a grave danger to a nation when the vote is cast at the bidding of a Pope either hostile to it or indifferent to its interests.

In accordance with their relationship to the State, Churches can now be divided into three groups: Established Churches; Free Churches in a free State; and Churches in a totalitarian State.

(*a*) *Established Churches*. Of these it is unnecessary to say much, as the rest of this book will be devoted to the relation between Church and State in England. Most of them are survivals of the day when there was only one Church in the nation. They are at their strongest in the Scandinavian countries, in England and in Scotland. It is more difficult to justify their existence now that there are several Churches in the same nation, and this difficulty is increased when neither executive nor legislative consist of members of the Established Church. Mr. Gladstone in his writings on the State and Church defended "the marriage" between them, but he assumed that the State was then Christian; in a speech in Parliament in 1847 he declared: "There are several senses in which a legislative may be called Christian. For example: either because all its members profess a known and definite body of truth constituting the Christian faith, or because they all adopt the designation of Christians, or because from the great preponderance of Christians in its personal composition . . . a Christian spirit pervades their legislation."[1]

But though in England much recent legislation has been Christian in spirit, neither all the members of Parliament, nor even a "preponderance" of them, call themselves Christians nor profess the Christian Creeds. Mr. Gladstone considered

[1] Quoted by A. Vidler in "The Orb and the Cross," p. 96.

that a State should choose one Church from all the others as the national Church on account of the superior truth of its teaching. But this would now mean that a secular State would judge the degrees of truth possessed and taught by the different Churches; at all times this would have been a position difficult for a Churchman to accept, and now quite impossible when the State is not necessarily Christian. There are really two questions: Should there be any one Church with a special and unique relationship to the State, and, if so, which Church should be chosen for this responsibility and privilege? Those who believe in the value of an Established Church would answer by saying that the State has responsibility for the spiritual and moral welfare of its people, but as it cannot discharge this duty by itself, it should therefore hand it over to a Church. If it is agreed that the State should recognise the Sovereignty of God, it can do this best through a Church which hallows its rulers, blesses its assemblies, and ministers the Word and Sacraments to its people. It is also of value to the State that over against it there should be a Church which has the right both to exhort and warn it to follow in the ways of righteousness, truth and mercy. "The State which does not recognise the Church as the organ of, or witness to, an absolute and transcendent kingdom of God, tends ineluctably to exalt itself into an absolute and to make transcendent claims for itself. And again because the State must strive to embody justice, but can achieve only a rough justice at the best of times, it needs to recognise and provide scope alongside itself for an institution which will declare the State's own limitations so that it shall neither idealise nor rest content with them."[1] If the Church is to do this fearlessly and impartially it must have sufficient liberty. The State, notwithstanding its power, must stand back so as to give the Church freedom to criticise and exhort.

But the question still remains—which Church among several should be chosen for this position? In England this is easily answered, for if it must have an Established Church, the Church of England has claims such as are possessed by none other. Historically it is the ancient Church of the land, closely connected with the State and nation through the centuries; it is the Church which has the comprehensiveness which should be found in a national Church and makes room within its wide borders for both Catholic and Protestant; it is the

[1] Ibid., p. 134.

only Church which provides spiritual ministrations for the whole nation and in every parish; and though its numbers have decreased, it still has a larger membership than any of the other Churches in England. If there should be an Established Church, the claims of the Church of England are unanswerable.

(*b*) *The Free Churches*. The Established Churches are now few in number; by far the larger number of the Churches in Europe and America have no connection with the State, and are free and independent of its control. Their members as citizens are under the laws of the country in which they live, and changes in the trust deeds by which their Churches hold their property require the sanction of the State. But the Churches are as free as any other voluntary association. They can choose their own officers, constitute their assemblies, make their own rules, and discipline their members. They are Free Churches, as independent of and as separate from the State as was the Church in the first three centuries. They claim that this liberty is essential to their very life if the Word of God is to have free course through them, and if they are to proclaim it without let or hindrance. In England when we speak of the Free Churches we think chiefly of those which once belonged to the Anglican Church and are now separated from it; but most of the Churches on the Continent and all the Churches of North America are independent of the State, and all the Churches which form the Anglican Communion are, with one exception, free from State control; but the one exception is the Mother Church—the Church of England.

The complete separation between Church and State in the United States is regarded as a principle of the greatest importance, and in practice is carried out most scrupulously. This is partly due to the importance of preserving equality between the many sects which are found in America, and partly as a defence against undue political pressure which might be exerted in sectarian interests against the State. The Federal Convention of 1787 adopted for the Constitution the provision "that no religious test shall ever be required as a qualification to any office or public trust under the United States," and in 1791 the First Amendment declared "Congress shall make no law respecting an establishment of religion, or prohibiting the free exercise thereof." The United States is not content with mere toleration, which assumes the inferiority of the religion tolerated, but aims at complete religious freedom and equality for all religions and denominations, provided that the law is obeyed and that public peace is not disturbed. In the words of a Judgement of the United States Supreme Court (1871), "The law knows no heresy; it is committed to the support of no dogma, the establishment of no sect." This strict separation between Church and State has led to refusal to allow in the State schools any religious observance or teaching, or any Bible reading or instruction. A series of Judicial decisions have prevented many of the States from giving any help, either direct or indirect, to the private schools belonging to different churches, frequently even free transport allowed for the children of State schools has been refused for the children who attend schools in which religious teaching is given. It is worth also noticing that, notwithstanding the complete separation between Church and State, there have been many appeals to the legislature and the judicature to decide disputed religious problems, especially in connection with the schools. But the States as a whole are convinced that the separation of Church and State is both a principle to uphold and a practical necessity to enforce. "We have staked the very existence of our country on the faith that complete separation between the State and religion is best for the State and best for religion."[1]

(*c*) *The Totalitarian State and the Church.* All Churches, both Established and Free, are now threatened by the emergence of the Totalitarian State. Nothing has been more remarkable in modern days than the vast extension of the powers of the State. In the past the functions of the State were largely regarded as negative; it had to suppress disorders, violence, dishonesty, injustice and crime. It interfered with the activities of the individual as little as possible. Now the emphasis is laid upon its positive duties; it is not sufficient for it to protect the weak; it must provide for the well-being of all its citizens; it must provide their food, houses, education, recreation; it must see that they have work under favourable conditions, and that they can earn a living wage. It cares for them from the cradle to the grave, both in sickness and in health. Until recently the State always had as its aim the welfare of the individual citizen; with the rise of the Communist and Nazi States this has been replaced by a new conception, revolutionary in character, namely, that the State does not exist for the good of its citizens, but the citizens exist for the State; their individuality is no longer to

[1] Judgement of the Supreme Court (1947) quoted by Johnson and Yost in "Separation of Church and State in the U.S.A."

be regarded as of any value, for they are the tools of the State to be used by it as its interests dictate. At the same time the State has extended its claims far beyond the outward actions and words of its citizens, and in its more extreme forms it now aims at moulding their characters and entering into the recesses of their being, so that their thoughts, aims, and motives are alike inspired and controlled by it. The State has become an all-absorbing, all-possessive force, emptying as far as it can its citizens of their individuality, undermining all sense of responsibility, and depriving them of liberty.

The Totalitarian State is thus in direct opposition to the Christian Church which teaches that all men are of value in the sight of God and, therefore, must be free if they are to fulfil His purpose for them. In country after country totalitarianism has found itself opposed by the Church. Goebbels' diaries show how greatly the gangsters round Hitler hated it, and Ciano's reveal the scorn which Mussolini felt for the Church with which he had made a concordat. When all other resistance against the Totalitarian State collapsed, the Churches on the Continent continued in various degrees of intensity to oppose its claims for absolute obedience. The Totalitarian State uses three methods to destroy this opposition. Sometimes its weapon has been undisguised brute force. In the years after the Revolution in Russia the Orthodox Church passed through a time of fierce persecution; thousands of its bishops and clergy were murdered or imprisoned, churches were closed and pillaged of their goods, and its lay members penalised in various ways. The Soviet State looked upon the Church as a dangerous political enemy, for it had been whole-hearted in its support of the old regime. The attempt to crush the Church failed, and now it has been given considerable freedom to manage its own affairs, to choose its own bishops, and to regulate its worship. In Germany, repeated attempts were made to weaken the Church, though Goebbels' diaries make it clear that the decisive attack on it was postponed until the war should be over.

More dangerous than direct attack is the creation of an atmosphere which is hostile to all religion. The party in control of the State has powerful means to create this. The censored press, the wireless, the cinema, the schools, and the armed forces with their young conscripts give the State the opportunities for creating an atmosphere of hostility to religion, and for inculcating fanatical and unquestioning obedience to the commands of the State. When from school days onwards religion is treated as an outworn superstition, and in a hundred different ways the Christian faith and ethics are either ignored, attacked, or criticised, it is only the few with very strong, well-grounded convictions who can escape from the prevalent agnosticism. "The great danger that we have to meet is not the danger of violent persecution, but rather that of the crushing out of religion from modern life by the sheer weight of a State-inspired public opinion, and by the mass organisation of society on a purely secular basis."[1] Only a Church with clear-cut convictions and with complete freedom can hope to resist these insidious and persistent attacks upon its faith.

Lately Communism had adopted a third method of weakening religion and of rendering more remote the possibility of the Church offering any opposition to its policy and plans. In Russia, and in most of its satellite States, open persecution has been abandoned. Freedom of worship is permitted and in some cases help is given by the State towards the training of priests and the maintenance of theological colleges. The Communist claims that freedom both of religion and of atheism is equally allowed; but his conception of religious freedom is very different from that which is held in the west. Encouraged by the fact that the Russian Church has always concentrated on faith and worship, the Communist regards religious freedom as freedom of worship within the churches. But any freedom over and above this is not permissible, and there is no recognition that Christianity is concerned with social, economic, and political conditions. Any attempt, therefore, by the Church to criticise the policy of the State is treated at once as dangerous and treasonable. There is little fear of a clash between Communism and Orthodoxy, but conflict is certain to arise when Communism comes into contact with Roman Catholic and Reformed Churches which claim the right to take an active part in political and social issues. Confronted with this possibility in Poland, Hungary, Bulgaria, Czechoslovakia and elsewhere, the Communist party has been deliberately striking blow after blow at leading ecclesiastics likely to resist it. It arrests and sentences them on charges of treason; it sends them to prison for long periods, and by so doing not only removes formidable critics, but hopes to intimidate others from following their example. The charge of treason against the State is

[1] Christopher Dawson, "Religion and the Modern State," p. 57.

stretched to include what in democratic countries would be regarded as constitutional opposition and legitimate criticism. The Churchman in a country under Communist control who objects to the teaching of atheism in the schools may find himself arrested for an offence against the State. The immediate aim of Communism is, therefore, not the suppression of the Church by means of open persecution, but the intimidation of its clergy and laity so as to compel them to confine their religious activities to narrow channels. Communism is prepared to tolerate the Churches provided it has tamed them so that they are unlikely to offer resistance to the State. Frequent arrests and savage sentences are the whips which are used to domesticate the Church into subservience to the State. The Roman Catholic Church is bravely resisting this policy, and by so doing is defending human freedom against tyrannical totalitarianism.

We should be foolish to treat these dangers as possibilities in all other countries except our own. Great Britain is very far from being a Totalitarian State such as those which have been established on the Continent, but year by year the influence of the State is rapidly spreading; its voracity for planning is far from satisfied, and the tendency towards centralisation is steadily increased; fields of education, charity, and recreation once occupied by the Church are now largely monopolised by the State; in this country, as elsewhere, the Church must be alert and vigilant, ready to resist all attempts to expel the spiritual from the life of the nation.

II

PAPAL SUPREMACY

If the question is asked, " When was the Church of Scotland established ? " the answer is simple—" By the Act of Union passed in the sixth year of the reign of Queen Anne." But when the same question is asked about the Church of England it is impossible to give a clear-cut answer. The phrase " the Church of England by law established " is first found in the Canons of 1603. Fifty years earlier the second Act of Uniformity speaks of " the establishing of the Book of Common Prayer." As far back as the reign of Edward III the phrase occurs in a statute that it is " ordered and established " that elections to bishoprics should be without papal interference. But though the term " establish " is used frequently, nowhere does the Statute Book contain any Act establishing the Church of England ; and nowhere in the whole of recorded English history can there be found any statute, ordinance, or decree which so establishes it.

If dates for the establishment must be given they would be those on which the first Anglo-Saxon kings were converted. In British days the Church was too weak to attract serious notice from the State, though at one time there seems to have been persecution, when the soldier Alban was martyred. With the Anglo-Saxon invasion the Church was driven back to the west. With the arrival of the Roman missionaries the conversion of the new settlers commenced. Bede gives vivid accounts of the more important of these conversions. In 597 Augustine and the monks with him approached in procession the city of Canterbury, bearing a silver cross for their banner and the image of the Saviour painted on a board, and singing a litany of penitence and intercession. The king had already heard them while he sat under a tree in the open air, lest their magic might have effect under a roof. He allowed them to use a church dedicated to St. Martin, and here they met to sing, to pray, to preach and to administer the Sacraments, until at last King Ethelbert " induced by the unspotted life of these holy men and their delightful promises," was converted and baptized. And though he coerced none of his subjects into the acceptance of Christianity, we are told that he encouraged and showed " more affection to believers, and to his fellow-citizens in the heavenly kingdom." Thirty years later there followed the conversion of Edwin, King of Northumbria. At first, like Ethelbert, he hesitated to accept the new teaching, so to help him in his decision he took counsel with the chief men of his kingdom. One of them compared man's life to the swift flight of a sparrow from the darkness outside through a brightly lighted room again into the rain and storm without, " so this life of man appears for a short space, but of what went before, or what is to follow we are utterly ignorant." The king then allowed the missionary Paulinus to preach the Gospel, which he did with such effect that Coifi, the high priest, riding a horse, dashed a spear against the idols he had served and ordered their temple to be burnt. And the king " with all the nobility of the nation, and a large number of the common sort received the faith and the washing of regeneration." Before many years passed other kings in different parts of England were converted, and their example was imitated by many of their subjects.

Since those days there has been close relationship between Church and State. For over thirteen centuries the Church of England has been accepted by the State as the national Church. The relationship between Church and State has passed through various phases; often there has been happy and peaceful co-operation, sometimes there has been bitter controversy, frequently there has been uneasy tension. But during all this time, with the exception of a brief period under the Commonwealth, there has never been a complete breach, still less any occasion when the State rejected one Church and substituted for it another of its own creation. For better or for worse the connection between Church and State has survived to our own day. Great changes have taken place since the early kings were converted; side by side Church and State have grown together, influencing one another for evil as well as for good. In numerous ways they have become so interwoven that often it has been difficult to distinguish their special provinces. The growth has been so gradual that it is impossible to give accurate dates to its different stages. " The 'Establishment' (so understood) of the Church in England grew up gradually and silently out of the relations between moral and physical power natural to an early age of society: not as the result of any definite act, compact, or conflict, but so that no one now can trace the exact steps of the process by which the voluntary recognition of moral and spiritual obligation passed into custom, and custom into law."[1]

Anglo-Saxon Centuries

In the four hundred and seventy years between the coming of Augustine and the Norman Conquest, the connection between Church and State was very close. The Church made great contributions to the creation of an united nation and the good order of the State, while the State extended its protection to the officers and property of the Church. There were occasional clashes between individual kings and archbishops, but there was as yet no sharp division between the ministers of the Church and of the State, for the ecclesiastic more often than not was one of the officers of the king in charge of some vaguely defined department of civil affairs. In four directions we can observe the close partnership between Church and State.

(1) This is seen most clearly in the relationship of the Crown to the bishops and higher ecclesiastics. In the earliest days the kingdom and the diocese were co-terminous, though as the size of the kingdoms increased it became necessary to create new dioceses. The bishop lived near the king, sometimes in the same building; when the king was at the wars, the bishop remained at home administering the diocese-kingdom. "In all cases, for a short time, the diocese coincided with the kingdom and needed no other limitation: the court was the chief mission-station, and sent out monks or priests to convert the outlying settlements."[2] As the bishops and clergy were usually the only educated men in an illiterate age they naturally became the secretariat of the Court; and the ecclesiastic who had proved useful to the king received his reward by promotion to a bishopric. The bishops and the abbots of the more important monasteries were summoned to the national Councils and sat side by side with the great nobles; on the other hand when an ecclesiastical synod was held, the king and his nobles seem to have been present. The laws passed by either assembly concerned both clergy and laity. The later practice by which certain assem-

[1] Selborne. "Defence of the Church of England against Disestablishment" (1886), p. 10.

[2] Stubbs, "Constitutional History," Vol. I., p. 245.

blies represent only special classes in the nation—the Convocations consisting of the clergy only, and in recent days the Church Assembly exclusively of members of the Church—was unthought of in an age when Churchman and citizen were the same. "The affairs of Church and State were, in fact, interdependent, and no king or bishop of the eighth century would have understood an argument which tried to show that ecclesiastical legislation or the protection of ecclesiastical interests was a matter for Churchmen alone."[1]

As the bishops took a large part in State affairs and proved of great use to the king in national administration, it was important to him that they should be chosen not only for their piety, but also for qualities which would enable them to take part in public life—even in our day Archbishop Lang used repeatedly to urge that some at any rate of the bishops should be specially qualified in this way. It was for this reason that the Anglo-Saxon king intervened in the choice of bishops; it was natural he should do so, for everywhere else he appointed the chief officers of the State, and though the clergy or the cathedral Chapters claimed the right to elect their bishop, the influence of the king was often decisive. Occasionally the king accepted the man chosen by the electing body, but more frequently the clergy elected his nominee. On account of the political importance of the see the appointment to Canterbury was made by the king, but the custom was established by which the Archbishops of Canterbury and York received[2] from the Pope the pallium (a narrow scarf of wool which loosely encircles the neck and hangs down before and behind, forming the letter Y). In the four centuries before the Conquest there was considerable variation in the manner in which a bishop was appointed, but by Edward the Confessor's reign it was usual for a bishop to be appointed by the king with the approval of his Council, and it is uncertain if the chapters or any assembly of clergy were still given opportunities either of nomination, election, or approval.

(2) The clergy were gradually granted special privileges and protection which distinguished them from the rest of the community. In 749 they had been given freedom of all burdens,

[1] F. M. Stenton, "Anglo-Saxon England," p. 236.

[2] There was no established custom of the Archbishop of Canterbury going to Rome until 927; and for the Archbishop of York, 1026. Earlier the pallium was normally sent. (See Levison, "England and the Continent in the Eighth Century," Appendix III.)

except the duties of repairing bridges and maintaining fortresses. The word of a bishop in a civil or criminal action was accepted without dispute, it was not necessary for him to bring, like a layman, compurgators, that is, neighbours who would swear with one voice and joined hands that the word of the witness could be accepted with confidence. In the same way the value, measured in money, of the life of one of the clergy was greater than that of a layman, and that of an archbishop higher than that of one of the clergy: for the murder of a priest the blood money required was six times as much as that for a simple freeman; that for a bishop and ealdorman four times as much as that for a priest; and for an archbishop six times as great as that inflicted for the killing of a priest![1] In fact the value of an archbishop estimated in the terms of the penalties for his murder was accounted as great as that of a king!

(3) Gifts of money and of land to the Church were encouraged and protected by law. Apart from grants of land there were four main sources of income: plough-alms which consisted of a penny paid within a fortnight of Easter for each plough team in the parish: soul scot, a voluntary offering made to the priest at the open grave for the soul of the departed: and Church scot, a payment in kind levied on all who were free men in proportion to their holding. These payments were authorised by an Ordinance of King Athelstan who directed that their payment should be enforced. But in addition there was the payment of tithe, which gradually replaced Church scot. Tithe had originally been a voluntary gift of one-tenth of the annual produce of land; it was taught as a religious duty, but it was not enforced by law; it could be given to the relief of the poor, for the help of pilgrims, or the support of churches, and then not necessarily to the church of the parish in which the donor lived or possessed land. It was not until the tenth century that penalties were attached to the failure to pay tithe; by that time it was used for the support of parish churches, and the other purposes to which it had once been applied had been gradually dropped. But in actual practice the owner still kept considerable discretion over its payment, and frequently diverted it from the parish church to some monastery in which he was especially interested. As time went on large gifts of land

[1] W. Hunt, "A History of the English Church, 597–1066." But there is considerable confusion and uncertainty on the amount of the "wergild" attached to the lives of those belonging to different classes.

were made to the chief ministers, to parishes, and to monasteries.

(4) While the State protected the Church, the Church contributed towards the formation of an united England. Its organisation ignored and stepped over national boundaries. Long before England was one, its Church included the rival kingdoms which divided it. By example and precept the Church pointed the way to national unity. Under the supremacy of the Archbishop of Canterbury the bishops of the different kingdoms kept in touch with one another and thus encouraged a unity larger than that which could be possessed by a tribe or a small kingdom. The Synod at Hertford in 673, over which Archbishop Theodore presided, was the first national council assembled in England. Only four of Theodore's suffragans attended in response to his summons, but it was a national instead of a tribal assembly. The canons which it passed were of no great importance in themselves; they were the re-statement of the accepted law of the Church, but the fact that they were promulgated by an assembly which represented the whole of England under the chairmanship of the Archbishop of Canterbury was an important stage in the movement towards unity. Many years had to pass before complete national unity was attained. It was delayed by disputes and wars between the kingdoms, by the revival of the archbishopric of York which created a challenge to the primacy of Canterbury, and by the dislocation caused by the Viking invasions. But these last helped to weld the nation into one, for local patriotism and tribal ambitions yielded to the conviction that only through unity could the nation survive. Without the example and influence of the Church the attainment of national unity might have been indefinitely postponed: "The unity of the Church in England was the pattern of the unity of the State; the cohesion of the Church was for ages the substitute for the cohesion which the divided nation was unable otherwise to realise. . . . It was to an extraordinary degree a national Church; national in its comprehensiveness as well as in its exclusiveness. Englishmen were in their lay aspect Mercians or West Saxons; only in the ecclesiastical relations could they feel themselves fellow-countrymen or fellow-subjects."[1]

In these four hundred and seventy years Church and State were related too closely for serious disputes between them to

[1] Stubbs, "Constitutional History," Vol. I, p. 266.

arise. It was unnecessary, therefore, to frame theories to explain their relationship or to define their respective spheres of influence; their close association was taken for granted by all concerned. The cry of Church freedom had not been raised, for the Church was not aware that it had anything missing from the spiritual freedom necessary for its welfare. On the Continent great controversies were rising between the Pope and Emperor; these so far had not reached the English Church. But with the Norman Conquest changes were pending which would affect for many centuries the relationship between Church and State.

The Norman Conquest

At the time of the Conquest both Church and State were weak. The kingdom had been exhausted both by the Danish invasions and by internal strife between great parties in the State. King Edward may have been a saint, but he lacked the qualities of a ruler, and in a wild age simple goodness and piety are no substitute for wisdom and strength; he failed to control his unruly subjects, and his unpopularity had been increased by his partiality for the foreigners with whom he filled many of the most important posts in the State. The Church had not altogether escaped from the general debility of the age; discipline and learning alike needed strengthening; too many of the bishops neglected their dioceses for administrative posts in the State; and one of the results of the Viking invasions had been to accentuate the insularity of the Church by separating it from the Continent and from the reform movements which were sweeping over it. The Conqueror was a complete contrast in character to Edward. Vigorous, strong, and determined, he intended to make his rule felt throughout his new dominion. While not naturally cruel, he could be utterly ruthless when his will was crossed, or the security of the State endangered. He was a strong Churchman, and his invasion was blessed by the Pope as a crusade against a country whose archbishop had been excommunicated. He brought to England the outlook of a Continental ruler, and from the start began to re-model both Church and State in accordance with principles to which he had been accustomed; though he had proclaimed he would respect the ancient customs of the kingdom, it was soon discovered that the old bottles would not contain the new wine poured into them. If at first there was no outward change in the administration of the Church, its administrators were quickly changed. Archbishop Stigand of Canterbury was deposed and Lanfranc appointed in his place. Sees vacant by death or deposition were soon filled by Normans. Centralisation both in Church and State was the keynote of William's policy. To carry this through it was important that the see of Canterbury should be occupied by a man in whom he could have complete trust and whose ends were the same as his own. Such a man was found in Lanfranc: he had the reputation of being one of the best scholars of his time, but William knew him chiefly as a most capable administrator. Probably never since has the see of Canterbury had an archbishop so great in the work of organisation and administration. More gentle than William, as befitted a Father in God, he was as clear sighted and determined. Never in this country have king and archbishop worked together so well—two oxen yoked equally together was the description later given of them.

William kept to the practice which prevailed in the time of his predecessor in the appointment of bishops. He retained this in his own hands, though there is no doubt he consulted Lanfranc. Regardless of the disputes on the Continent over the question of investiture, he vested the men he chose with staff and ring, and required their homage for the lands which they held from him as their over-lord. And though Lanfranc received the pallium and was appointed papal legate, the King was determined that the Pope should not interfere with the archbishop or ecclesiastical affairs within the kingdom. This was not because William rejected the spiritual supremacy of the Pope; this he fully accepted, but that "The Pope should of his own initiative interfere in such a way as to limit the king's authority over any of his subjects, must obviously be prevented at all costs. This was the normal position of a tenth or eleventh century ruler."[1] To secure this freedom from papal interference he refused to allow anyone to go to Rome without his permission. A legate from the Pope was only to be admitted as an envoy to the king, and was not allowed to have any authority over the archbishops or bishops. When the Pope demanded that William should pay him fealty for his kingdom he was told by the king that he had never promised this, nor had this fealty ever been paid by any of his predecessors. He made it

[1] Z. N. Brooke, "The English Church and the Papacy," p. 186.

clear that the customary offering of Peter's Pence was a voluntary gift and not a compulsory tribute. It is not surprising that the Pope disliked this independence, and in 1079 wrote indignantly that " no king, not even a pagan king, has presumed to act against the apostolic see in the way William unblushingly has acted; no one has been so irreverent and insolent as to prevent archbishops and bishops from coming to the threshold of the apostles."[1] But though the Pope protested he avoided an open breach with the king.

Free from the interference of the Pope and with the full support of the king, Lanfranc carried out his plans for reform. It was first necessary to deal with the claims of the Archbishop of York, for centralisation was impossible while the northern province claimed to act independently of the south. Not by any means for the last time the bureaucratic mind decided that the north should both in spiritual and temporal matters be administered from the south. But at that particular stage in English history there could be no unity if the north went its own way independently of the south. An enquiry was made into the claims of the two archbishops. The monks of Canterbury by forged documents lent decisive aid to their archbishop, and the primate of the north made very reluctantly his submission to the primate of the south. How bitterly this was felt by the northern primate was shown by an interruption he made in the next reign at the consecration of Anselm: the mandate described the new archbishop as " Metropolitan of all Britain "; when this was read, the Archbishop of York interrupted with the indignant exclamation: " Metropolitan of all Britain! Then is the Church of York which all men know to be metropolitan, not metropolitan? "; and as a result of the protest the document was amended. With his supremacy firmly established Lanfranc held three great synods which gave new authority to old laws which had often been disregarded, and laid down new regulations to meet the special needs of the time. Discipline was tightened both over the clergy and over the monks. By another reform several rural sees were transferred from remote villages to the cities: among them Selsey was abandoned for Chichester, and Dunwich for Norwich.

More important to the future relationship between Church and State was the establishment of special courts for the hearing of ecclesiastical cases. In the Anglo-Saxon reigns all cases were

[1] Ibid., p. 137.

generally heard in the ordinary secular court: spiritual matters were thus often decided with the assistance of laymen, and the condemnation of the clergy for crime was pronounced by the laity as well as by their ecclesiastical superiors. To William and Lanfranc, accustomed to special courts for the clergy in Normandy, this seemed most unfitting; humiliating to those who were in the sacred ministry, and open to the practical disadvantage that men unversed in ecclesiastical law might have to administer it. The king, therefore, ordered that in the future no bishop nor archdeacon should hold pleas of episcopal law in the assemblies of the Hundred "but whoever shall be impleaded by the episcopal laws for any cause or crime, let him come to the place which the bishop shall choose and name for his purpose, and there answer for his cause or crime, and not according to the Hundred but according to the canons and episcopal laws."[1] A fine was appointed for every refusal to obey the bishop's summons; the bishop could pass a sentence of excommunication and the king would see this was enforced. The laity as well as the clergy could be brought before these courts, though disputes over patronage were carefully excluded from their jurisdiction. The establishment of these courts led to endless friction between Church and State: they were intensely unpopular with the laity, who disliked clergy passing judgement on them for moral offences; they were viewed with suspicion by the secular judges, who frequently issued injunctions to withdraw cases from their control; and later on they became a byword for incompetence and dilatoriness. Only in subsequent centuries were these defects clearly revealed, but their establishment at once opened the door to foreign influences "which though present in pre-Conquest England, had been kept there within a narrow range. By 1089 when Lanfranc died, an uninterrupted sphere had been provided for the operation of the canon law through the creation of separate ecclesiastical courts."[2] As canon law depended upon the Pope these courts led to the spread of papal influence and to repeated appeals to Rome to decide disputed points.

Papal Supremacy

The strong hand of the Conqueror had protected both Church and nation from papal encroachments, for William was

[1] Gee and Hardy, "Documents Illustrative of English Church History," p.58.
[2] F. M. Stenton, "Anglo-Saxon England," p. 667.

determined that the Pope should not interfere in his realm without his permission. But the appointment of Norman bishops, contemptuous of the Anglo-Saxon Church and sympathetic with the reform movement on the Continent, and the creation of separate spiritual courts, prepared the way for the assertion of papal claims. William's weaker successors had neither the will nor the power to make a resolute stand against the continuous pressure of the Pope. Rufus had to give way to the Pope and Anselm, by abandoning the custom by which the king invested a newly appointed bishop with staff and ring. In the anarchy of Stephen's reign, papal legates and bulls freely entered the country, and frequent appeals were made to Rome without the royal permission. The resistance and martyrdom of Thomas Becket forced Henry II to accept defeat in the controversy over the Church courts. The depths of degradation before the Papacy were reached when John surrendered the crown to the Pope, and as his vassal received it back. In the next three centuries the Church had to struggle, often in vain, to preserve any appearance of independence against the demands of both Pope and king.

The ecclesiastical disputes of this period fall into two groups. The struggle of the Church and often of the nation against the claims of the Pope; and the controversies of a more domestic character within the nation between the Church and the State.

The true nature of these controversies is often misunderstood. Those between the Church and the Papacy sometimes have been misinterpreted as the attempt of an indignant Church and patriotic nation to escape from thraldom to Rome. However much we might wish this had been so, the actual facts give no support to a theory so congenial to later-day Protestantism. Both Church and State accepted the spiritual supremacy of the Pope; they honoured and respected him as the lawful successor of St. Peter, holding the keys for the opening and closing of the gates of heaven, possessing authority to bind and to loose, and to judge both individuals and nations. Only those who were in faithful communion with him could hope for salvation. To die excommunicate meant the loss of eternal life. Papal authority and jurisdiction were accepted in England as in the rest of Western Christendom; the controversies arose only over the extent and limits of their exercise. Papal authority was not denied, but its application was frequently opposed and rejected. English kings who would have been indignant at any suggestion that they were cutting themselves adrift from the papacy, and who would have condemned to a cruel death any of their subjects who attempted it, saw no inconsistency in stoutly resisting the Pope when he overstepped the bounds of his lawful authority, as they understood it.

It is very widely assumed that the medieval conflicts between Church and State in England are comparable to the struggles which now take place on the Continent between Church and State arrayed against each other as separate and hostile societies. This comparison would have been impossible to men of the Church and of the State in the Middle Ages, for they were members of the same Church and of the same State. The disputes were within the Church between two groups of its members; and within the State between two groups of citizens. Every Churchman was a citizen, and every citizen was a Churchman. A member of the State who did not belong to the Church was a heretic and must be liquidated with the same deadly efficiency which the Totalitarian State of to-day uses against citizens whose hostility it suspects. The confusion over the controversies between Church and State is partly due to ambiguity over the use of the word Churchman: in the Middle Ages it was given a narrower and more precise meaning than it now conveys. To us it means any baptized member of the Church who has neither left the Church of his own will nor been excommunicated from it; but in the Middle Ages it meant a man who had been admitted to one of the Orders of the Church, not necessarily as a deacon or priest, but as a sub-deacon, an exorcist, or as a member of some minor order. There were large numbers who claimed in this sense to be Churchmen and the right to the benefit of clergy, though they were always in a minority compared with the great mass of laity who had never been ordained. A Churchman in the meaning of the Middle Ages was therefore a man who had been admitted either to Holy Orders or to one of the minor Orders. It was in this sense that Viola in "Twelfth Night" uses the term when she asks the clown, "Art thou a Churchman?" In our modern sense of the term he could not have been otherwise, and the question would have been pointless. A boy who to-day told his vicar that he was "going into the Church" would probably receive a heavy rebuke and be reminded that by his baptism he had already been made one of its members. But in the Middle Ages it would have been understood at once that the boy intended to say he was a candidate for ordination. To describe a man as a Churchman meant that he belonged to the governing body of the Church—an ecclesiastic, as the word implies.[1] Disputes between Church and State were between two sets of officials, both members of the same Church and nation, but one set acting in the interests of the Church, the other of the king and Parliament. These disputes can be more conveniently compared with those which arise between different departments of State, rather than with the more dangerous disputes between different States. Even in our more civilised days great anger and irritation are caused by inter-departmental disputes. Some years before the war one of the permanent staff of an important ministry told me he had had a nerve-wracking week. "Germany, I suppose?" I asked. "No, no, far worse; a first-class row with another ministry—these inter-departmental rows are far more trying than an international crisis!" In the Middle Ages the strain of such disputes must have been much greater, when one set of officials threatened the other with dire penalties for high treason, while the other retorted with the graver menace of damnation both in this world and the next.

The occasions of these disputes were many and different, fundamentally the causes were the same: the claims of either the Pope or the king upon the Church; sometimes the king helped the Church in its resistance, on other occasions the king made an agreement with the Pope at the expense of the Church. From time to time the dispute was directly between Church and State, and then either one or both appealed to the Pope for support.

(1) Both popes and kings did all in their power to secure the appointment of bishops who would further their respective interests and support their policy. In theory the bishops were elected by the Chapter of the cathedral, but in practice the king claimed that his nominee should be accepted. At one time successive kings promised freedom of election, but as they often insisted that the election should be held in their presence and in their chamber, they were able to bring pressure on any elector who threatened to take an independent line. If, however, the election was disputed or there had been some defect in the procedure an appeal could be made to the Pope, and

[1] For all this paragraph see J. N. Figgis, "Churches in the Modern State," pp. 186–192.

this gave him the opportunity of setting aside the elected candidate and making an appointment of his own. He appointed also to the vacancies caused by translation. It became the custom to apply to the Pope, and not to the Metropolitan of the Province, for confirmation of the election; this meant both expense and delay, and sometimes the Pope declared an election invalid, and filled the vacancy thus caused with his own nominee. On the whole papal interference in episcopal elections of the thirteenth century was an advantage to the Church. The king was the chief danger to freedom of election, and would press upon a timid Chapter the name of one of his servants whom he wished to reward. In such cases the Pope had the power to encourage and help the Chapter in their opposition, and frequently chose a good and capable man as a bishop in the place of the man he had refused to accept. Professor Powicke gives a favourable verdict on papal interference in the reigns of Henry III and Edward I. "In general the Pope's increasing supervision of ecclesiastical elections helped in this period to maintain the freedom of electoral bodies against intrusion by the royal power. In England at any rate it upheld the common law of the Church on behalf of those brave or rich enough to fight for their rights and appeal to Rome. . . . Indeed the superiority of the English episcopate in this century to that of the later Middle Ages was mainly due to the maintenance of the electoral system, which while it gave full weight to, and often bowed before, the interests of the king, did impose, as a barrier to his will or caprice, the force of an organised Church. This was a fact of great political no less than ecclesiastical significance. It gave the bishops an independence in the realm such as they had rarely had before, and except in the peculiar reign of James II have never exercised since."[1]

As the reforming age of the papacy passed away it became more corrupt and unscrupulous. No longer did the Pope think chiefly of the needs of a vacant diocese, but of the opportunity it gave him to fill it either with some foreigner he wished to reward, or the relative of some rich noble who offered a sufficiently large bribe. Not only did he create vacancies by translations but claimed that he had the right to "provide" bishops according to the number of sees which he demanded should be placed at his disposal. Against this system of provision which applied to every kind of benefice Church and State united in

[1] F. M. Powicke, "King Henry III and the Lord Edward," Vol. I, p. 274.

their protests. The king, however, gradually reached an agreement with the Pope that he should accept his nominee. It became understood that the Pope must do so whether he approved or not: one of the Popes contemptuously remarked, "If the King of England asked for an ass to be made bishop we must grant his request." The mockery with which the Papal Court treated some of these requests was shown shortly after the appointment of an Archbishop of Canterbury, when an ass was led to the Pope with a petition tied to its neck asking that it also might be given a see. At the end of the fifteenth century the election by the Chapter had become a mere formality—the Chapter went through the procedure of electing the king's nominee; the king sent the name to the Pope; and the Pope gave his approval. The fifteenth century "marks a steady growth in the influence of the Crown over the choice of the spiritual rulers of the Church."[1] Thomas Gascoigne in the middle of the fifteenth century wrote bitterly of the collusion between the king and the papacy, "There are three things to-day that make a bishop in England—the will of the king, the will of the Pope or of the court of Rome, and the money paid in large quantities to that court; for thousands of pounds of English money are paid here in England to Lombards for exchange to the impoverishment of the realm."[2]

It was a matter of great importance to the king that his bishops should be men whom he could trust and employ. Unfortunately this meant that the ablest among them had to spend years at Court to the almost complete neglect of their diocese. Bishop Fox had never visited two of his dioceses, Exeter and Bath and Wells; only after thirty years in the king's service did he withdraw to his see at Winchester to care for the souls, "whereof I never see the bodies." Wolsey never visited Winchester or Durham, and only spent a few weeks in the diocese of York after his disgrace, and was arrested before he reached his metropolitical cathedral. The king was anxious that the bishops should be loyal subjects as they had great influence in Parliament. In the House of Lords there were twenty bishops and twenty-six abbots (though the latter were very irregular in their attendance), while the average number of lay lords was forty. If the bishops had been nominated by the Pope and not by the king, the foreign element in Parliament would have been dangerously large.

[1] A. Hamilton Thompson, "The English Clergy," p. 31.
[2] Quoted by A. Hamilton Thompson in "The English Clergy," p. 24.

(2) The Pope was not content with attempting to secure the right to appoint diocesan bishops. He claimed also the next appointment to various deaneries, canonries, and rich benefices. The pretext was that he could in this way at once provide a suitable priest for the vacancy without the inconvenience caused by a long delay. By this system of "provisions" he was able to provide profitable posts for his favourites and courtiers, and at the same time to secure large sums of money as bribes from those he appointed. Archbishops and bishops were ordered to set aside benefices for the Pope to fill at his pleasure on the next vacancy. This iniquitous policy was carried to extraordinary lengths, with complete lack of consideration either for the lawful patrons, the clergy, or parishioners.[1] In 1240 the Pope required the Bishops of Lincoln and Salisbury alone to provide benefices for three hundred foreigners! Widespread indignation was caused by this method of filling cathedral canonries as well as parishes with aliens who would never visit their cures, and if they did would be unable to understand a word spoken by their parishioners. The action taken by the Pope to carry out his orders was almost incredibly high-handed. In the middle of the thirteenth century three strangers entered York Minster. They found a worshipper and asked which was the Dean's stall. When he pointed it out they went up to it, and two of them, placing the third in it, said, "Brother, we install thee by the authority of the Pope." The Pope in this way had given the stall to an Italian cardinal named Jordan.[2] Various attempts were made to stop these usurpations. In an unexpectedly vigorous letter Henry III rebukes a papal collector who in 1244 attempted to interfere with presentations to stalls in Peterborough Cathedral: "Your stone heart is too hard to receive our words. . . . We will allow no interference with the presentations aforesaid, and we shall in no wise allow them; our magnates protest with no uncertain voice against our toleration of your practice." But protests by themselves were unavailing. So in 1351 the Statute of Provisors was passed forbidding any person to accept a papal provision. But the value of this Statute was destroyed by the king and Pope acting together to evade it, when this collusion was to the advantage of both.

(3) Through taxation the Pope made heavy claims upon both

[1] Professor G. Barraclough in his book on "Papal Provisions," (1935), strongly defended the system. It is true that *sometimes* the Popes "provided" better and more learned men than otherwise would have been secured.

[2] J. Raine, "Lives of the Archbishops of York," p. 298.

Church and nation. He regarded the English nation as a milch cow which he could milk at pleasure. His demands increased the difficulties experienced by the clergy in paying their taxes to the king. Over this there were frequent disputes. The clergy claimed the right to tax themselves in Convocation. The king attempted to overcome this difficulty by summoning the clergy to attend Parliament. They refused however to take this opportunity of sitting with the National Assembly. It is interesting to speculate what the results would have been if the clergy had regularly elected some of their number to represent them in Parliament, though probably long before the twentieth century this right would have been taken from the Church. But in the early days of Parliament, it was not regarded as a privilege to sit in it. Instead of the modern enthusiasm to secure election by many speeches and lavish promises, there was great reluctance on the part of those who were chosen; fines and threats had to be used to compel their attendance. They disliked this public duty, for they knew that they were summoned to vote taxation, that often they would be bullied into granting a sum far larger than they had expected would have been required, and that when they returned home they would have to face great unpopularity for giving their consent to taxation which would have to be paid by their neighbours as well as by themselves. The clergy, perhaps not unwisely, absented themselves from Parliament, but by so doing they did not escape from heavy taxation, for they were compelled to vote it in Convocation. And sometimes their difficulty in doing this was increased through the tactless and unwise intervention of the Pope. In 1296 Boniface VIII published a bull forbidding the clergy to pay, and the laity to demand, taxes on the property of the Church. Excommunication was the penalty for disobedience. This would be comparable to Moscow ordering all communists in this country to refuse, under pain of expulsion from the party, to pay any taxes. Edward I's anger would correspond to that which would be felt now in this country if a foreign power thus attempted to interfere with its taxation. When the clergy in obedience to the Pope refused to pay the required tax, they were outlawed by the Courts, and were thus liable to be robbed and beaten without redress until they reached an agreement with the king. There was trouble again for the clergy over taxation in Edward III's reign, when the Pope demanded a subsidy from England on the ground that he was the lord paramount. A council of the lords spiritual and temporal was summoned to consider the request. The Archbishop of Canterbury was asked if the Pope was indeed lord of the realm. As he hesitated in replying the Black Prince lost his temper, and shouted at him: "Answer, ass; it is your duty to instruct us all." When the Archbishop replied "the Pope is not lord here," the assembly agreed with him, and the grant was refused.

The clergy, therefore, were not only called upon to pay their just share of taxes as citizens, but they were also required by the Pope both to tax themselves and to raise large sums of money for his benefit. The papal collectors travelled up and down the country squeezing donations from the clergy. They were the most unpopular officials in the nation; they were hated by all, and went in danger of their lives. The payments made were the more disliked as it was suspected that they found their way into the coffers of the King of France, often at war with England. On many occasions Church and State stood together in resistance to papal taxation, but occasionally the king in return for concessions reached an agreement with the Pope over the subsidy demanded, and the clergy were compelled to pay it.

(4) Through the ecclesiastical courts the papacy was able to extend its power. The law they administered was the Canon Law which depended upon the Pope, and in the case of dispute could only be finally determined by him. Two sets of law thus had authority in the same realm, the Common Law and the Canon Law. Occasion was given for repeated appeals from the royal courts to the papal courts, causing much delay and heavy expenditure. The ecclesiastical courts were a persistent cause of friction between the clerical and lay elements in the State. The lay judges watched their proceedings with dislike and suspicion, repeatedly granting injunctions to withdraw cases from their jurisdiction; the clerical judges jealously guarded their rights and were always anxious to extend the scope of their authority; the king both regretted the diversion of fines from the secular to the spiritual courts and deplored the obstacle they offered to the punishment of crime. Among the criminal class they were naturally popular for the penalties they inflicted were light compared with the savage punishments ordered by the State judges. By pleading benefit of clergy criminals escaped severe punishment, and this privilege was claimed not only by priests and deacons, but by a host of minor officials, by door keepers,

readers, exorcists and by all who asserted they had received some kind of Orders. The claim became so common, and the refusal to allow it caused such controversy with the judges of the spiritual courts, that eventually the fact that a man could read was accepted as a sufficient proof that he was in Orders. Many criminals were let loose to rob and murder. Various attempts were made to check this laxity. Under Henry VI an offender charged before a secular court was tried and convicted, even if he pleaded benefit of clergy, before he was handed over to the bishop. Early in Henry VII's reign convicted clerks were branded under the thumb and excluded from claiming privilege if another charge should be brought against them.

It would, however, be mistaken to imagine that the clerical and lay members of the Church and State were engaged in perpetual controversy. A common faith held them together. Side by side more often than not they worked for the spiritual welfare and the good government of the people. The people were probably untouched by, and often completely unaware of, the controversies which we have been discussing. They tilled the ground, gathered the harvest; went to Mass every Sunday and Holy Day, and with some grumbling paid their tithes and taxes. The main body of the clergy were probably as unpolitically minded as they are to-day; they carried out their duties faithfully, all the time complaining of increased expenses and taxation, criticising innovations, fearing the archdeacon as the devil, and, unlike the clergy of to-day, praying devoutly that the bishop might not visit their parishes, for they looked upon him as a disciplinarian rather than as father in God. Occasionally there were dangerous outbursts of mob violence, in one of which Archbishop Sudbury of Canterbury lost his life. Occasionally, too, an archbishop was in violent and fatal conflict with the king; Thomas Becket was murdered at Canterbury as a result of his quarrel with Henry II over ecclesiastical courts; and in the room next to that in which I am writing Archbishop Scrope was condemned to death for rebellion against Henry IV, at the block he called upon all men to witness that he perished "for the sake of the law and liberties of England." But these were the exceptions to the rule that during the greater part of the Middle Ages Church and State worked together.

In one direction the co-operation between authorities of Church and State led to tragic results. Alarm was felt both by the king and the clergy at the growth of Lollardry. The Archbishop and the Convocation of Canterbury urged the king to suppress it by force. The detestable Statute *De heretico comburendo* was passed. By this anyone convicted of heresy was handed over for execution to the sheriff of the county or the mayor of the city. Punishment by burning was at that time very rare in England, though for some time past it had been used on the Continent as the penalty of heresy. Toleration was still unknown, and heresy was looked upon as a sin against God and a criminal offence against society. Under this statute those who were convicted of Lollardry were burned to death unless they made sufficient abjuration. Many simple folk were put to death by the officers of the State at the request of the Church and with the approval of popular opinion.

From the Conquest onwards the liberty of the Church was threatened by the Pope and by the Crown. If for complete spiritual liberty it is necessary that a Church should freely appoint its own officers, this right was never exercised by the Church of England over a long period of years. In Anglo-Saxon days in some of the dioceses there may have been free elections, but later the rights of the electing body were overruled, first by the Pope, sometimes by Pope and king, and finally by the king. In actual practice no doubt the clergy of the Church had great freedom; to parishes difficult to reach the visits of the archdeacon, and still more those of the bishop, were rare. In the isolation of the country the clergy went their own way; only in London and in the great cities were they caught up in the ecclesiastical and political movements of their time. But it cannot be rightly claimed that in the Middle Ages the Church of England was able to control its own life and to administer its own affairs without external interference. At one time the danger was that it might lose its freedom to the Pope, who exercised his supremacy through an Italian bureaucracy a thousand miles away; but as papal claims were resisted, the authority of the king grew greater, and the outward respect paid to the Pope only thinly concealed the fact that ecclesiastical jurisdiction in England was passing into the hands of the king.

III

THE ROYAL SUPREMACY

THE Reformation brought great changes to Church and State. In this chapter no attempt will be made to describe or to discuss those which concerned doctrine and worship, but it will be confined to the constitutional and political changes which were made in a very short time in the relationship of the Church both to the Papacy and the State. The rapidity and decisiveness with which they were carried through were due to the strength of two monarchs, to the weakness of a third, and to the fanaticism of a queen. Henry VIII and Elizabeth were autocratic and capable; Edward VI a sickly and priggish boy governed by his Council; and Mary a bitter and narrow bigot who by the burnings at Smithfield caused a violent reaction from Rome towards the reformed faith.

But no monarchs however strong could have made such great changes in England, unless behind them they had the support and good will of its people. Historical sense is lacking if it is imagined that the Reformation in England can be explained solely by the determination of an autocrat to change his wife for another woman. Actually Henry's treatment of his wife was so unpopular with his subjects that it prejudiced them against him. The so-called divorce, in reality a demand for a decree of nullity, was the occasion but was not the cause of the Reformation. If Henry and Katherine had been happy in their marriage and no question had ever arisen of an appeal to the Pope for its annulment, reformation nevertheless would have come sooner or later. For many years events had been moving steadily towards a crisis in the affairs of the Church, and especially over the claims of the Pope.

The causes which immediately led to the Reformation in England were political and social rather than doctrinal. The path taken by the Reformation in this country was very different from what had been followed in Europe, where doctrinal changes preceded those which were political and administrative. In

England there was first an awakened nationalism which accentuated the dislike of papal interference so frequently shown in the past by protests and statutes. The king and his judges objected to the perpetual appeals from the national courts to a seat of justice a thousand miles away. The great landowners were jealous of the immense amount of property owned by the Church. The bishops were irritated by the exemption of the monasteries from their control. The clergy and laity both resented the filling of vacant benefices by Italians and French. The mass of the people, very insular in their outlook, disliked the presence of foreign priests in their parishes, and were angered at the frequent papal appeals for grants of money. Suspicion of the Papacy was increased when the Pope was in the power of the French king at a time when England was at war with him. We can sympathise with this attitude, for in this country there was much indignation when the Pope congratulated the armies of Italy after a successful war of aggression against Abyssinia, when he sent an ambassador to Japan in our darkest hour of defeat, and when he protested vehemently against the mere possibility of attack from the air on the enemy city of Rome, though he had been silent when London, Liverpool and other English cities had been bombed. Not all the causes of discontent were operative at any one time, and by the eve of the Reformation some of the worst abuses had been removed; and though national feeling was hostile to papal policy and exactions, there had never come from any responsible quarter the demand that the Pope's spiritual jurisdiction should be renounced root and branch.

Anti-clericalism on the eve of the Reformation was as strong as anti-papalism, perhaps it was stronger, as it was directed against evils close at hand. The absorption of so many of the higher ecclesiastics in politics, the wealth of the monasteries, the abuses of the ecclesiastical courts, and the alleged avarice of the clergy were frequent causes of complaint. In almost every century since the Conquest protests of the laity against the clergy had been made. In 1529 this resentment was once again simmering. "To prove a single will, in which I was executor," one Member of Parliament declared, "I was compelled to pay a thousand marks to the Lord Cardinal and the Archbishop of Canterbury." Wolsey's ostentation and pomp attained heights which were almost fantastic: when his cardinal's hat arrived it was carried in solemn state through the city to the Abbey, where it was laid on the altar until the Sunday, when a ceremony at Mass like a coronation took place, with three archbishops, eight bishops and eight abbots assisting; then a sermon on humility was preached! When as Chancellor he regulated the nation's apparel and diet in the interests of economy, his critics complained that while burgesses were restricted to homespun, the clergy were encouraged to appear publicly in silk and velvet; and while three dishes a meal was the limit set to ordinary gentlemen, and six to lords, the Cardinal fixed nine as the limit for himself.[1]

The laity complained of the offerings exacted by the clergy at the burial of their parishioners, and it was commonly said that they would beggar orphan children by taking from them their dead father's only cow, rather than go without their due. There was no need for Henry VIII to create anti-clericalism; it was already in existence, but he fanned it into flame and used it to promote his purposes. On one occasion he told the Papal Nuncio "that the great concourse of people present had come solely and exclusively to request him to bastinado the clergy who were hated by both nobles and people."[2] Without the existing unpopularity of the bishops and clergy the king would have been powerless. It proved the greatest factor which made successful his attack on both the Pope and the Church. "This anti-ecclesiatical bias on the part of the laity was the dominant sentiment in the Reformation under Henry VIII"; it was "indeed neither more nor less than a violent self-assertion of the laity against the immunities which the Church had herself enjoyed, and the restraints which she imposed upon others."[3]

These anti-Papal and anti-clerical movements were strengthened and encouraged by the Lollardry which still lingered on, though secretly, in various parts of the country. The Bible was better known to the laity through partial translations passed from hand to hand, and its contents were compared and often contrasted with the doctrine and practices of the Church; its reading created doubts about teaching and ceremonies which for centuries had been accepted without question. It is impossible to know how far the Lollard movement had any direct influence on the opening stages of the Reformation, for it was mainly the simple and unlettered who had been most influenced

[1] A. F. Pollard, "Wolsey," p. 71.
[2] Spanish Despatches, October 15th, 1530.
[3] A. F. Pollard, "Henry VIII," p. 267.

by the teaching of Wycliff and his followers; any open expression of heretical views was almost impossible, but underground the movement was smouldering and ready under favourable conditions to burst into flame.

The king's matter, as it was called, was like a spark to dry timber. Holbein's portraits of Henry reveal his character; if the rich and picturesque clothing in which he is painted were stripped from him, and he was shown in the loud check suit of a racing man, we should recognise him at once; blusterous, noisy, hearty, boastful, talkative, with a force of personality which makes it impossible to ignore him, he occupies the central place on the stage, whether he is at the bar of a public house, or in the smoking-room of a club, or at a committee meeting. He has plenty of ability, and always knows his own mind. He will express his opinion loudly and decisively, but when contradicted he becomes sulky or bad-tempered.[1] He is good-natured up to a certain point, but those who know him best are uncertain of his temper, for there is something crafty about his eyes which makes them cautious. He can be a good friend, lavish and generous while his liking lasts, but it is bad to have him as an enemy. He enjoys his food and drink in plenty, and is attracted by women when they have some of his own vitality. Give such a man almost unlimited power, set him on the throne in Tudor days, and we have Henry VIII. He might call himself a good churchman, for the Pope himself had described him as Defender of the Faith; the last thing he wanted was a breach with the Pope who had so honoured him, and he had no intention of deserting historic Christendom for new-fangled ideas in religion. Faggots and the stake seemed to him the only sensible way of arguing with those who questioned the faith of his fathers.

The difficulty which troubled him and eventually changed him from an obedient son of the Pope into an inveterate enemy was at first a cloud no larger than a man's hand. For what appeared to him good reasons he wished to be free of his present wife Katherine, and to marry Ann Boleyn in her stead. For his own satisfaction and for the safety of the kingdom he passionately desired an heir, and Katherine had failed to give him one. As she was his elder brother's sister he had no reason to think that the Pope would refuse to the Defender of the Faith a decree of nullity; then, as a bachelor he could marry.

[1] "The Archbishop of Canterbury spoke much against the King, who was very angry and used foul language to him." (Venetian Despatches, March 21st, 1532.)

Such decrees of nullity were easy to obtain from Rome if they were asked for by the right kind of person and were supported by sufficient money or political concessions. In his own family Henry had examples of the ease with which such decrees were granted. His sister Mary had married Louis XII of France, who by dispensation had been married to Jeanne of France related to him in the fourth degree; later Louis obtained a decree of nullity from Jeanne, as he wished to marry the widow of his former wife's brother, Anne of Brittany (to unite Brittany to the Crown of France). When Anne died he married Mary of England, who on his death soon afterwards, married Charles Brandon, Duke of Suffolk. He had had also a chequered marriage career; he had obtained a dispensation to marry his first wife, but was set free from her by a decree of nullity! If the fortune of his sister Mary were not sufficient to give Henry hope that the Pope would grant, almost as a matter of form, his request, he had only to think of another sister, Margaret—with a dispensation she had married James IV of Scotland; on his death she married the Earl of Angus, and later divorced him—Wolsey described this judgement as "a shameless sentence." No wonder then that Henry thought he would meet with no serious difficulty in obtaining a decree of annulment for causes which were religious, political and personal.[1]

There is every reason to believe that the required decree would have been granted, but for one obstacle. At the time it was asked the Pope was in the power of Charles V, the nephew of Katherine, and as Charles made it plain he would regard an insult to his aunt as an insult to himself, the Pope dare not agree to Henry's request. He did all he could to help the King of England, even going so far as to suggest he might have two wives! He delayed as long as he could any definite decision. He sent a commission to hear the case in England; but as this made no progress it was adjourned indefinitely and the Pope made the fatal mistake of citing Henry to appear before the Court at Rome. The whole episode is discreditable to all concerned, with the exception of the Queen who throughout behaved with quiet dignity. The real guilt lies with the Pope; if in the past he had not repeatedly granted or refused these decrees as political expediency dictated, Henry would never have made his application. It was because the Papacy was notoriously corrupt that the king made his request with confidence.

[1] For this paragraph see Creighton, "The Church and the Nation," p. 203.

The refusal of the Pope to give a decree of nullity came with a shock of surprise, and it was the more infuriating as he knew it was due to the influence of his enemy, the Emperor Charles.

The Rejection of Papal Jurisdiction

The outstanding event of the Reformation under Henry was the denial of all papal jurisdiction in the kingdom. For centuries the Church had been under both the Pope and the king, henceforward it was to be under the king only. The Pope had been the final court of appeal in cases ecclesiastical; he had bestowed the pallium on the two archbishops; he had interfered in the appointment to vacant sees; he had exacted an oath of obedience from every bishop; he had filled benefices with his nominees; he had received sums of money from taxation, from bribes and special subsidies as well as from Peter's Pence. He was the visitor of monasteries. Through the bishops and mitred abbots in the Lords he had been able to influence Parliament. By the weapons of excommunication and of interdict he had brought either terror or inconvenience to thousands. Now this was all ended. There were undoubtedly losses in this rejection of papal authority. The Pope had kept an insular Church in contact with the great religious movements on the Continent, and by his appointments had occasionally given to it men of greater experience and culture than would have been found at that time in a small island; and often the Pope had supported the Church in its resistance to unreasonable demands made by king or Parliament. But since the great reforming popes the Papacy had steadily deteriorated; it had become a secular State intriguing with diplomatic weapons to extend its territories, and when these failed resorting to alliances with States which with temporal weapons would fight its battles. A succession of immoral popes had made the Papacy despised by the truly religious, and a subject of flattery or intimidation by kings and statesmen who either courted or feared its power.

Characteristically in the English manner the first Statute of Parliament dealing with a great constitutional change was concerned with taxation. In 1532 the payment of annates to the Pope was suspended—and it was ordered that if the Pope in retaliation refused bulls for the consecration of bishops they were to be ignored. The Statute was intended as a threat in the hope that it would show that the king intended to press forward with his demand for a decree of nullity. A year later there followed an Act for the Restraint of Appeals, and though the Pope was not mentioned it was plainly intended to apply to him. The preamble is worth quoting: it declared that the king has the right to do justice to all manner of folk within the realm "without restraint or provocation to any foreign princes or potentates of the world," and the English Church is "sufficient and meet of itself, without the intermeddling of any exterior person or persons, to declare and determine all such doubts, and to administer all such offices and duties, as to their rooms spiritual doth appertain." Any person obtaining sentences from Rome would incur the penalties of *præmunire*; in future appeals were to go no further than the archbishops, except in cases concerning the king himself when they would go to Convocation. In 1534 the Suspension Act against annates was made permanent, and all payments to the Pope of annates or first fruits were prohibited. In this Act the Pope is no longer called "the Pope's holiness" but "the Bishop of Rome, otherwise called the Pope." In the next Act forbidding the payment of Peter's Pence, the language becomes stronger; it speaks of "exaction paid to the see of Rome," and of the "intolerable exactions" which the Pope had made on the realm. A third Act of the same year confirmed the earlier Acts forbidding appeals to Rome and declared that Convocation was only to be assembled by Royal Writ and could only make canons with the royal assent. In May of that year the Northern Convocation received a royal brief requiring it to deliberate and determine whether by Holy Scriptures the Bishop of Rome had greater jurisdiction in the realm of England than any other bishop. In June the Convocation gave its reply against the supremacy of the Pope, and at the end of the year the Southern Convocation reached the same conclusion. In the same year the bishops were ordered to erase from all books used in church the mention of the Bishop of Rome—that his name and memory "except to his contumely and reproach, might be extinct, suppressed and obscured."

With these decisive Acts the Church and realm repudiated the Pope and his claims. For a brief period in Mary's reign his power was restored, and with Parliament kneeling in penitence before him Cardinal Pole gave absolution and reconciliation from the Pope to England. Since that time neither Church nor State have accepted papal authority. Much of the old anti-Roman bitterness and fear have now gone; the utterances of the Pope are listened to with interest and respect by many who have no intention of acknowledging his claims; only occasionally from the underworld of bigotry is he now assailed with coarse abuse. But the people of England as a whole stand behind the statement made concisely and uncompromisingly in Article XXXVII, "The Bishop of Rome hath no jurisdiction in this Realm of England," and at greater length in the first canon of 1603 on the king's supremacy in which it is asserted that "all usurped and foreign power (forasmuch as the same hath no establishment nor ground by the laws of God) is for the most just cause taken away and abolished."

The Submission of the Clergy

To secure his position against the Pope, the king at the same time took steps to render the clergy powerless. From time immemorial the Church had its provincial synods or convocations. In England they consisted of bishops, deans, archdeacons, canons and representatives of the parochial clergy. In the Middle Ages the two Convocations of the south and of the north were summoned separately by the two Metropolitans, the Archbishops of Canterbury and of York, either on their own initiative or after they had received a Royal Writ requiring them to do so. They were the Parliaments of the Church; they made canons; they condemned heretical opinions; they authorised forms of worship, and for some centuries their consent was necessary for taxation of the clergy either by the Pope or by the king. As they were autonomous bodies they might easily become a rallying ground for those who supported the papacy and were hostile to the policy of the king and the Parliament. To remove any possibility of this danger the king with the support of Parliament made an attack as unscrupulous as it was vigorous on the ancient rights of the clergy in Convocation.

There were three stages in this attack. First the king accused the clergy of breaking the Statute of Præmunire by acknowledging Cardinal Wolsey's legatine authority. The Statute, under pain of heavy penalties, forbad the entry into the kingdom of papal legates and bulls without the king's express permission. The charge against the clergy was absurdly unjust, for Wolsey would never have exercised his authority of legate unless this had been authorised by the king. The king himself was the chief offender against his own law. But regardless of consistency Henry threatened the whole body of clergy with a charge of high treason for doing what he himself had done, and only pardoned them on their promising to pay a heavy fine and to recognise him as the Supreme Head of the English Church and clergy. Two years later the next stage opened when the king resumed the attack, declaring that the clergy in Convocation made laws and constitutions without the approval of the king or of the laity. When Convocation returned a reply which the king regarded as unsatisfactory, he announced to the Speaker and twelve members of Parliament that he had discovered the clergy are " but half our subjects—yea and scarce our subjects. For all the prelates at their consecration made an oath to the Pope clear contrary to the oath that they made to us so that they seem his subjects and not ours." There had never been any secret about this oath; it must have been known to the king as well as to any of his ministers, but the fact that this oath had been taken was now used to intimidate the clergy. The Convocations, after much debate, made their submission to the king in a document in which they promised they would never make or promulge any canons or even meet in Convocation without his previous licence and writ. In the third stage of his attack the king asked Parliament to confirm the victory by an Act in which the submission of the clergy was embodied, and which also contained the important provision that existing canons " which were not contrariant to the laws of the realm, nor prejudicial to the prerogative royal " should continue to be observed until the canons had been revised by a commission expressly appointed for this purpose.

It is difficult not to censure the bishops and clergy for their weak submission and for thus surrendering the ancient freedom of Convocation; their timidity and weakness are in painful contrast to the resolution shown by Bishop Fisher and Sir Thomas More, who chose death rather than disobey conscience; but we should keep in mind the verdict of Dr. G. M. Trevelyan who says: " The attitude of the English clergy, though not heroic, was more patriotic, more useful and more morally sound than fanatical intransigence and the preaching of civil war in defence of outworn privileges. Because the clergy accepted much which they could not be expected to like, they saved England from a war of religion, and they soon recovered what they had long lost, a great place in the affection of the country, under a new regime, suited to modern times."[1]

[1] Trevelyan, " The History of England," p. 303.

Other humiliations followed. The bishops again had to promise to observe all the laws which had been made against the papacy, and to promise that in the future they would only speak of the Pope as the " Bishop of Rome " or " Brother " ! They were given orders as to the manner in which they were to preach and provided with a model sermon on the divorce. The justices of the peace were commanded to see that both the bishops and the clergy were obedient to these directions. And as a crowning insult (though perhaps not so regarded in those days) the bishops were ordered to send up to the Court the sermons they had preached. Many of the methods adopted by the modern police State to spy upon and intimidate a Church of dubious loyalty were thus used four hundred years ago. Later on all preaching was forbidden for three months, except by the bishops or in their presence. This was during the preparation of the Ten Articles, which have been described as the first English Confession bearing " the character of a compromise between the Old and the New Learning."[1] Meantime the visitatorial powers of the bishops were suspended to enable a lay commission to visit the universities and the monasteries. A year later the Canterbury Convocation was insulted by one of Cromwell's doctors presiding over it in the place of the Archbishop of Canterbury.

The Royal Supremacy

The humiliation of the clergy was made possible through the autocratic powers claimed by the king. Previously the Church had been under both the Pope and the king ; but now the king with the support of Parliament had taken to himself the authority which had once been shared by them both. Before the clergy were granted pardon by the king for the offence of *præmunire* they were required by him to accept his assumption of the title " the only Protector and Supreme Head of the Church and Clergy of England." The Archbishop of Canterbury proposed the insertion of the words " as far as it is allowed by the laws of Christ." This was not seconded, so the Archbishop said, " Whoever is silent seems to consent," to which one of the members replied, " Then, are we all silent," and the article and amendment were both passed. In the Northern Convocation greater courage was shown, and the Bishop of Durham

[1] For this and much of the preceding paragraph, see Dixon, " History of the Church of England," Vol. I.

protested against the title; this drew from the king a conciliatory explanation in which he denied any intention of intruding into the sacerdotal functions. In 1534 Parliament passed an Act giving the king the style of Supreme Head of the Church of England, without however the amendment suggested by the Convocations; the Act moreover recognised that the king as Supreme Head had the right to "visit, repress, redress, reform, order, correct, restrain, and amend all such errors, heresies, abuses, offences, contempts and enormities whatsoever they be which by any manner spiritual authority or jurisdiction ought or may lawfully be reformed." This gave the king the power to act as Visitor. It proved to be no formal claim; it was used to the full, and the king issued orders and proclamations giving directions to the clergy, without any previous reference to Convocation. To do this the more thoroughly he appointed Thomas Cromwell as his Vicar-General to visit "all Cathedral and Collegiate Churches as well as others, correct and punish their presidents and prelates although archbishops and bishops."

The unconditional claim to supremacy was not made by Elizabeth, who deliberately refused to renew the title. In the first public document of her reign she used an "etc." after her name to avoid committing herself hastily to a title which she disliked, but which once used might be difficult to discard; very soon, however, she decided to describe herself as "Supreme Governor of this realm . . . as well in all spiritual or ecclesiastical things or causes as temporal." She disliked the title "Supreme Head," holding that this "honour is due to Christ alone, and cannot belong to any human being whatsoever." To make her position clear she added to the Injunctions of 1559 an explanation for the benefit of "simple men deceived by malicious" that the Oath of Supremacy was nothing new but was a recognition of the "authority" "which is and was of ancient time due to the Imperial Crown of this realm; that is under God to have the sovereignty and rule over all manner of persons born within these her realms, dominions and countries, of what estate, either ecclesiastical or temporal, soever they be, so as no other foreign power shall or ought to have any superiority over them."

The supremacy of the Crown was used in four ways:

(1) The Sovereign sometimes acted directly in ecclesiastical affairs without any intermediary. Henry had obtained from Parliament an Act decreeing that proclamations made by the

king should be obeyed. This gave the royal edicts concerning Church and State the force of law. For years past kings had issued proclamations dealing with matters both great and small. The practice was now confirmed with the important proviso that proclamations must be made with the advice of the Council, with the exception of those dealing with heresy when the king was given complete authority. The method of rule by proclamation gave the king despotic and unconditional power; by it he could dispense with consulting the bishops and Convocations on matters which directly concerned the Church. The only justification of this high-handed policy was that it enabled swift action to be taken in an age of crisis.

Under Edward VI proclamations were freely used in the cause of reform. But as the king was a minor the Council transferred to itself a power which had been the personal prerogative of the king. Erastianism reached its height. Never before and never afterwards was it so undisguised. The rights of the Church were ignored and the Council issued homilies, ordered a general visitation, suspended the visitatorial rights of the bishop, authorised an Order of Communion, enjoined the disuse of the traditional gestures by the priest in celebrating, added to the Second Prayer Book (against Cranmer's wishes) a rubric that kneeling did not imply adoration, and promulgated the Forty Two articles.

Elizabeth used freely the same method of proclamation for the regulation of ecclesiastical affairs. If order was to be secured action had to be taken very promptly, for on her accession there was no Archbishop of Canterbury, and the attitude of both Parliament and Convocation was doubtful; so the Queen in Council issued proclamations on worship and preaching, on communion in both kinds, and a number of injunctions. These last were a modified form of those issued in the reign of Edward but with considerable additions—among them the strange regulations that no priests or deacons should marry until their fiancées had been approved by the bishop and two justices; while for the marriage of a bishop, the approval of his Metropolitan and some royal commissioners was necessary! Happily this soon was regarded as a dead letter, and the modern bishop is not called upon to approve or criticise the matrimonial ventures of his clergy. Of singing and music it was directed that "a modest and distinct song" should be used in all parts of the Common Prayer, while a hymn or song of praise was allowed at the beginning or end of the service "having respect that the sentence of the hymn may be understanded and perceived." No altar which had survived the previous demolition should be taken down without the oversight of the curate and churchwardens. The holy table should be set where the altar had been, and so stand save when "the communion of the Sacrament" was administered and then it should be placed in the chancel. In the days of Edward VI common fine bread was used for the Sacrament, now it was ordered "for the more reverence to be given to these holy mysteries, being the Sacrament of the Body and Blood of our Saviour Jesus Christ" that the sacramental bread be "made and formed plain, without any figure thereupon, of the same fineness and fashion round though somewhat bigger in compass and thickness, as the usual bread and wafer, heretofore named as singing cakes, which served for the use of the private mass." These quotations from the Injunctions illustrate how thoroughly the queen used her visitatorial powers. The regulations about the holy table and the bread go beyond the directions of the Prayer Book and come under the discretion given to her by the Act of Uniformity of 1559 by which in the case of any contempt or irreverence in the use of ceremonies and orders of the Book,—"The Queen's Majesty may by the like advice of the said commissaries, or Metropolitan, ordain, and publish such further rites as may be most for the advancement of God's glory, the edifying of His Church, and the due reverence of Christ's holy mysteries and sacraments."

(2) The Crown also exercised its authority over the Church by means of commissions, either temporary or permanent. It was through commissions that Henry first enquired into the condition of the monasteries and then secured their dissolution. Repeated commissions which apparently never met were appointed to revise the canons. But while in the past commissions had been temporary in character, appointed for some definite purpose, Elizabeth in the Supremacy Act had in view a commission which would permanently exercise some of the ecclesiastical powers which belonged to the Crown. Thus there came into existence what was afterwards known, and hated, as the Court of High Commission. But as action was urgently required if disorder was not to degenerate into anarchy, Elizabeth almost immediately appointed temporary commissioners to visit the dioceses, to administer the oath of allegiance, and to enforce the Royal Injunctions. However, before they had com-

pleted their work the High Commission had been set up. This was a standing court with ecclesiastics at its head, and lawyers and other laymen sitting with them. Its duties were to enquire into the working of the new Acts and to exercise the visitatorial powers of the Crown. York had its Commission which corresponded to the " High " Commission in London: " it tended to become something of a reinforced and superior Court of the Archbishop, because he was permanent President of the Commission and could avail himself for his own purposes of its wide powers and authority based on his Royal Commission."[1]

(3) Thirdly the Crown used Parliament both to control the Church and to protect it. We have already seen how Henry took action against both the Pope and the English clergy with the full co-operation of Parliament. With remarkable political skill he enlisted its aid in the difficult and dangerous operations in which he was engaged. The measures against both the Pope and the clergy, as well as the assertion of the Royal Supremacy found their way into the Statute Book. Under Edward action was frequently taken by means of Proclamation; but authority for the two Prayer Books was given by Parliament, though it is doubtful if the first received the approval of Convocation, and it is certain that it was neither asked for nor given in the case of the second. On the accession of Elizabeth, Parliament gave its support to her policy and with a few alterations the Prayer Book of 1552 was re-issued and its use throughout the kingdom made compulsory by a new Act of Uniformity.

Parliament also by Statute confirmed and encouraged a policy of persecution. Before long it was clear that there was a life and death struggle between the papacy and the Elizabethan State, so increasingly severe repressive methods were adopted by the Queen and her Council. As Mary had burnt those whom she regarded as heretics, so Elizabeth punished recusants by fines and imprisonment, and Jesuits and proselytising priests by death for high treason. No satisfaction can be obtained by comparing the extent and degree of the religious persecution of these two reigns; but under the Elizabethan penal laws there were no holocausts of victims: " only some two hundred and fifty perished during twenty years, including those who died in prison—a notable fact, when we consider that in the five years of Mary's reign more than three hundred Protestants

[1] J. S. Purvis, " Tudor Parish Documents of the Diocese of York," p. xv.

were put to death."[1] It is unprofitable to discuss whether in Elizabeth's reign the sentences were for political or religious opinions; some of the victims were a danger to the Queen, for she had been excommunicated and deposed by the Pope, and with his approval a few Roman Catholics were ready to remove her by murder. The Cardinal Secretary had written: "There is no doubt that whosoever sends her out of the world with the pious intention of doing God service, not only does not sin, but gains merit."[2] But among those executed were men and women of noble character and deep devotion, who had no thought of murder in their minds, and gave their lives in an attempt to win their fellow countrymen to a Church outside of which they were convinced there was no salvation. The execution of men and women for their faith, whether they were Anglicans, Protestants, or Roman Catholics, was the melancholy and tragic result of an age when toleration was unknown, when religion and politics were intermingled, and when it was firmly believed that the fires of hell would be the penalty awaiting those who denied the faith held by their persecutors. In our own day the Totalitarian State has proved how the flower of toleration is still very fragile. Some day it is to be hoped that Anglicans, Nonconformists, and Roman Catholics may unite in a great service of penitence and thanksgiving for all who have suffered for religious conviction; of penitence and shame for the share our different Churches took in persecution, of thanksgiving and honour for all who obeyed the voice of conscience rather than the voice of man.

Though both Henry and Elizabeth asked for the help of Parliament in ecclesiastical affairs they resolutely held to the claim of personal supremacy. They held this as strongly as the Pope had done in the Middle Ages. They had no intention of allowing Parliament to share their jurisdiction. When Parliament acted it was at their wish and request; Henry either took the initiative in approaching Parliament or secretly prompted it, but both he and Elizabeth were determined that it should not encroach on their prerogative. Elizabeth in her fourth Parliament informed the Commons through the Speaker that it was her pleasure that henceforth no bills concerning religion should be received into the House, unless they had first been considered by the clergy. On another occasion she rebuked

[1] J. B. Black, "The Reign of Elizabeth," p. 151.
[2] J. B. Black, Ibid, p. 144.

Parliament for deciding to hold a public fast " not for that they desired fasting or prayer, but for the manner of presuming to indict a public fast without order and without her privity, which was to intrude upon her authority ecclesiastical." A gradual change can be discerned during Elizabeth's reign in the relationship between the Crown and the Church ; by the close of her reign she is protecting the Church against the interference of Parliament. An alliance between the Church and the Crown was beginning which in later reigns would lead to results disastrous for both.

(4) The Crown also exercised its supremacy through the bishops. Before the Reformation the cathedral Chapter accepted the name sent to it by the king, and before consecration the bishop-elect had to ask the Pope to confirm his election. There was thus nothing new in Henry's claim to appoint to vacant sees. The Statute of Annates actually regularised what for some time had been the usual practice—the king sending the Chapter the name of the man he wanted appointed, but by this Statute if the Chapter failed to elect him they were liable to the terrible penalties of *præmunire* ; in future the Metropolitan and not the Pope confirmed the election, and then the consecration took place. In the next reign for a short time even the semblance of election was abandoned, and the appointment was made by letters patent. But Elizabeth returned to the older custom of nomination and election, though like her father she expected her nominee to be approved. She treated the bishops with little respect, but more as servants whom she could direct and chide as she thought fit. She rebuked them sternly when she felt they were failing in their duties. In a letter to Archbishop Parker complaining of the increase in diversities of religious opinion she sharply blames him and the bishops. " Through lack of regard given by such superiors as you the Primate and other the bishops of your Province, there is crept into the Church open disorder," and she closes her remonstrance by ordering him to report to her any persons who obstruct reform " for so the sovereign authority which we have under Almighty God would be made frustrate, and we might be thought to bear the sword in vain. Use all expedition ; that we be not occasioned for lack of your diligence to use further sharp proceedings, whereof we shall impute the cause to you." She suspended Archbishop Grindal from his ecclesiastical functions for six months, and, though twelve bishops petitioned in his favour,

seriously considered the possibility of depriving him. It is said that to one of the bishops, who protested against some request she had made, she wrote as follows: "Proud prelate, you know what you were before I made you what you are. If you do not immediately comply with my request, by God I will unfrock you!" Even if she did not write this letter, it is not an unfair illustration of the high-handed line she took with the bishops.

Disendowment

History shows that any serious change in the relationship between Church and State almost invariably means that the Church loses some of its possessions. The Church in Henry's reign lost both in political influence and in wealth through the dissolution of the monasteries. By the dissolution of the larger monasteries twenty abbots lost their seats in the House of Lords, thus giving the lay peers a clear majority over the spiritual. There were various precedents for the closing of monasteries and the appropriation of their funds. Early in the fifteenth century (1411) the alien priories had been suppressed and handed over to the Crown.[1] Cardinal Wolsey had also suppressed some small monasteries, used their funds for the building of Christ Church, Oxford, and had transferred their inmates elsewhere. By the sixteenth century the monasteries had largely outlived their usefulness, many of them were dangerously near bankruptcy, several were far below the number of monks for which they had been intended. Often their discipline was unsatisfactory. But most of the charges brought against them as centres of gross immorality can be dismissed as false—they were the cruel slanders invented by unscrupulous men and gladly accepted as true by those who for various reasons desired to see the destruction of the monasteries. Probably most of those living in them at the time of the dissolution were quiet, elderly folk who had sought a peaceful shelter from the world. Monasticism had behind it a great and noble history; it had preserved much of the culture which otherwise would have perished in the collapse of the Roman world, it had brought under cultivation many waste and desolate places, and had given hospitality to many. Even some of its critics at the time of the Reformation recognised that, especially in the north of England, the monasteries were a resting place for travellers and wayfarers. At their

[1] A good many had passed into royal control still earlier.

best they were homes for those who had a vocation to a life of meditation and prayer, and from them there rose a continual round of praise and intercession; while at their worst among the monks and nuns there would still have been found some who never forgot the high ideals of the original founders. But the king wanted money, and his nobles wanted more land, and both needs could be met by the spoliation of the monasteries. In addition, the king feared the communities as possible strongholds of the Pope, while the bishops disliked them as exempt from their jurisdiction. The monks had few friends among the clergy, who looked upon them as rivals; and though as landlords they may have been slightly better than the lay owners of land, the difference was so slight that neither tenant nor labourer was likely to rally to their defence.

The king used Cromwell as his Vicar-General to bring about their destruction. As a first step commissions of enquiry were sent out to visit the religious houses—the reports were unfavourable to all the smaller monasteries, though the larger were exempt from blame. The second step was the suppression of the smaller monasteries. The third step was the "voluntary" or compulsory surrender of the larger religious houses. In all about five thousand monks, sixteen hundred friars, and two thousand nuns[1] were evicted from the religious houses. Recent investigation has shown that they were not treated as inhumanly as once it had been thought: many received a bonus, others a pension, some were appointed to benefices, some married and for this had to make further penance in Mary's reign.[2] The nuns had the hardest lot, though many of them were given small pensions. In addition to the monks and nuns there was a large number of servants, attendants, and hangers-on at all these houses; they either had to find work elsewhere or join the ranks of the sturdy beggars who roamed about in gangs and were a terror to law-abiding persons—"the beggars are coming to town." There were a few monks, notably among the Carthusians, who suffered a savage death at the hand of the executioner. The abbey churches were despoiled of their treasures, the lead stripped from their roofs, their fabrics exposed to wind and storm, and often used as the quarry of the neighbourhood when houses or walls had to be built or

[1] G. M. Trevelyan, "English Social History," p. 108.

[2] G. Baskerville, "English Monks and the Suppression of the Monasteries," Chapter X.

repaired; while their lands were forfeited to the king, who sold what he did not retain for himself. Few will deny that the monasteries required reformation, but there are still fewer who will now attempt to defend either their wholesale suppression or the means by which this was carried out. But the king acquired the money he wanted, taxation was relieved, and those who obtained monastic property by gift or purchase were closely bound to the Crown through fear of any reactionary movement which might restore their new possessions to the original owners.

In the following reign Henry's intention of suppressing the chantries was carried out. Again property devoted to religious purposes was diverted to the Crown. The Act suppressing them suggested that their funds might be better employed in the support of schools, universities, the poorer clergy, and other charitable purposes; but in fact the money thus secured was squandered, and a few educational establishments allowed to survive were called "Edward VI Grammar Schools," which led three centuries to imagine they had been founded by a boy king interested in the education of his subjects. Bishop Latimer indeed protested in one of his sermons against the misuse of funds which might have been used to establish a national system of education; after deploring the lack of the study of divinity in Cambridge, he goes on: "Here I will make a supplication, that ye would bestow so much to the finding of scholars of good wits, of poor men's sons, to exercise the office of salvation, in relieving of scholars, as ye were wont to bestow in pilgrimage-matters, in trentals, in masses, in pardons, in purgatory matters."[1]

Though there were no longer monasteries to sack, there were still churches to pull down. The Lord Protector proposed to destroy Westminster Abbey and to use the materials and site for the building of a great palace for himself; he was only turned from his intention by the Dean and Chapter buying him off with twenty of their manors; he then attempted to destroy St. Margaret's, but the parishioners put up a good fight and drove off the wreckers with sticks and stones; so he had to be content with the destruction of two city churches in whole or in part, of some chapels and cloisters attached to St. Paul's, and of the London residences of three bishops. With the material thus obtained he ordered the building of Somerset House, but before it was completed he had been beheaded.

[1] Fifth Sermon preached before Edward VI.

Losses and Gains

The political revolution in Church and State was on the whole a squalid story of tyranny, violence, corruption and greed. It was redeemed by the heroism of those who suffered death rather than act against their consciences. We can only pass a fair judgement on these years if we contrast the comparative moderation shown in this country with the cruelties of the Inquisition in Spain, the wholesale persecution in the Netherlands, and the massacre of St. Bartholomew's Day in France. England was released from the interventions and exactions of an ecclesiastical bureaucracy over a thousand miles away. No longer had the bishops to make the long journey to Rome or to obey the commands of a Pope who often understood little about the Church of England; no longer were the clergy called upon to raise for his benefit large sums of money; no longer were appeals possible from the English Courts to a tribunal at Rome; State and Church were alike freed from the open interference of the Pope with their domestic affairs. But this did not mean that the Church had secured freedom. What the Pope had lost had been gained by the Crown and not by the Church. The appointment of its bishops was made on the nomination of the king without reference to the Pope; money once paid to the Pope was paid now to the king; and the Convocations had lost the right to meet on the summons of their archbishops and to pass canons at will. The greatest loss of all was that by the rejection of papal supremacy the Church of England was separated from the rest of Western Christendom, and for three centuries became spiritually as well as literally an insular Church.

The Reformation was not forced upon the Church by a foreign power. It was a movement on the part of some of its laity against papal and clerical domination. The clergy and laity belonged to the same Church. It was the climax of a struggle which since the days of the Normans had been waged with varying success between the clergy and the laity. "The Reformation was in short a lay revolution carried by Crown and Parliament —more especially by Crown and Commons—against the will of the Church authorities."[1]

The spiritual gains of the Reformation were great. Hence-

[1] G. M. Trevelyan, "History of England," p. 329.

forth there was free access to the Bible, which was taken as the authoritative standard to test all that was claimed to be necessary for salvation. The public worship of the Church in future was in a language understood by the people. Both clergy and laity were given larger spiritual freedom than they had possessed for many centuries. Through all these changes the Church had retained unbroken continuity with the past. The bishops continued to consecrate and ordain. The episcopal succession had been carefully preserved. The great mass of the clergy remained in their parishes through the changes.[1] The Convocations met with the accustomed forms, though restricted in their action. The ecclesiastical courts held their sittings with minor changes in procedure, though murderers and robbers could no longer claim benefit of clergy. Throughout the Reformation the Church was still called by the old title " Ecclesia Anglicana," and its theologians made their appeal to the ancient Catholic Church of undivided Christendom. But when losses and gains have been weighed and judged, it is impossible to claim that the Reformation brought complete freedom to the Church. It was freed indeed from the Pope, but it was now controlled by the Crown. The supremacy of the Crown had been substituted for the supremacy of the Pope. And though the spiritual gains were great, there were also losses in addition to the separation from Catholic Christendom on the Continent. Simplicity in worship was sometimes won at the cost of awe and mystery. The vivid awareness of the communion of saints through prayer for the departed and the thankful commemoration of the saints in glory became dim and uncertain. And in the anxiety of the reformers to win complete spiritual freedom for the individual Christian much of great value in the ordered discipline of the Church was for a time cast aside. But when the storms of the Reformation had died down, the Church of England, notwithstanding many changes, stood firm and strong as the Catholic Church of the land, possessing the Scriptures, the historic creeds, the sacraments instituted by Our Lord, and the unbroken succession of bishops, priests and deacons.

[1] Some of the clergy were evidently confused over the nature of the changes. The York Diocesan Registry records a case for defamation in 1597 when two clergy riding on Garrowby Hill got into dispute, and one of them—James Randall—" said unto John Otes Clerke, ' Thou arte no prieste nor any that was maid priests in Quene Maries tyme as thou wast '." I am indebted for this quotation to the Rev. J. S. Purvis, D.D., the archivist of the York Diocesan Registry.

IV

THE SUPREMACY OF PARLIAMENT

TOWARDS the end of Elizabeth's reign there were signs of the Crown and the Church drawing together in opposition to the growing power of Parliament. In the next reigns Crown and Church stand and fall together to the great injury of the Church. On the one side were the king and the Church, on the other Parliament and the Puritans; the former represented absolutism, the latter constitutionalism.

The Divine Right of Kings

James I had left Scotland carrying with him a profound dislike of Presbyterianism. He had suffered much at its hands. He had been lectured and scolded at great length by its divines, who had told him he was "God's silly vassal." He was thankful to migrate to a kingdom where episcopacy was the accepted form of Church government, and he hoped that through the bishops he would control the Church. Very early in his reign he had made clear his views on Presbyterianism; at the Hampton Court Conference one of the speakers made some reference to the bishop and presbyters, and the king retorted, "If you aim at a Scotch presbytery it agrees as well with monarchy as God and the devil." He had almost an equal dislike of the House of Commons; he told the Spanish Ambassador that it was a body without a head; that the members gave their opinions in a disorderly manner, and at their meetings nothing could be heard but cries, shouts and confusion. "I am surprised that my ancestors should ever have permitted such an institution to come into existence. I am a stranger and found it here when I arrived, so that I am obliged to put up with what I cannot get rid of."[1] He was a strong upholder of the doctrine of the divine right of kings. He had been appointed by God

[1] Quoted by G. Davies, "The Early Stuarts," p. 17.

and was responsible to God alone. He was above Parliament and could act without it even against its expressed wishes. He could suspend laws and dispense his subjects from keeping them. It was not only treason, but it was sin to dispute the will of the king. But though the king was supreme and his power absolute, yet it was his duty to rule well and to give good laws to his subjects. Charles I did not lecture his subjects so frequently as his father on the doctrine of his divine right, but he held it with equal tenacity. He insisted that the commands of the king should be at all times obeyed. Disobedience to the king was almost as sinful as disobedience to God. He told the Secretary of State about to negotiate with the Parliamentary Commissioners at Uxbridge, that it might do good if in private discourse he put them in mind that "they were arrant rebelles, and that their end must be demnation, ruine and infamy, except they repented."[1]

Unhappily this doctrine was welcomed warmly by large numbers of the clergy. The attitude of the clergy to the king, both in Tudor and Stuart days, is partly explained by the semi-sacred prestige he had in our older history and in ancient days "the deeper we delve into the origins of our civilisation and of every civilisation, the larger is the place that kingship holds in both the religious and the social pattern of life and thought."[2] In 1627 Dr. Robert Sibthorpe preached at Northampton a sermon supporting the royal request for a loan; in it he stated "if princes command anything which subjects may not perform, because it is against the laws of God, or of nature, or impossible, yet subjects are bound to undergo the punishment without either resistance or railing and reviling; and so to yield a passive obedience where they cannot exhibit an active one." In the first of the proposed canons of 1640 the doctrine of divine right was formally proclaimed by Convocation—"The most high and sacred order of kings is of divine right, being the ordinance of God Himself, founded in the prime laws of nature, and clearly established by express texts both of the Old and the New Testaments." The canon was to be read aloud at morning prayer once a quarter. Not all the clergy held to the extreme application of the doctrine. It is said that James I asked Lancelot Andrewes and Bishop Neile: "Cannot I take my subjects' money when I want it without all this formality

[1] Ibid., p. 32.
[2] C. Dawson, "Religion and Culture," p. 109.

of Parliament ?" Neile replied at once: "God forbid but that you should." As Andrewes remained silent the king pressed him for an answer: "Sir," he replied, "I think it lawful for you to take my brother Neile's money, for he offers it." When Charles demanded that Archbishop Abbot should licence Sibthorpe's sermon, he met with a refusal. The king was so annoyed at this that he made the primate withdraw from the Court to Canterbury.

The Church and the Crown

While the Church taught the divine right of kings and the duty of passive obedience, the king patronised and protected the Church. James, on his arrival in England, soon received a large number of petitions from those who desired still further changes in the Church. The best known of these was the Millenary petition, supposed to come from a thousand ministers. It was moderate in tone, and asked for various changes in the Prayer Book, such as the abolition of the sign of the cross at baptism and the ring at marriage; the removal of "dumb" ministers; the condemnation of pluralities; and various reforms in administration and discipline, such as giving up the practice of excommunicating lay officials for trifling offences. There were other memorials more violent and revolutionary in their demands. The king held a conference at Hampton Court early in 1604 to consider the various grievances mentioned in the memorials. Most of the requests of the petitioners were rejected, but a number of minor changes and additions were made in the Prayer Book, the most important of these being the completion of the Catechism by the addition of a section on the Sacraments, and the Prayer Book thus revised was authorised not by Convocation but by royal letters patent and by a proclamation.

The most important decision was that a new translation of the Bible should be made. This was carried through in seven years. Though called "The Authorised Version" it never received the authority of Convocation, but on the title page it states that it has been "compared and revised by His Majesty's special command" and is "appointed to be read in Churches." Its dedication to the king by the translators affords a good example of the relationship between the king and the Church, the former is praised for his writings in defence of the truth and his zeal manifesting itself "every day at home, by religious and learned discourse, by frequenting the house of God, by hearing the Word preached, by cherishing the Teachers thereof, by caring for the Church, as a most tender and loving nursing Father." But though the king took the initiative in promoting the new translation of the Scriptures, it was the Church which carried it through, and by its use in its services made it familiar to all. The Authorised Version of the Bible has had an unique influence both on the formation of the character of the English people, and on setting the highest standard for the use of the English language: dignity, beauty and simplicity are the characteristics of the Authorised Version; it is significant that while Shakespeare employed eighteen thousand different words, and Milton twelve thousand, for the Bible only six thousand were used by the translators.[1] It has been truly said that "the intensive private study of that book by many hundreds of thousands of persons otherwise unlearned had more to do with the character, the mind, and the imagination of our ancestors than we moderns can always understand."[2]

In the same year as the Hampton Court Conference the Church at last received the long-promised revision of the canons. In the previous year, 1603, the King had given his licence to the Canterbury Convocation to meet for the purpose that they "might conferre, treate, debate, consider, consult, and agree of and upon such Canons, Orders, Ordinances, and Consultations, as they should think necessary, fit and convenient for the honour and service of Almighty God, the good and quiet of the Church, and the better government thereof." Convocation acted with great speed, and in the following year the Royal Assent was given to the new canons "according to the forme of a certaine Statute or Acte of Parliament made in that behalfe in the 25th year of the Reigne of King Henry the eight, and by our sayd Prerogative Royall, and Supreme Authority in cause Ecclesiastical." These canons, though drawn up by Convocation and authorised by the King, were never submitted to Parliament and therefore have no authority over the laity. The proclamation authorising them ordered that they should be read once every year "upon Sundayes or Holy dayes, in the afternoone before Divine Service."

[1] G. Davies, "The Early Stuarts," p. 404.

[2] G. M. Trevelyan, "An Autobiography," p. 23.

The Church needed the help of the State against the attacks made upon it both from without and within. The Roman Catholics had only a small minority of adherents left in the country; it has been estimated that they numbered only 8,570, less than one for every parish.[1] Most of these were prepared to live as loyal subjects, if only they were let alone and allowed to follow their religion. But the suspicion with which they were regarded flared up into open hostility after the discovery of the Gunpowder Plot in 1605, and again in 1610 after the murder of Henry IV of Paris. Rome was uncompromising against attempts made by some of its adherents to reach an accommodation with the Government. The State tightened its precautions against any possible dangers from the Roman Catholics in its midst: its clergy were sentenced to banishment, some were executed, and its laity often had to pay large fines.

The most dangerous of the attacks on the Church came from within it. Roman Catholicism might be the most feared, but was no longer the most dangerous enemy. The real danger came from clergy within the Church who had been influenced by continental Protestantism and were determined to root out any vesture, rite, or ceremony which the Church of England had in common with the Church of Rome. They detested episcopacy as contrary to the Word of God; they despised the Sacraments; they disliked set forms of prayer, and they regarded the most harmless symbolism as superstitious and idolatrous. They exalted preaching far above all liturgical worship. In promotion of their views secret presses produced a stream of abusive and libellous pamphlets and tracts. In Elizabeth's reign their bitter and slanderous invective had reached heights hitherto unattained even in a century when violent abuse was the stock in trade of every controversialist. From an underworld the Archbishop of Canterbury was described as a "bloody tyrant," and the bishops as "incarnate devils and cozening knaves," while the clergy were called "dolts, hags, drunkards." But strong language was not confined to one side alone, and it was often returned with equal vigour and the same lack of charity. Both under James and Charles opposition to the hierarchy and the Church was inflamed by pamphlets and broadsheets as scurrilous as those which had been common in the time of Elizabeth. By fines, by imprisonment, and by the pillory, the State attempted to suppress these attacks upon the Church.

[1] W. H. Frere, "History of the English Church, 1558–1625," p. 290.

More dangerous than open attack and violent invective was the attempt to change from within the character of the Church. The prescribed vestments were not worn, the Holy Table was a mere board on trestles, the symbolism ordered was not used, and the statutory services were often hurriedly and perfunctorily taken by a curate as a mere prelude to the great and central event, the sermon by the minister clad in Geneva gown and wearing his bands. There was risk that unless drastic action was taken the Reformation settlement would be destroyed and a Church refashioned on an extreme continental model would be substituted for the ancient, but reformed, Ecclesia Anglicana.

Against these attacks both Church and State combined. From the Church there came a series of learned treatises on its position as against both Rome and the Puritans. Richard Hooker, Jewel and other divines built up a massive structure of theological argument, justifying the position of the Church of England by appeals to the Scriptures, the ancient fathers, and to common sense. But learned argument can never by itself quell the flames of religious fanaticism, so the bishops enlisted the aid of the State to help them in repressing disorder; on the other hand when the bishops seemed to be lax they were incited to further efforts by the king and Council. At the end of 1604 the Council urged the bishops to take steps to secure conformity to the Prayer Book and the canons, reminding them that persistent nonconformists were liable to deprivation and that trustworthy ministers should be put in their place. The archbishops hesitated at taking action, and gave further time to those ready to conform even if they refused to subscribe. But eventually some of the ministers were deprived, their number is a matter of much controversy—Bishop Frere estimates it at forty-nine,[1] but according to other authorities this would be a considerable understatement, though it is certain that the figures were greatly exaggerated by Puritan writers.

The breach between the Anglican and Puritan parties in the Church was deepened by different views on the observance of Sunday. The Puritans had transferred to the first day of the week, a day of rejoicing for the Christian Church, the stern and rigid rules which the Jews had made for the Sabbath. The Puritans indeed observed the Sunday as a day of rest, but it was to be kept with the utmost solemnity; games and work

[1] Ibid., p. 321.

were alike an offence to Almighty God. James in 1617 issued a declaration, commonly known as the Book of Sports, in which it was laid down that certain sports and games were lawful after Divine Service. The compulsory reading of this declaration caused the greatest offence to a large body of opinion, who disliked many harmless games at any time, and who abhorred them on Sunday. Before the storm of protest it was eventually withdrawn; but the odium which it excited fell upon the bishops even more than upon the king.

Under Charles I it was plain that between the Anglicans and the Puritans a life and death struggle was imminent. It was precipitated by the character and policy of Archbishop Laud, though it is doubtful if the wisest and most tactful of archbishops could have steered the Church in safety through the tempest. Laud had devotion, conviction and courage, but he had neither wisdom nor tact. His portraits show his character more clearly than any number of biographies. The powerful face, with florid complexion, obstinate mouth partly concealed by the pointed beard, and penetrating eyes with arched eyebrows raised quickly to express astonishment or indignation, belong to a very familiar clerical type. They are found in the cleric who rises at a meeting with some technical point which he will continue to press notwithstanding all attempts of the chairman to call him to order; persistently and doggedly he sticks to his point; defeated, he will raise it again on the next occasion, and eventually the chairman realises that it saves time to allow him to proceed, for nothing will shake his obstinacy; he is a faithful parish priest, respected by most, feared by many, hated by a few, and loved by none; his sermons are sound, but dull; the laity write complaining of his rigidity to the bishop, who invariably finds that the accused is well within the letter of the law. If he is made rural dean, his deanery will be the best worked in the diocese; he will repeatedly visit the clergy, send them numerous notices, and make them fully aware of their sins of omission. His bishop carefully avoids embarking on an argument with him; for he has a streak of impish humour which finds delight in proving that his bishop has forgotten some obsolete rubric or canon. And then when all agree that he is almost impossible he is taken ill, and for the first time another side of his character is seen as he suffers with quiet heroism, and the clergy and parishioners begin to tell one another how, when they were in great trouble, he had come to their help with tender sympathy and secret generosity. As I look at Laud's portrait this is the kind of character I see; but in days of difficulty and opposition, to those who only knew him from without, he seemed the rigid and intolerant disciplinarian. In his Province and diocese he applied the regulations laid down in the interests of decency and order: he once said " 'Tis superstition now-a-days for any man to come with more reverence into a Church, than a tinker and his bitch come into an ale house": resolutely he determined to set this right, but he could only do this with the help of the king, the Council and the Court of High Commission. To carry out his policy he used the Court of High Commission and his visitatorial powers as Metropolitan. The Court, from which there was no appeal, dealt with almost every kind of ecclesiastical problem. Writers and printers as well as lecturers and clergymen were summoned by it, and by the so-called *ex officio* oath were called upon to give evidence about their opinions as well as their actions. Under Laud this Court lost the merits it once possessed and came to be detested by all; vigorous protests were made repeatedly against it. But Laud was not only concerned with the ecclesiastical offences. He used his position on the Star Chamber to punish those who oppressed the poor. "When an Essex farmer came before the Star Chamber in 1631 on a charge of increasing the price of corn by keeping it until a time of shortage, Laud declared him guilty of 'a most foul offence which the Prophet hath in a very evangelical phrase grinding the face of the poor.' He fined one of the Queen's Court for making an enclosure, telling him he had devoured the people with a shepherd and a dog."[1]

In addition the Archbishop claimed that he had the right as Metropolitan to visit, either personally or by delegation, not only his own diocese, but the whole of the Southern Province. He used this power to see that his regulations were acted upon by the different diocesan bishops, and where there was neglect he took strong action.

In almost every direction Laud's policy of thoroughness made itself felt. Greater reverence was enforced in the worship of the Church, and the arrangement of its buildings. The Press was placed under a stern censorship; Laud had the weapon at his hand to make this possible, for in Elizabeth's reign the Star Chamber had made a regulation that no book should be printed

[1] H. B. Trevor-Roper, "Archbishop Laud," pp. 168, 169.

without the licence of the Archbishop or the Bishop of London. The preacher, too, who had been outspoken in his sermon was liable to be called before the High Commission. Chaplains and lecturers engaged by gentlemen and municipalities, dissatisfied with the sermons of the incumbent of the parish, were forbidden to preach. But it was not only the unlicensed preacher who was in danger; for with the same resolution Laud used the Church Courts for action against the rich adulterer.

The resistance grew in strength and found expression in vehement protests. Laud's policy could never have been enforced if he had not been assured of the support of the Crown. Parliament was bitterly hostile, the lawyers were angered at illegal and high-handed action, the landed gentry were alienated, and from the great mass of the people, especially in London, there was slowly rising a roar of discontent. But Laud was undeterred; resolutely he went on his way indifferent to hatred and unpopularity. The Church and Crown were now so closely associated that the fall of one must mean the ruin of the other. At last the storm burst, and loyalty to the king drew many who detested Laud to the Royal Standard. In the troubled years which followed men fought and died in defence of the Church and king, steadfast to the end in resisting the hatred directed against both. As they had stood together in days of prosperity, so now together Church and Crown were overwhelmed by the flood of anger and unpopularity they had evoked. Laud went to the block with the words "I was born and baptized in the bosom of the Church of England. In that profession I have ever since lived, and in that I am now come to die"; and some years later Charles met the same death with equal calm and dignity, forgiving those who had caused his death, and declaring: "He did not believe the happiness of people lay in sharing government, subject and sovereign being clean different."

It is not necessary to dwell on the relationship between the Church of England and the State during the Protectorate. Cromwell for his century was singularly tolerant of diversity in religious belief, but toleration was extended to neither Anglicans nor Roman Catholics. The massacre of Roman Catholics in Ireland is an indelible blot on a great name. In England episcopacy was abolished by law, the use of the Prayer Book was forbidden not only in churches but also in private houses under the penalty of a year's imprisonment; some three thousand clergy were ejected from their livings, many were imprisoned, others sought voluntary exile, many were in danger of actual starvation. The remainder of the clergy were hedged in with restrictions and threatened with severe penalties if they broke them. The Prayer Book Service for the burial of the dead was not allowed, and its use was harshly forbidden even at the burial of the body of Charles I at Windsor. No religious rite was allowed at a marriage; it was simply a civil ceremony conducted by a Justice of the Peace. Christmas Day was kept as a fast day. The utmost harshness was used by the triumphant Puritans not only to humiliate Anglicans, but also to banish and destroy their order and worship. The policy of repression was set forth in the Solemn League and Covenant which was imposed upon all Englishmen over eighteen years of age. After declaring that all who signed it would endeavour to bring the churches of God to such uniformity in religion that "we and our posterity after us may as brethren live in faith and love, and the Lord may delight to dwell in the midst of us," it continued: "That we shall in like manner without respect of persons, endeavour the extirpation of popery, prelacy (that is Church government by archbishops, bishops, their chancellors and commissaries, deans and chapters, archdeacons and all other ecclesiastical officers depending on that hierarchy), superstition, heresy, schism, profaneness, and whatsoever shall be found to be contrary to sound doctrine and the power of godliness." The persecution of the Church gained for it both respect and popularity. The hardness of the Puritan regime pressed on all sections of the nation, so when Cromwell died, the restoration of both Church and king was certain.

The Re-Establishment

The restoration of the king saw the re-establishment of the Church. The Statutes severing its connection with the State were quickly repealed. The bishops again took their seats in the House of Lords, the Convocations were summoned, and the work of revising the Prayer Book was undertaken by a committee representing both the Southern and Northern Provinces. In less than a month the revision was completed, some six hundred alterations were made, most of them of minor importance, and the Book thus amended was accepted by both Houses of the Convocations. There is no doubt that, whatever may have been the case with the earlier Prayer Books, the Book of 1662 was fully sanctioned and approved by the Church through its constitutional assemblies. After an interval of two months it was presented to Parliament; in neither House were the amendments debated, though the House of Commons passed a resolution affirming its right of discussion. On May 19th an Act of Uniformity was passed making the use of the new Book obligatory and ordering it to be read in all churches and chapels on St. Bartholomew's Day, 1662. It had thus the authority of both Church and State.

An immediate problem had to be faced. The Restoration led to the return to their benefices of over a thousand clergymen who had been ejected. But there were also still large numbers of Puritan and Presbyterian ministers occupying benefices which had become vacant through the death, resignation, or deprivation of the previous incumbent. It would have created a position impossible for the Church if among its ministers there were men who had never been episcopally ordained, who denied its doctrines, who denounced its worship as papistical and superstitious, and who refused to conform to its rules for reverence and good order. All these ministers were required to receive episcopal ordination and to declare their acceptance of the Prayer Book. Some twelve hundred refused, and were compelled to vacate their benefices. All honour to the men who for the sake of their convictions chose poverty and loss of position. But it is hard to say what other course could have been taken by Parliament. There would have been no chance of peace and order within the Church if some of its ministers were left free to speak of episcopacy as an invention of the devil, of the Prayer Book as a popish document, and of the surplice as a badge of Rome. As colleagues they would have angered the loyal clergy, and as parish priests they would have alienated faithful laymen who had suffered for their religion under the Puritan regime, and whose hardships had deepened their devotion to their Church.

Unhappily the State was not content with this. In violent reaction from the harshness of the rule of the Puritans and fearful lest they might rise again to power, Parliament passed a number of severely restrictive Acts. Henceforward the Puritans, once within the Church, became Nonconformists beyond its borders. Previously by their prophesyings and their system of classes they had worked within the Church in an attempt to change it in accordance with their views as to what was truly

Scriptural. Now Church and State saw it was useless to attempt to compel them to remain within the Church; and the Puritans for their part after the failure of the Savoy Conference retained little hope of making a home for themselves in the Church. They therefore formed congregations and Churches independent of the Church of England. But this did not save them from persecution. Parliament was afraid that they might prove a subversive element in the State, and to prevent this danger passed a series of enactments intended to weaken them and make them politically harmless. By the Corporation Act of 1661 all existing holders of municipal office had to take the oaths of allegiance and supremacy, and in the future holders of office had to receive the Sacrament within a year of their election; it was a detestable Act which encouraged hypocrisy and profaned the Holy Communion. In 1664 there followed the Conventicle Act which made every person present at a religious service other than that of the Church of England liable to fine and imprisonment, and on a third conviction to transportation. In 1665 the Five Mile Act was passed against Puritan ministers and schoolmasters; unless they took an oath denying the lawfulness of bearing arms against the king and against promoting changes in Church or State, they were not to come within five miles of any town in which they had acted as parsons. By these Acts it was intended to secure that national and local government was placed firmly in the control of the members of the Church of England, and at the same time to weaken and suppress nonconformity. The last of these Acts did much to deprive Puritans who were living in towns of education. The Acts were not mere formal gestures to satisfy the more extreme cavaliers; magistrates who had suffered during the Commonwealth saw they were enforced, and they were assisted by a crowd of informers and spies who sought for reward or revenge. "Some magistrates spent a good part of their lives surprising midnight conventicles; trapping teachers and clergymen who had strayed out of bounds; crowding the plague-stricken gaols with hundreds of priests and prophets, and thousands of men and women; creating day by day the martyrology of dissent, and the political tradition that has handed down through long generations of English Puritans an attitude of vigilant criticism and protest towards the powers that rule society and the State."[1]

[1] G. M. Trevelyan, "England Under the Stuarts," p. 362.

Though in the early years of the Restoration persecution of the Roman Catholics had ceased, they were viewed with great suspicion by both Anglicans and Dissenters; the latter would prefer to remain victims of intolerance rather than see Roman Catholics set free from disabilities by an inclusive Act of Toleration. After the Great Fire baseless charges were brought against "the Papists" for causing it. The increasing number of Roman Catholics at the Royal Court deepened suspicion. It is now known that the suspicions generally entertained of an attempt being made to establish Roman Catholicism were more than justified, for Charles had entered into a secret treaty with Louis, by which the French king had promised money and military aid to enable him to declare himself a Roman Catholic as the first step towards the conversion of England.

In 1673, largely as the result of Puritan agitation, a Test Act was passed to prevent Roman Catholics from holding office; it was ordered that every holder of office must receive the Holy Communion according to the rites of the Church of England, take the oath accepting the Royal Supremacy, and abjure the doctrine of transubstantiation, affirming that in the Sacrament after the Consecration there is the substance of bread and wine. This Act was made the more insulting by the regulation that certificates declaring that communion had been received must be obtained from the clergy. All these Acts of intolerance were hateful, whether directed against Romanist or Puritan. While nothing can be said in defence of them, the fears and passions of the age in which they were passed must be understood before we judge too harshly those responsible for them. On all sides there were rumours of plots; the Cromwellian regime was vividly in the minds of the mass of the people, and from mouth to mouth there went reports of papal intrigue. Titus Oates with the alleged Popish Plot had excited popular feeling to frenzy against the Roman Catholics. Only a few enlightened men knew the meaning of toleration, and even their interpretation of it would seem to us very narrow. Church and State alike accepted as natural a policy which now we should all condemn.

It was not only by measures against Puritans and Romanists that the State attempted to make the position of the Church secure. By the Licensing Act of 1662 it protected both Church and State from hostile broadsheets and pamphlets. The number of Master Printers was gradually to diminish until there were not more than twenty; every new appointment was to be made by the Archbishop of Canterbury and the Bishop of London; no book was to be published unless it had been passed by the civil or ecclesiastical censor; and there were to be no printing presses outside London, Oxford and Cambridge. With the intention of strengthening the Church a Royal Proclamation ordered the observance of previous Statutes which had made church attendance compulsory; those who abstained from public worship without good cause were to be fined a shilling for each offence. The same Proclamation condemned Sunday trading and dissolute behaviour.

The Church was not, however, completely restored to the position it had held in the past. The Ecclesiastical Courts were re-established, but the most unpopular of them—the Court of High Commission—was abolished though it was revived for a short time under James II. An Act of Parliament also declared illegal the canons passed by Convocation in 1640 and against which there had been strong protests. More important was the surrender by Convocation of its traditional right to tax the clergy. By a private agreement made between the Archbishop of Canterbury and the Chancellor, the Convocations gave up the privilege of taxing the clerical body. In the future the clergy with the rest of the realm would be taxed by Parliament. Though from a practical point of view there was everything to be said for bringing to an end what had become an anachronism, the new arrangement had serious results for the Church. As long as the clergy could only be taxed by themselves in Convocation, it had to be summoned regularly; when this privilege was surrendered, its meeting was no longer necessary for the financial machinery of the State. So from 1664 to 1689 Convocation did not sit, and in the following century its sittings were suspended for a hundred and fifty years; but this could not have been foreseen at the time when an agreement so much in accordance with common sense was reached.

The Restoration Church was wholehearted in its support of the Crown. There was no question of the Crown browbeating the Church as in Tudor days. The Church and the Crown acted together; the Church taught the duty of loyalty, and the Crown gave support and protection to the Church. Immediately after the Restoration, Parliament ordered the anniversary of the execution of Charles to be kept as a day of humiliation and mourning; two years later Convocation prepared forms of prayer for use on that day and on the anniversary of the Restoration. The earlier Form was entitled " A Form of Prayer with fasting to be used yearly upon the thirtieth of January, being the Day of the Martyrdom of the Blessed King Charles I to implore the mercy of God, that neither the guilt of that sacred and innocent blood, nor those other sins, by which God was provoked to deliver up both us, and our king, into the hands of cruel and unreasonable men, may at any time hereafter be visited upon us or our posterity " ; and the Minister was instructed to read the first and second parts of the Homily against disobedience or to preach " a sermon of his own composing upon the same Argument." The Homily in the most uncompromising manner declared the divine right of kings and the duty of passive obedience, and stigmatised rebellion as sinful at any time or under any circumstances.

Loyal as the Church was to the Crown in Stuart days it never degenerated into complete subservience. Archbishops Sheldon and Sancroft had both protested to Charles II against his manner of life. Stillingfleet had preached before him on the text " Lest any of you be hardened through the deceitfulness of sin." And when Charles was staying at Winchester, Canon Ken refused to allow Nell Gwynne to live in his house of residence—the closed-up door in the wall can still be seen through which Charles is supposed to have visited Nell when he was at the Deanery. To the credit of the king it should be added that when Ken was nominated to a bishopric, Charles agreed to the appointment with the remark, " Isn't he the little black man who refused a lodging to poor Nell ? " When James II revived the Court of High Commission Archbishop Sancroft made a public declaration that he would take no part in its proceedings. And when James issued his Declaration of Liberty of Conscience by which all penal laws in matters of religion and all tests and oaths were abolished, seven bishops headed by the Archbishop refused to read it in Church and presented a petition to the king giving their reasons why they could not do this. " This is the standard of rebellion " was the king's reply. " We will honour you, but we must fear God " was the answer. The imprisonment of the bishops made them the champions of public opinion which regarded the Declaration as an illegal instrument to prepare the way for the restoration of the Church of Rome. But though Sancroft had led the protest, he rebuked with great anger his chaplain for praying in Lambeth Palace

Chapel for William and Mary as King and Queen, saying that "as long as King James was alive no other persons could be sovereigns of the country."[1]

Erastianism Triumphant

With the accession of William and Mary a new chapter opened in the relation between Church and State. It was no longer possible to teach the divine right of kings and the duty of passive obedience, after a king had been deposed and another chosen in his place. Some of the bishops and clergy refused to accept the lawfulness of the change; Archbishop Sancroft and five other bishops were deprived for refusing to take the oath of allegiance and went into retirement; their example was followed by four hundred of the clergy. The bishops were deprived solely by the authority of the State, and appointment to sees not canonically vacant was contrary to Church law. Among the deprived was Ken, who wrote for the inscription on his tomb "uncanonically deprived." This secession of the non-jurors was a great blow to the Church. It lost some of the ablest and most devoted of the clergy, and their departure greatly weakened its resistance to the Erastianism which treated the Church as a department of the State. As a result of the Revolution much of the authority which had belonged to the Crown passed over to Parliament; the sovereignty of Parliament was in sight, though for another century it would be controlled or managed by the executive. It was in the future Parliament, and not the Crown, which controlled the Church. This was a constitutional change of vital importance; though more gradual and less sensational it eventually affected the freedom of the Church to an extent comparable only to the action of Henry VIII in annexing to the Crown powers previously possessed by the Pope. As long as Parliament consisted chiefly of Churchmen, it could still be treated as representing the laity of the Church, but if the House of Commons should become predominantly nonconformist or secularist, then a position of the utmost gravity to the Church would be created.

[1] See for much of this paragraph W. H. Hutton, "A History of the English Church from the Accession of Charles I to the Death of Anne," p. 232.

One of the immediate results of the Revolution was the passing of the Toleration Act. The Nonconformists had stood solid with the Anglicans in their opposition to the toleration which James had offered to all—for they saw this was really intended for the benefit of the Roman Catholics. Their resistance entitled them to consideration from the new regime. William at first was anxious to widen the borders of the Church so that room within it might be found for the Nonconformists. A Bill for Comprehension was passed by the House of Lords, but it was opposed so strongly by Convocation that it had to be dropped. If its proposals had been accepted they would have changed the whole character of the Church and its Prayer Book; comprehensiveness would have been purchased at the cost of catholicism; and one of the immediate results would have been very large secessions to the non-jurors. The well-intentioned proposals of the Bill were due to William's ignorance of the special nature of the Church of England. Instead of the Bill for Comprehension an Act of Toleration was passed; this allowed within certain conditions dissenters from the Established Church to worship in their own chapels without any penalty, and their ministers were freed from the limitations of the Five Mile Act. Though this was a step towards religious freedom, it was timid and hesitating—Nonconformists remained excluded from all public office for a century and a half. Happily in the next century these restrictions were largely ignored, and with general good will Acts of indemnity were passed to save Nonconformists from the penalties they had incurred by acceptance of public office. Roman Catholics and Unitarians were excluded from even the limited toleration granted by this Act.

The Church still had great political influence in the country, and the cry that "the Church is in danger" was a threat to the security of the Government. So much was this the case that in 1705 in Anne's reign both Houses of Parliament found it advisable to pass the following resolution that "the Church which was rescued from the extremest dangers by King William III of glorious memory, is now by God's blessing, under the happy reign of her Majesty, in a most safe and flourishing condition: and whoever goes about to suggest and insinuate that the Church is in danger under her Majesty's administration is an enemy to the Queen, the Church, and the Kingdom."[1] It was therefore important for the State to

[1] Quoted by Winston Churchill in "Marlborough," Vol. III, p. 36.

continue to use the Church for political ends, but the methods employed were different from those which once had been adopted. For many centuries the Crown had looked to the ranks of the clergy for its secretaries, treasurers and ambassadors. From time to time protests had been made by the laity against this policy, but with brief intervals this continued to be the practice until the eve of the Reformation. Since then it had been almost completely abandoned, though in 1621 Williams, Bishop of Lincoln, later Archbishop of York, was Lord Keeper; in 1636 Juxon of London was Lord Treasurer; and as late as 1711 Harley appointed Robinson of Bristol to the post of Lord Privy Seal. A few years later Bolingbroke intended to make Atterbury of Rochester Lord Privy Seal, but the ministry went out of office before this was done, though the bishop had prematurely given the order for a magnificent State carriage which was for many years an object of amusement and curiosity to Londoners. These were, however, rare survivals of an obsolete policy. The political influence of the episcopal bench was in future to be found in the House of Lords rather than in ministerial posts.

Though the Upper Chamber did not possess in the eighteenth century the power of the Lower, its importance was very great. A Government defeated in it would have suffered a serious blow; the ministry was, therefore, always anxious to have a secure majority of peers upon whom it could depend in any critical division. The House had a membership of about two hundred and twenty, and of these between a hundred and twenty and two hundred were regular in their attendance, so the votes of two archbishops and twenty-four bishops were of considerable value. The ministry of the day therefore did its best to nominate to vacant sees the men most likely to give it regular support. Occasionally however the Crown intervened decisively and made the appointment regardless of the advice of its ministers. Queen Anne was on the side of the Tories—she once said to the Duchess of Marlborough, "As to my saying the Church was in danger in the late reign I cannot alter my opinion. For though there was no violent thing done, everybody that will speak impartially must own that everything was tending towards the Whigs. And wherever this is I shall think the Church beginning to be in danger." During the next two reigns the bishops were deliberately chosen as supporters of the Whigs and with such care that in 1735 the high water mark of Whig control of the bench was reached when twenty-four episcopal suffrages were cast for the Government![1]

Usually the nominee of the ministry was appointed first to a diocese with a small income; if by attendance and vote in the Lords he proved he was a good and sound party man he could look forward with confidence to translation to one of the more important sees. Regular attendance was necessary if his hopes of preferment were to be realised. This meant that the bishops had to spend most of the year away from their dioceses. Usually they would go to their London house in October and remain there more or less continuously until Parliament adjourned in May; the summer months were given to their dioceses. During the time they spent in their dioceses they entertained in a truly royal manner. Parson Woodforde describes in his diary under the date of September 4th, 1783, a dinner given by the Bishop of Norwich in his palace. "There were twenty of us at the Table and a very elegant Dinner the Bishop gave us. We had 2 courses of 20 Dishes each course, and a Dessert after of 20 Dishes. Madeira, Red and White wines. The first Course amongst many other things were 2 Dishes of prodigious fine stewed carp and Trench and a fine Haunch of Venison. Among the second a fine Turkey Poult, Partridge, Pidgeon, and Sweetmeats. Dessert—among other things—Mulberries, Melon, Peaches, Nectarines and Grapes." A modern archbishop whose meagre ration makes entertaining on a large scale impossible feels a slight twinge of envy as he reads of those spacious days!

In the winter the country roads were so appalling that often episcopal visitation was impossible. Most of the bishops felt that they were more usefully employed in London, especially as many of them regarded their duty to the State as more important than their duty to their diocese. When age or ill-health made regular attendance in the Lords impossible we find apologetic letters written to the minister the bishop looked upon as his patron. For instance, in 1739 the Bishop of Chester writes to the Duke of Newcastle explaining that age (he was 72) and ill-health made it difficult for him to bear the long and cold journey to London, but heroically he adds, "If there be any necessity for personal attendance, I will venture all and be at the house in time though I travel but ten miles in the day." The House appreciated the attendance of the bishops,

[1] Norman Sykes, "The Church and State in the XVIII Century," p. 51.

and on one occasion adjourned over the Trinity Sunday week-end to enable them to travel to their dioceses for their ordinations and to return in time for the division the next week.[1]

The suspension of Convocation deprived the Church of its spiritual Parliament. The high church view of Convocation is clearly stated by Bishop Gibson in his Introductory Discourse to his Codex of the Canon Law of the English Church: "England is governed by two distinct Administrations—one Spiritual, for matters of a spiritual nature; and the other Temporal, for matters of a Temporal nature. And for the same ends, hath it two Legislatives—the one consisting of persons Spiritual, and the other of persons Temporal; whose business it is to frame the laws for the Government of Church and State: and these Laws being enacted and confirmed by the Prince, as Sovereign and Supreme Head, become obligatory to the people." But since the Reformation Convocation had lost much of its power. It was humiliated by Henry VIII, largely ignored by Edward VI's Council, abolished during the Commonwealth, and though revived at the Restoration it was enfeebled by the voluntary surrender of its powers of taxation, and for the greater part of the reigns of Charles II and James II it held no sitting sessions. The claim that it was a partner with Parliament in legislation had long been dropped. But it remained the constitutional council of the Church, to which the bishops and clergy were summoned to discuss matters that concerned its welfare, and its right to be consulted before Parliament legislated on ecclesiastical matters had been repeatedly recognised. In 1628 Charles I had issued a Royal Declaration in which he stated "that of our princely care that the churchmen may do the work which is proper unto them, the bishops and clergy from time to time in convocation upon their humble desire, shall have licence under our broad seal to deliberate of, and to do all such things as, being made plain by them, and assented unto by us, shall concern the settled continuance of the doctrine and discipline of the Church of England now established."

The suspension of a sitting Convocation for over a hundred and fifty years was largely due to the quarrelsome spirit of the Lower House of Canterbury: it had embarked on a series of acrimonious disputes with the Upper House, challenging the

[1] For much of the above paragraph I am indebted to Dr. Sykes' important book on "The Church and State in England in the XVIII Century," especially Chapter II.

authority of the archbishop, and advancing extreme Tory views.[1] When in 1717 it launched an attack on Bishop Hoadley, it was adjourned by high-handed action on the part of the Government. The York Convocation shared the same fate, though it had shown little interest in the controversies which were agitating so violently the Southern Houses; possibly there may have been at that time some truth in the caustic remark of Thomas Fuller that Convocation was like a clock, of which the face was York, but the works Canterbury! The suspension of the sittings of Convocation was a heavy blow to the Church. Some of the bishops complained that it deprived them of a useful field for developing qualities of debate which might serve them well in the House of Lords: in fact one of the bishops gave as his excuse for not speaking in Parliament that he had no training in Convocation.[2] But the real losses were graver. The gulf between the bishops and the rest of the clergy became wider, as there were no longer opportunities for discussing together matters which concerned them all. Most serious of all, the suppression of Convocation led to the assumption that Parliament was the assembly of the Church with the bishops in the Lords and the laity in the Commons, and therefore competent to make decisions on spiritual as well as temporal affairs. The Church came to be regarded simply as a department of the State under the control of Parliament. There were a few churchmen who realised how greatly the Church was injured. Boswell discovered this to his cost when, as an illustration of the absurdity of stories which were told of Dr. Johnson, he said to the doctor that it was reported that he would face a battery of guns in defence of Convocation. "Little did I apprehend that he had actually said this: but I was soon convinced of my error; for with a determined look, he thundered out, 'And would I not, Sir? Shall the Presbyterian Kirk of Scotland have its General Assembly, and the Church of England be denied its Convocation?'"

The State and the Parish

So far I have written chiefly of the relationship between Church and State on what would now be called the highest level, namely, of disputes between the hierarchy and the great men of State,

[1] For a full account, see E. Carpenter's "Thomas Tenison," pp. 248–271.
[2] Sykes. "The Church and State in England in the xviii Century," p. 313.

and between the Convocations and Parliament. But on another level Church and State were all the time quietly and harmoniously working together. The parishes—and most of them were rural—were comparatively little affected by the storms which occasionally raged overhead, and as through the changes of the Reformation most parish priests continued their pastoral work without interruption, so, in the eighteenth century parish, Church and State worked smoothly and happily with only the occasional conflicts which are bound to occur in all human relations. In various ways the State used the parish priest, the parochial machinery, the pulpit and even the church door for the purposes of good government. In the Middle Ages the parish was primarily ecclesiastical. " As a unit of civil government, the parish began its history only after the Reformation."[1] The Tudors used it for poor relief, and in 1572 gave it power to impose a compulsory rate and to appoint overseers. It developed gradually an organisation used for civil purposes such as the upkeep of highways.

In most of our old churches there can still be found many documents which witness to this close co-operation of Church and State. The ancient registers are the most obvious illustration of this. For several centuries the Church did the work of registration of births, marriages and deaths for the State. In the Middle Ages it was not customary to keep registers, but in 1538 Thomas Cromwell ordered every parson to enter in a book christenings, weddings and burials of his parish. This order was imperfectly observed: many of the entries seem to have been made on loose sheets of papers, which were often lost or destroyed; about eight hundred registers survive from this period, but there are few original entries; most of them seem to be in the hands of the incumbents of 1598, in which year Queen Elizabeth ordered[2] that all names on the earlier registers should be copied on parchment, especially from the first year of her reign. From that time the registers were kept with greater care, though many by now have perished through damp or age. From those which survive it is possible to learn much of the history of a parish and its people. One of the most interesting set of entries I know is to be found in the registers at Hursley: Richard Cromwell is described on his

[1] D. Lindsay Keir, " The Constitutional History of Modern Britain, 1485–1937," p. 128.

[2] This was in approval of a provincial constitution of Canterbury of the previous year.

marriage in 1649 as "The Right Worthy Richard Cromwell Esquire"; in 1654 as "The Rt. Hon. the Lord Richard Cromwell"; in 1658 as "his High: Richard, Lord Protector of England Scotland and Ireland"; but in 1712, the entry of his burial describes him simply as "Richard Cromwell Esquire." By an Act in 1678 the clergy were made responsible for the enforcement of a measure of indirect taxation for the encouragement of the woollen trade, for they had to declare that the Act had been observed by which under a penalty of £5 "no corpse of any person (except those who shall die of plague) shall be buried in any shirt, shift, sheet, or shroud of anything . . . other than that made of sheeps wool only," and the fact of "burial in woollen" had to be entered in the register.

In days when few could read and nearly all came to church the pulpit was invaluable for instruction and information. There were times, as we have seen, when the Government of the day either silenced the pulpit or tuned it to its own ends. Homilies were provided and instructions issued by the Council as to the subjects on which the clergy could preach most profitably to the good of the common weal. In the old parish chests which can still be found in many churches there survive proclamations ordering national days of prayer, humiliation and thanksgiving: exhortations from the Government for amendment of morals, especially for less swearing: and briefs with the royal arms asking for money for some good cause, such as the relief of those who had suffered by flood or fire—these were read from the pulpit at the end of the service, and the clerk stood by the door to take the collection. "Before the people of the countryside were generally literate, any notice, information, or advice, which the central authorities thought well to bring to public attention, could best be published by reading in church. National events were so registered in proclamations; ecclesiastical decrees and citations were made public in the same way, and Parliament often by express enactment, ordered notices affecting the parish generally to be read out in church, when all the parishioners were, or should have been present."[1]

The pulpit of the parish church was in the seventeenth and eighteenth centuries the substitute for our daily press and

[1] W. E. Tate, "The Parish Chest," p. 151. An interesting book on the inter-relation of Church and State in parochial administration.

wireless, and, especially since 1837,[1] the great door of the church porch, still covered with nail marks, was the board for official notices which concerned the parish.

The incumbent and churchwardens had special responsibility for the poor of the parish. To describe the forms this took would require a separate volume. It is sufficient here to say that the State expected the officers of the parish to assist in providing charity for the poor and destitute and in suppressing vagrancy. The harshness with which the State until comparatively recent years treated the poor is one of the dark blots in our English history. An occasional entry in the records of vestry meetings shows how hardly beggars and the destitute were treated, and how they were passed from place to place lest they should become a charge upon the parish. But the duty of the Church to the poor was always taught; at his ordination the deacon has to promise the bishop that he will "search for the sick, poor and impotent people of the parish, to intimate their estates, names, and places where they dwell unto the curate, that by his exhortation they may be relieved with the alms of the parishioners and others"; and the bishop at his consecration promises to show himself "merciful for Christ's sake to poor and needy people, and to all strangers destitute of help"; and at the Holy Communion the "Alms for the Poor" are given and offered. In one of the canons of 1603 the duty of helping the poor and needy is insisted upon, and in the churchwarden's accounts of the eighteenth century there are frequent entries dealing with the relief of the poor, money grants, payments for food and clothing, as well as for the cost of their burial.

Many secular matters were dealt with by the parochial machinery. The minute books and other documents which have been preserved in the parish chest still found in many parishes, show how various were the duties which fell upon incumbent, churchwardens and the vestry. Regulations dealing with open field cultivation, the allotment of lands to different farms, the responsibility for the keeping clean of the ditches, were often decided at meetings held in the church. Notice of a bill of enclosure was given in the parish church, to the dismay of those who often found that without their previous knowledge their common rights on which they largely depended for their livelihood, were likely to be taken from them.

[1] In this year an Act was passed forbidding the publication of notices on secular affairs during the service. The practice then became common of posting public notices on the church door.

A few hours spent in looking over the records of an ancient parish church will reveal how Church and State were closely associated for many centuries in local government. It is hardly an exaggeration to say that the decisions made at Westminster would have been largely ineffective if there had been no parochial machinery through which they could be conveyed to an illiterate population. In the parish even more than in Parliament there can be seen the close co-operation between Church and State. It became even closer as the clergy gradually rise from the low social position they had occupied in the seventeenth century. As they take their place as country gentlemen they become to a large extent officers of State, though retaining their independence. "They took their share in every side of the work of each of the two fundamental organisations of English local government, the parish and the county. On the county bench the clerical Justice of the Peace was a prominent figure during the eighteenth century, often acting as chairman of quarter sessions, and displaying not only an unusual knowledge of the law, but an even more unusual humanitarian spirit, though his zeal as a magistrate was apt at times to outrun his charity as a Christian minister."[1]

The Nineteenth Century

In the following century the State shows diminishing interest in the affairs of the Church. The Church retires to the background of the political life of the nation compared with the place it once had held in it. It is only necessary to contrast the small space given to the Church in a history of the nineteenth century, with the chapters it occupies in those dealing with earlier periods. This does not mean that the Church had lost all influence either in the parishes or over the lives of individuals. The churches were usually full on Sundays, and most of the people were still nominally members of the Church. It was possible for a historian of the last twenty years of the century to write that "no one will ever understand Victorian England who does not appreciate that among highly civilised, in contradistinction to more primitive, countries it was one of the most religious that the world has known."[2] And this was

[1] D. Lindsay Keir. "The Constitutional History of Modern Britain, 1485–1937," p. 428.

[2] R. C. K. Ensor, "England, 1870–1914," p. 137.

true of most of the century. But the State is no longer occupied with the affairs of the Church as in the past. For most of the century Church and State each go their own way; the Church occasionally resisting what it regarded as dangerous attacks on its privileges and rights, and the State looking upon the Church as a somewhat awkward and badly managed branch of the civil administration. From time to time, however, the State actively intervened; the most important occasion was in the years 1836–40 when a number of valuable administrative reforms were carried, and the Ecclesiastical Commission was brought into existence. Much later, in 1860, the Public Worship Regulation Act was an unfortunate and futile interference of the State in an attempt to regulate the worship of the Church.

The nineteenth century saw a gradual decrease in the privileges which once were possessed by the Church. It lost its special position in national and local government, and in the universities and in education. The Test Acts were at last abolished and public offices were open to Nonconformists without the danger of incurring heavy penalties. After a long struggle the universities were freed from religious tests and Nonconformists could enter them and take degrees without difficulty. Compulsory Church rates were abolished, and Nonconformists allowed to be buried by their ministers in churchyards. Roman Catholics were freed from various disabilities, and, with the exception of the Lord Chancellorship, all government offices were opened to them. These reforms gave freedom to the different Christian Churches to hold their worship, to teach, and to take their full share in the social, political and religious life of the nation. The long struggle between the Churches had at last taught the nation the value of toleration, and that without it there could be no true civic freedom.

The Church also lost its privileged position in marriages and in education. In 1836 Parliament passed an Act allowing civil marriages, and dispensing Nonconformists from having their banns called in churches. Twenty years later a more serious step was taken by the passing of the Divorce Act. Before this divorce had been only possible by a special and expensive Act of Parliament, but in the future secular courts could grant divorce to the man for the adultery of his wife, and to the woman for adultery and cruelty on the part of her husband. This new Act made it plain that the laws of the Church and State were not identical, for it allowed a clergyman to refuse to take the marriage of divorced persons if one of them was the guilty party. This was the first stage in a process which has gradually brought the marriage laws of the Church and of the State into opposition.

Education had also in the past been almost entirely the responsibility of the Church. It was the Church which first had made provision for the education of the poor; but it was impossible for it to cover the whole country with its schools, and to meet the heavy expenditure required by an ever-rising standard of education. Moreover on the part of the Nonconformists there were strong objections to their children being compelled to attend the schools in which Church teaching was exclusively given. By the 1870 Act, State schools, under the name of Board Schools, came into existence, and the continuance of the Church Voluntary Schools created the Dual System. As the years passed an increasing number of children attended schools in which the religious teaching, though acceptable to the Nonconformists, was satisfactory neither to Anglicans nor Roman Catholics.

The political disputes between the Church and Nonconformists, which had their origin in the intolerance both of the Churchmen and Puritans of the seventeenth century, continued to injure throughout the nineteenth century the cause of religion. The political parties used these quarrels for their own advantage. Churchmen and Nonconformists separated into the Conservative and Liberal camps. The demand for disestablishment and disputes over the schools were the causes of bitter controversy. Nonconformity was the background of Liberalism, while the Church was taunted with being the "Conservative party at prayer." It was assumed that every Nonconformist was a Liberal, and every churchman a Conservative; there were exceptions to this, for it was a devoted Churchman, Mr. Gladstone, who disestablished the Church of Ireland; but, generally speaking, religious and political preferences coincided. Anthony Trollope in his autobiography says that when in 1868 he was standing as a Liberal candidate for Beverley he proposed to go to the Minster on Sunday; but his chief supporter told him it would be useless, as the Church party were all certain to support the Conservative, "so I stayed away and omitted my prayers. No Church of England church in Beverley would on such an occasion have welcomed a Liberal candidate."

In the nineteenth century there was taking place within the

Church a revival which already has had great, and may have decisive, influence on the relationship between Church and State. The Oxford Movement renewed the conception of the Church as a spiritual society with a divine origin and vocation. At the end of the eighteenth century John Wesley had brought the Gospel to multitudes who were living in paganism; in the first quarter of the nineteenth century the Clapham sect not only cultivated personal piety, but obtained through Parliament the abolition of the slave trade; and later another Evangelical, Lord Shaftesbury, succeeded in persuading Parliament to remove some of the worst crimes of the industrial revolution. But neither the Clapham sect nor Shaftesbury attached much importance to the Church as a divine society; their religion chiefly stressed the relation between the individual and his Maker. The contribution which the Oxford Movement made to the Church was that it proclaimed that it was the historic Catholic Church, the chosen body through which Christ worked in this nation. Those who accepted this view no longer thought of the Church of England either as founded at the Reformation or as a department of State, but as possessing a supernatural life of its own independent of the State. One of the first results of this revival of the sense of a corporate spiritual life was the restoration of the sittings for debate of the Convocations. Since 1717 they had formally met at the commencement of Parliament, and then had adjourned without the transaction of any business until at the end of the session they were prorogued by the archbishop. There was a vigorous agitation in favour of Convocation meeting for business; after some hesitation Bishop Wilberforce of Winchester came out strongly in favour of this course. But the archbishop hesitated, and Prime Ministers of both parties withheld permission. "Nothing shows more clearly the subjection of the Church of England to the State than the situation in 1853. A Prime Minister well disposed to the Church is so apprehensive of danger, or at least disquiet, if the smallest measure of self-government should be granted, that he refuses to allow the synodical assembly of the Church to debate or even to ask leave to debate, beyond a single day's sitting, lest Puseyites, Liberals, and Evangelicals should bring a disturbing element into Parliamentary politics."[1] But at last Lord Aberdeen changed his mind and allowed Convocation to meet for the

[1] F. Warre Cornish, "The English Church in the Nineteenth Century," p. 41.

transaction of business which could not be properly discussed by any other body. This took place on February 6th, 1855. It was felt at the time that a body consisting solely of clergy could not fully represent the Church of England; there were prolonged discussions over this, and it was not until 1885 that the constitution of a House of Laymen was agreed upon; the first meeting of the Canterbury House was held in the following year, but six years passed before a similar House met in York.

The centuries since the repudiation of papal supremacy show remarkable contrasts in the relations between Church and State. At first the Church is under the personal control of the Crown; but soon the hostility of Parliament to both the king and the Church forces them into alliance for self-defence. With the constitutional Revolution of 1688 power gradually passes from the Crown to Parliament, and by the eighteenth century the supremacy of Parliament has been substituted for the supremacy of the Crown. But the nineteenth century saw a great awakening of the Church to its spiritual heritage. Aware that it had an independent life of its own, it became restive over its subordination to the State. Tension between Church and State increases as the State becomes more powerful and secular, and the Church more aware of its divine origin and mission.

V

CHURCH AND STATE IN THE TWENTIETH CENTURY

THE first half of the twentieth century has seen remarkable changes in Church and State. The influence of the Church on national life has decreased, but at the same time it has become more conscious of its spiritual rights as the divine society through which Christ works. The State, on the other hand, has gained unprecedented power and intervenes actively in almost every department of national life.

The Great Leviathan

In pre-Reformation days Parliament was powerless when confronted by an alliance between the Church and the Crown. At the Reformation the Crown and Parliament together asserted their supremacy against the clerical element in the Church. Later Parliament secured the supremacy once possessed by the Crown. To-day Parliament on account of the amount of legislation which requires enactment and subsequent administration has abdicated some of its authority to an executive which steadily increases in power. The business of Parliament is now largely arranged by the Government, and little room is left for initiative by private members. But in the last resort the executive is controlled by the House of Commons, and illegal action can always be checked by an appeal to the Courts of Justice.

Either through the agency of Parliament or of the executive, the State to a degree hitherto unknown in English history has extended its authority in every direction. The old liberal conception of the State has long vanished—its action is no longer confined to the preservation of good order and the protection of the individual citizen from violence. Year by year it increases its power and enters into fields until recently occupied by private enterprise and individual effort. The change, revolutionary in nature, from a negative to a positive conception of the duties and responsibilities of the State, has been hastened by two great wars. The necessity of rapid action when the nation was fighting for its very life, and the vital importance of making full and equitable use of all the resources of the nation, resulted in the setting up of a huge bureaucracy, which through a vast army of civil servants and by a never ending spate of orders and regulations, now casts like a gigantic octopus its acquisitive tentacles into every nook and cranny of industrial, agricultural, educational, and even domestic life. In the last few years over twenty-five thousand orders have been issued. Parliament itself is unable to control the formidable monster it has created, and its activities have not been reduced by the end of the war. In Tudor days State interference was often autocratic and capricious, but usually its action was negative, and only a small minority came under its tyranny; its edicts passed over the heads of ordinary citizens, and struck at the great and powerful. To-day the new Totalitarian State for good or for ill, and often unquestionably for good, regulates and plans the lives of all its subjects.

Such an extension of the power and activities of the State is bound to affect the work of the Church. England so far has escaped the hostile action of a State determined to injure the Church. On the Continent religious persecution, which until recently civilisation seemed to have outgrown, has struck hard at both Protestant and Catholic Churches. In Great Britain the growth of State power makes itself felt on the Church in a different way. Gradually and almost inevitably, and without any hostile intent, the State takes over work which used to be the responsibility of the Church, and squeezes it out of fields which once it had occupied. Education, the relief of the poor, help for the unemployed, welfare work of various kinds, clubs for youth, and most of the duties of the old vestry have been taken over by the State. Usually this has meant gain in efficiency, for the material resources of the State far exceed those possessed by any voluntary societies, but the Church has been crowded out of spheres of work previously regarded as especially belonging to it. Only in one direction has the State increased the social work of the clergy, and that is by the enormous number of forms and papers concerning pensions, grants, and applications of all kinds, which must be signed or witnessed by a minister of religion, a doctor, or a magistrate! In large parishes an appreciable amount of the time of the clergy is occupied in dealing with these papers.

Elsewhere reduction is very notable in the number of public and semi-public duties for which the clergy were once responsible. This is no disadvantage if it enables the clergy to concentrate on their special duties as the spiritual pastors of their people.

Political Weakness of the Church

The Church meantime has become politically weaker both in Parliament and in the country.

(1) In the eighteenth century the bishops looked upon attendance at the Lords as one of the most important of their duties. During most of the nineteenth century their attendance was fairly regular, and on great occasions the episcopal benches were crowded. In the debates on Church Bills some of the bishops took an active part, both speaking and voting. But the House is never a very easy place for bishops who are accustomed both to a different style of oratory and a different kind of audience. Archbishop Benson in 1884 told a brother bishop: "I had to speak in the House of Lords last night. It was a really terrible place for the unaccustomed. Frigid impatience and absolute good will, combined with a thorough conviction of the infallibility of laymen (if not too religious) on all sacred subjects are the tone, morale, and reason of the House as a living being."[1] Though the bishops wear their robes they must not preach, nor will they find their opinions received with the same agreement as in their diocesan conferences. In the Lords rhetoric and fluency are suspect, though the House prefers a speaker who does not keep his eyes the whole time on his manuscript; and it will always listen to a member who knows his subject and speaks out directly and audibly. The House likes best a speech delivered in conversational tones, with flashes of humour, well informed and not too long; in fact as different as can be from the ordinary sermon. No bishop to-day is likely to bring upon himself the rebuke described by Greville: "A certain bishop in the House of Lords rose to speak, and announced that he would divide what he had to say into twelve parts, when the Duke of Wharton interrupted him, and begged he might be indulged for a few minutes, as he had a story to tell which he could only introduce at that moment. A drunken fellow was passing by St. Paul's at night

[1] A. C. Benson, "The Life of Edward White Benson" (Abridged Edition), p. 294.

and heard the clock slowly chiming twelve. He counted the strokes, and when it had finished looked towards the clock and said, 'Damn you! Why couldn't you give us all that at once?' That was the end of the bishop's oratory!"[1] It is not bishops alone who are sometimes nonplussed by the Upper House; often new members from the Lower House are clearly disconcerted at the silence which follows their rhetoric, at the bored courtesy with which their most provocative statements are received, and at the low murmur which marks the end of their speech, and which will be described next morning by *The Times* as "cheers." Few bishops have the time, with their increased diocesan work, to attend the House so regularly that they become really familiar with its ways.

During this century there has been a marked decrease in episcopal attendance; though the same could be said of the lay peers, for out of a total membership of over six hundred not more than fifty to sixty attend regularly, and even on a great occasion the members would rarely reach the two hundred mark. Archbishop Davidson was one of the most regular of members; only absence from home, illness, or the most urgent business kept him away. He was a real House of Lords man. He valued his membership as an opportunity of expressing the mind of the Church on some of the subjects which were debated, and also for the opportunities it gave him of contact with the lay peers in the library or lobbies. He was not an eloquent speaker, but his common sense, practical wisdom, and his long experience of public affairs always gained for him an attentive hearing. He made his influence felt not only in public debate, but in private counsel with the leaders of both parties. His influence in the Lords has never been approached by any other member of the Bench. Archbishop Lang had greater gifts of oratory, and his speeches on important occasions made a deep impression. His speech urging the Lords not to reject Mr. Lloyd George's budget was both courageous and eloquent. When he became Archbishop he told me he did not propose to attend the House as regularly as his predecessor "who," he said, "would go there if the heavens were falling"; but as a matter of fact he became very regular in his attendance and frequently intervened in the debates. Archbishop Temple did not often speak in the House; he found in war time regular attendance was very difficult,

[1] "The Greville Diary," October 8th, 1920: Vol. I., p. 384. (Edited by Philip Whitwell Wilson.)

as he was overwhelmed with every kind of problem during his brief archiepiscopate; when he did speak he was listened to with interest and attention. When Bishop Hensley Henson of Durham spoke the House generally filled; he rarely convinced, but his brilliancy and his command of language were greatly admired. One of the most regular of the lay peers said after listening to him, "I always enjoy listening to the little man; I wouldn't miss it for anything, but I am damned if I shall ever vote with him!"

When some important subject is under discussion one at least of the archbishops or bishops is usually present, and if the debate is of exceptional interest, there may be half a dozen bishops or more on their benches; and when the Prayer Book was debated there was a full attendance of bishops. But politically the attendance and votes of the bishops are no longer of importance, though on one occasion they excited considerable influence in a grave constitutional crisis. It looked as if the Parliament Bill of 1911, reducing the powers of the House of Lords, would be rejected; this would have meant in all probability the creation of five hundred new peers who would carry the Bill within a few weeks of its re-introduction. Towards the close of the debate, Archbishop Davidson in a speech of only a few minutes, gave his reasons for voting with the Government. The Archbishop of York and eleven bishops followed him into the Lobby in support of the Bill, and afterwards several peers said that this speech had persuaded them to vote for it. As it was the Bill was only carried by a small majority. Occasionally, but rarely, the Whips make enquiries as to which way the bishops are likely to vote, though often they are consulted before a Bill is introduced which might affect the Church. Only once have I been urged by the Whips to vote, and that was under unusual circumstances; shortly after I had become a member of the House, another bishop and I were listening in a small House to a dull debate; one of the Government Whips asked me if I was intending to vote; I said "No," as I had no interest in the Bill. He replied that the Government would be very grateful if I would do so, and also ask my colleague to do likewise; they were indifferent as to which way we voted, but if we did not vote there would not be the necessary quorum of thirty, and the Bill would then have had to be postponed to another session! While the bishops can still make useful speeches on matters of which they have some special knowledge, their political influence no longer has its old importance.

In the House of Commons the decline in the political influence of the Church has been equally marked. It cannot now be described as a House of Church laymen. At the Reformation it consisted exclusively of members of the Church of England. At the Restoration it had a few members who were not Anglicans, but then and for the next two and a half centuries the overwhelming majority of its members were Churchmen. With the removal of religious disabilities Nonformists, Roman Catholics, Jews and agnostics were elected to Parliament. To-day Churchmen are in a small minority both in the Government and in the House of Commons; it is even possible that Churchmen, Nonconformists, and Roman Catholics taken together might now prove to be a minority compared with the members who stand apart from all institutional religion. The House of Commons is not unfriendly either to religion or to the Church, but it cannot reasonably be expected to take an active interest in the affairs of a Church to which only a minority of its members are attached. This is a grave matter for the Established Church which is compelled to ask Parliamentary approval for many necessary reforms.

(2) The political influence of the Church in the constituencies is also less than it was in the nineteenth century. Controversies over the schools and the dread that the Church of England might share the fate of the Church of Ireland by disestablishment, kept the clergy within the Conservative fold. In the eighteenth century the Whiggism of the bishops in the Lords was not really representative of the Church of England; most of the clergy and laity were born and bred Conservatives. All through the nineteenth century the influence of the parochial clergy was on the side of the Conservatives; the political sermon became rare; though it was apparently more common among the Roman Catholic priests in Ireland, and the Nonconformists in England and Wales than it was among the Anglican clergy of the last quarter of the century. Only once have I heard a political sermon during an election—and that strangely enough was by a future archbishop—Cosmo Lang, during the time he was vicar of Portsea. The Conservative candidate had agreed to all the demands of the local brewers. On the following Sunday, immediately before polling day, Dr. Lang exhorted a large congregation to show their independence of the Conservative party. It was generally thought that this sermon had a decisive influence on the election. But though political sermons

were rare, the influence of most clergy both in town and country was used on behalf of the Conservatives.

In the twentieth century a definite opinion has been formed against using the pulpit for party purposes, and most of the clergy have scrupulously avoided appearing on political platforms. Moreover the clergy are no longer of one opinion about the merits of the parties. With the collapse of Liberalism the political foe of the Church has gone; fear of its victory is now no reason for voting for the other party. Many of the clergy, especially those who have worked in the great industrial cities, are in sympathy with the Labour party, and some of them are as ready to support it by speech and vote as their predecessors supported Conservatism. William Temple was for many years a member of the Labour party, and though I never joined the party as a young curate I occasionally spoke on its platform in support of social reform. Temple's political influence was considerable, especially over the younger men and women. His speeches and his writings led many to support Labour, long after he had given up his own membership of the Party. A reviewer of his "Life" in *The Times Literary Supplement* wrote: "The sweeping Labour victory in the General Election of 1945 will certainly not be counted least among the forces that have shaped contemporary British life; and without consciously intending it, William Temple probably contributed as much to that result as any one man . . . to him as much as to any man is due the fact that on July 5th, 1945, hundreds of thousands of middle class homes decided to 'give labour a chance' . . . although he always distinguished the Labour movement from the Labour party, he made the Labour party respectable."[1]

The happier relationships with Nonconformists have also helped to turn the Church from political partisanship. Disestablishment and religious education are no longer burning controversies which make co-operation impossible between Churchmen and Nonconformists. On a large number of subjects they can act together and frequently join in deputations to Ministers of State on moral and social problems which areof equal concern to all Christians. This is a most welcome development which would have been quite impossible at the beginning of the century. The political influence of the Churches is not used now in rivalry, but together for the same ends. Representa-

[1] August 28th, 1948.

tion made unitedly by the different Churches carries much greater weight than that by a Church acting by itself. The Churches united in policy may be successful, where divided they would fail.

(3) One of the chief causes for decline in the political influence of the Church is due to the decrease in its own membership. In the past politicians, especially when engaged in a contested election, were anxious to enlist the support of the clergy and the leading Church laity who were in touch Sunday by Sunday with a large number of those whose votes they were canvassing. Even if the Sunday congregations were apathetic over the election, a careless speech or an unwise pledge might awaken them to active hostility. The Conservative candidate could not always safely assume that every Churchman would take the trouble to go to the poll, and a number of abstentions might be fatal to victory; and the Liberal, though he could not expect to gain the Church vote *en bloc*, might with care avoid the whole of it being cast against him. But now with small congregations in most places of worship, the candidate finds he can disregard the views either of church or chapel, and concentrates on making his appeal to the great mass of the constituents. The one exception he must make is with the Roman Catholics; their congregations instructed by their bishops and priests, will vote solidly for the candidate who appears to be most likely to favour their Church.

Adverse Legislation

This decline in the political influence of the Church has weakened its power of resisting changes which might injure its work. A formidable list of such legislation in the present century might easily be compiled. Much of it was not deliberately hostile to the Church, but was intended to remove anomalies and grievances, or to improve social conditions. But the disestablishment and disendowment of the four Welsh dioceses were the result of a long agitation directed against the Church; and the earlier Education Acts were the result of Nonconformist opposition to the voluntary schools which were considered to give unfair advantages to the Church. These Acts and their administration have reduced very considerably the number of voluntary schools, so that it is now Anglicans and Roman Catholics who suffer from a sense of grievance in that they have to pay for the upkeep of schools in which the religion taught is satisfactory to the Nonconformists and not to themselves. But later Acts were passed for the purpose of improved education, without any intention of inflicting injury on the Church, and the Act of 1945 is based on an agreed settlement between Churchmen and Nonconformists on the religious teaching under a national system of education. The taking of so many of the old Grammar Schools from Church management, and the unjust prohibition against any of the clergy teaching in them when they have come under State control are the aftermath of ancient controversies.

Legislation has also reduced the income of the Church, though the Acts which were responsible for this were not anti-Church measures. The payment of tithe had for centuries been a cause of angry dispute between the clerical tithe owner and his parishioners; its abolition was therefore in the long run a gain to the Church; but it meant that at the next vacancy there would be a reduction of 20 per cent. in the income of parishes where tithe had been paid in the past to the incumbent. This has caused severe financial loss in many of the country parishes. Mining royalties had also been a cause of offence; their abolition was welcomed, especially by the clergy who had to work in mining districts, but they involved a loss of many millions to the Church. Again, the nationalisation of railways and the conversion of local loans to holdings with lower rates of interest have reduced considerably the financial resources of the Church.

Among the laws passed this century which have had an adverse effect on the relationship between Church and State, the Divorce Act of 1937 stands in a category of its own. It carries much further the Divorce Act of 1843; this had been defended as not really departing from the scriptural teaching on divorce. But no such case can be made for the more recent Act. The Church teaches that marriage is "a lifelong and indissoluble union for better or for worse of one man with one woman to the exclusion of all other on either side." The new Act allows divorce not only for adultery but for desertion, cruelty, incurable insanity, and on a petition on the part of the wife on the grounds of various forms of bestiality. The State has to legislate for all its citizens whether they are Christians or not. There is little doubt that the Divorce Act of 1937 met with the approval of the country as a whole. It made divorces more easy, and their number has greatly increased. It also made deeper the cleavage between Church and State, for the marriage law of the Church remains unchanged. It has made it clear beyond all misunderstanding that the laws of Church and State are not identical; what is allowed by the State is condemned by the Church. The Act recognises this by Section 12 which reads, "No clergyman of the Church of England or of the Church of Wales shall be compelled to solemnize the marriage of any person whose former marriage has been dissolved on any ground and whose former husband or wife is still living, or to permit the marriage of any such person to be solemnized in the Church or Chapel of which he is the minister." On this Mr Arthur Macmillan comments, "This provision appears to us to be supremely important; it is not only a full recognition by Parliament of the right of the Church to decide for herself on the question of re-marriage after divorce, but it also recognises that Parliament legislates independently of, and possibly contrary to, the laws of the Church."[1] The Church asserts its law by refusing to marry those whom the State permits to re-marry. The refusal is often a great shock to many who had never realised that the law of Church and State are not the same, and that the Church has a discipline of its own. The tension thus created between Church and State, and still more between the clergy and the loosely attached layman, may eventually result in a renewed demand for disestablishment. It is argued that an established Church has no right to oppose the wishes of the majority of the nation, and to refuse what the State permits. But though the Church cannot expect to impose its own laws upon citizens who do not belong to it, it has the right to exercise discipline over its own members. This right it must maintain at all costs. Archbishop Davidson speaking in 1920 in the House of Lords on a Divorce Bill, declared: "I yield to none in my sense of the value to the nation of the Establishment, for which I care with my whole heart: but there are higher considerations even than that if you do force us into the position of loyalty to the one thing or of loyalty to the other thing."[2]

Life and Liberty

The most serious disadvantage suffered by the Church through the increasing volume of business before Parliament and its own political weakness, was the difficulty in persuading the House of Commons to treat Church affairs as of sufficient importance to make time for their consideration. The time table

[1] A. T. Macmillan, "What is Marriage?" p. 117.
[2] G. K. A. Bell, "Randall Davidson," Vol. II., p. 1000.

of Parliament is always a problem for those who have to arrange its business. It is now very rarely that a Bill not sponsored by the Government has any chance of finding its way to the Statute Book. Bills introduced by private members have little hope of passing if they are controversial; and even if they are uncontroversial they can easily be blocked or talked out by prejudiced individuals. This was the fate of many Church Bills; they were either crowded out session after session through lack of time, or they were deliberately talked out by a small group who disliked the Church and purposed by their tactics to force Churchmen to ask for disestablishment.

At the end of the last century Archbishop Benson, after repeated failures, managed to secure the passing of a Clergy Discipline Bill; he could hardly have done this if it had not been for the help of Mr. Gladstone who was then in opposition. He was less fortunate with a Bill intended to remove some glaring abuses in patronage: "its enemies were however vigorous, and after two days spent on the first few clauses dealing with patronage, it was plain that the obstructive tactics of the so-called defenders of property could only be defeated by the Government taking up the Bill and either devoting a great deal of time to it or sacrificing a large portion of it."[1] Within a few years the difficulties of gaining a place for a Church Bill were far greater. Bills were held up for years, until they were sometimes abandoned in despair. It was not so much deliberate hostility, as lack of interest and pressure of other work which blocked the way to Church reform. "A bill to fix the stipend of the archdeacon of Cornwall required nine successive sessions for its passage into law. In thirty-three years, though only one Church Bill was negatived, nearly two hundred—six-sevenths of the whole—had to be dropped for lack of time."[2] The Church wanted these reforms; it was criticised bitterly by its enemies for tolerating ancient abuses and anomalies; many of the clergy and laity blamed the bishops for not setting right what was clearly wrong; but nothing could be done without Parliament, and Parliament had neither the interest nor the time to help the Church. Archbishop Davidson, speaking at the Representative Church Assembly, stated the case with authority and clearness: "Not once or twice, or five times, or perhaps ten times, have I brought before the

[1] A. C. Benson, "Edward White Benson." (Abridged Edition), p. 300.

[2] G. L. Prestige, "The Life of Charles Gore," p. 314.

ministers in power during the last quarter of a century matters which, big or little, I thought needed attention at the time in the Church's life, and the answer has been again and again the same: 'Probably you are quite right, but with the present pressure upon the time of Parliament and the present attitude of the House of Commons towards the varied work that lies urgently before it, we could never give up the days or the weeks that would be necessary!' They did not say: 'We are opposed to it,' or 'We are objecting to what you do,' but rather, 'You are asking a machine to do it which is already so clogged with work, and work of a different kind, that you are asking an impossibility.'"[1]

Strange and unsatisfactory devices were adopted to secure the passage of Church Bills. Money had been raised by the Church for the creation of three new dioceses, all difficulties had been removed, and there was no kind of local opposition. The Bishoprics Bill was, however, blocked in Parliament by a small group. Suddenly it went through, the supporters of the Bill told the promoters of some Nonconformist Bills that they would oppose them unless they dropped opposition to the Church Bill; the intention to move the Church Bill was kept secret until the last minute, so that some extreme Protestants from Liverpool might not return in time to oppose it. The tactics were successful, but it was regrettable that an obstructionist opposition rendered them necessary. The formation of two other dioceses was blocked in the same way, though the money for them had been raised, and the members of the proposed dioceses were enthusiastic in their support. But in this case an air raid came to the rescue, and the opponents sought refuge in the underground shelter, while the supporters of the Bill succeeded in passing it through a very small House!

It was becoming quite intolerable that all Church Reform should be held up indefinitely by the House of Commons either through lack of time, or through the opposition of small irresponsible groups. Dick Sheppard had been discussing the position with some of his friends, and in 1916 invited some twenty or more clergymen and laymen to meet at the Vicarage of St. Martin's-in-the-Fields. One by one we were asked the question: "What is the greatest need of the Church of England at the present time?" In different ways we all gave the answer that no Church Reform was possible unless the Church was given some powers of self-government. We then discussed

[1] G. K. A. Bell, "Randall Davidson," p. 968.

as to how far we ought to go in urging this, and we were almost unanimous in deciding that if we could not obtain self-government we should ask for disestablishment. As we knew that this demand might alarm many who would otherwise support us, it was agreed that we should at first lay all our emphasis on self-government and freedom, only advocating disestablishment in the last resort. The Report of the Archbishops' Commission on the relationship between Church and State had given a practical policy. But we were in the midst of war, and it seemed most unlikely that proposals of this nature would be seriously considered by responsible people already preoccupied with problems of vital importance. Certainly this was the view of Archbishop Davidson who, while he welcomed the Report, made it plain that nothing could be done to implement its recommendations during the war. This was not however the view of large numbers of the younger clergy and laity. We determined to launch a vigorous campaign throughout the Church of England; and if we failed to secure any measure of reasonable freedom for the Church, then we should ask for disestablishment. The leaders of the movement were William Temple, Dick Sheppard, F. A. Iremonger, now Dean of Lichfield, and Lord Wolmer; in the earlier meetings Bishop Gore gave wise counsel and support, but withdrew from the movement when it was decided not to adopt communicant status as the qualification for the Church franchise. It was resolved to call the movement "Life and Liberty," and a large meeting to inaugurate it was held at the Queen's Hall in London on July 26th, 1917. I was present at the main meeting only for a short time as I was taking the Chair at an overflow in the smaller hall; but I was there long enough to gain a general impression —the platform and hall were crowded, there were large numbers of clergy, and, considering war conditions, the attendance of laymen was remarkably good. There was not the enthusiasm which is sometimes noticeable at missionary or evangelistic meetings, but there was solid, steady determination, which was most impressive. Temple, who was suffering severely from an attack of gout, made a restrained and reasoned speech from the Chair, and with one dissentient the following resolution was carried: "That whereas the present conditions under which the Church lives and works constitute an intolerable hindrance to its spiritual activity, this Meeting instructs the Council (of the Life and Liberty Movement), as a first step, to approach the archbishops, in order to urge upon them that they should ascertain without delay, and make known to the Church at large, whether and on what terms Parliament is prepared to give freedom to the Church in the sense of full power to manage its own life, so that it may better fulfil its duty to God and to the nation and its mission to the world." Every word of the resolution had been carefully discussed beforehand. Shortly after the meeting a deputation went to Lambeth and received a cautious but friendly welcome from the archbishop, considerable stress being laid by him on what had already been done, and how difficult it was to do anything until the war was over. We expected, and we were not surprised at meeting with considerable opposition from large numbers of the clergy and laity. Dr. Hensley Henson, whose solitary hand had been held up against the Queen's Hall resolution, in a letter to *The Times* voiced the opposition and asked, " Is the religious settlement which was slowly hammered into shape in the course of 150 years (1529–1662) . . . to be hustled out of existence, during the desperate distractions of a great war, by a handful of enthusiasts who really have but little beyond their enthusiasm to put hand to the task ? " Not a very accurate description of a movement which had among its leaders some of the most experienced parish priests in England ! There were many who felt this was the wrong time, the most frequent of all objections to Church reform ; there were some who feared that the demand for self-government might bring disestablishment nearer ; there were many others who had an instinctive and conservative objection to any departure from well trodden ways.

Hard work was necessary if indifference and opposition were to be defeated, and sufficient influence brought upon Parliament. Temple resigned St. James, Piccadilly, with its £2,000 a year, and led the campaign in all parts of the country. I went with him for a week in the diocese of Durham, where we found much suspicion and still greater ignorance of the movement. I arrived one morning at a vicarage in a mining village ; I found the elderly vicar had forgotten the meeting arranged for the afternoon, but he managed hastily to collect some kind of audience, and introduced me in words such as these : " The Life and Liberty Movement—that's the right name, is it not, Canon Garbett ?—has some good objects in view, but I am afraid I don't really know what they are or anything about the movement." So with this introduction I had to do my best to interest my small audience in the crying need of freedom for the Church. Temple was tireless in speaking and writing for the movement, and interviewing personally many who held posts of influence. I had the honour of being the first member elected to Convocation on a Life and Liberty programme; a much more significant victory took place shortly afterwards when Temple was elected for the diocese of London. It was soon plain that there was very large support for the policy of the movement. The archbishops were asked to receive another deputation; this went seventy or eighty strong to Lambeth Palace. Unfortunately some of our spokesmen felt that rudeness and enthusiasm were the same, one of them said, that as both of the archbishops were from Scotland they were naturally out of sympathy with the Church of England!; and another, a naval chaplain, told the Archbishop of Canterbury that the Lower Deck did not even know his name! Many of us left the Palace feeling that more harm than good had been done. But Dr. Bell says, "the Archbishop (of Canterbury) was more impressed as to the need of a definite pronouncement than he showed at the time."[1] He did not however propose to be hurried, but would go forward when he judged the time was ripe.

The Church Assembly

Early in 1919 the time for a definite move had arrived and a scheme was presented to the Representative Church Council by which, under the name of the National Assembly of the Church of England, it would be given certain legislative powers. The scheme was opposed by a minority with great vigour, and many were doubtful, but the decisive speech in its favour was made by the Archbishop of Canterbury. At first it had on some of us a chilling effect; we had been appealing to a great principle, to the right of the Church of God to have freedom to determine its own affairs. Life and Liberty had been emblazoned on our banner; so there was a momentary sense of disappointment, and of suspicion that we were being "debunked" publicly and officially, when the Archbishop took the line that the Assembly was discussing the improvement of some obsolete machinery which had not been overhauled for many years, and now was causing serious inconvenience. It was the speech of an administrator appealing to practical men

[1] G. K. A. Bell, ' Randall Davidson," Vol. II., p. 967.

to repair machinery which was working badly. But though the matter of fact speech was somewhat of a cold douche to those who had hoped for a bold pronouncement on the inherent rights of the Church, it had a profound effect; it disarmed the opposition and convinced doubters. It was a remarkable performance, and the Archbishop was loudly applauded when he sat down.

In July of 1919 the Enabling Bill was introduced into Parliament. It did not set up the Church Assembly, that already was in existence; it had been deliberately decided not to ask Parliament either to create or to authorise a central Church Assembly. It was, however, asked to give to the Representative Church Council certain powers in regard to legislation. Under this plan when the Assembly had passed a Measure and an Ecclesiastical Committee representing Parliament had advised His Majesty to give His Royal Assent to the Measure, the Assent must be given within forty days, unless either House should direct to the contrary. An amendment in the Lords was, however, accepted by the Archbishop, by which it would be necessary for each House to pass a resolution asking that the Measure be presented for the Royal Assent; this meant that opportunities for debate had to be found for every Measure. The Archbishop throughout argued the case for the Bill on practical administrative grounds, and it eventually was passed by the Lords without a division. Lord Wolmer piloted it safely through the House of Commons, and on December 15th the Bill received the Royal Assent.

The Assembly to which the enabling powers were granted now consists of the two archbishops, forty-one diocesan bishops, about three hundred and twenty-three members of the Lower Houses of Convocation, and about three hundred and forty-seven laymen; the total number of members is rather over seven hundred. When a Measure has passed through all its stages it is sent to the Legislative Committee which consists of members of the Assembly; it decides when and how the Measure is to be forwarded to the Ecclesiastical Committee. This Committee has fifteen members of the House of Lords nominated by the Lord Chancellor, and fifteen of the House of Commons by the Speaker. It is responsible for scrutinising the Measure to see it contains nothing which affects adversely the rights of any citizen, and for preparing a report on it for Parliament. Each House must then pass a resolution in favour of the Measure being presented to His Majesty for the Royal Assent. Parliament has no power to amend a Measure, but it can debate it and reject it. The State thus agreed to a most important change in its relationship to the Church. It has delegated some of its powers to a body set up by the Church. An ordinary Bill must pass both Houses in all its stages ; it has three readings, a committee and report stage, and it can be amended and changed out of all recognition at the will of the House. Under the Enabling Act all these complicated stages are omitted, and, provided the Measure is confined to ecclesiastical affairs and has passed correctly through the Assembly, nothing is required except a resolution in each of the Houses of Parliament. The practical advantages of this are very great ; the difficulty of finding time in Parliament is overcome, for the Measures presented to it have already been subjected to careful examination by a body containing many who are especially qualified by lifelong experience of Church affairs. Since the Enabling Act was passed the Church has been able to secure a large number of reforms which for long had been asked in vain. Usually both Houses have been content with a brief explanation by the Member in charge, and the Measure has been approved without difficulty. So successful has been this partial delegation of its powers by an overworked Parliament that there are some who would like Parliament to apply the same method to other matters, and thus enable it to deal more quickly with an ever accumulating mass of Bills for which no time can be found.

There are three observations which should be made. First, through the Assembly and its request for the Enabling Act, the Church reaffirms the right of its laity to be consulted on ecclesiastical legislation. As we have seen the Reformation was a lay movement, and Parliament at one time the assembly of lay churchmen. There would not have been the slightest chance of Parliament granting enabling powers to any assembly on which the laity was not fully represented. No Church reform to-day would have any chance of approval by Parliament unless it was certain that behind it there was the support of the laity. The assured place of the laity in ecclesiastical affairs is a deep-rooted tradition in England which goes back to Anglo-Saxon days. It was for this reason that after much hesitation the Church franchise was made as wide as possible, so that its electors should consist of all who have been baptized and who declare that they are members of the Church of England and do not belong to any other religious body not in communion with it. The members of its various assemblies must have communicant status, but those who elect them need not have been confirmed. Many with Bishop Gore regretted the franchise is so wide, but it was unavoidable if Parliament was to give semi-legislative powers to the Assembly; there was great dislike of anything like a communicant test, and the fear that membership of the National Church might be unduly narrowed. The weight which Parliament will give to the wishes of the Assembly will depend very largely on the numbers of those whom it represents. The smallness of the electoral roll is at the moment a serious weakness. It will prejudice the influence of the Assembly, for when a controversial Measure is sent to Parliament, the question will be asked as to how far the Assembly is really representative. It is thus of importance that the roll of electors in every parish should be made as complete as possible, and that those who are elected should be truly representative of the laity. At present the laity either on the diocesan conferences or in the Church Assembly are not sufficiently representative of the working classes. This is a serious drawback. Those dependent upon a weekly wage cannot afford the expense caused by five days in London—this is especially true of those living in the north. The difficulty must be overcome if the Assembly is to be truly representative of the laity.

Secondly, the constitution of the Assembly and the Enabling Act have made it plain that citizenship is not the same as Churchmanship. In actual practice this has been the case since the Restoration, but with the illogicality which distinguishes our nation the claim still continued to be made that every citizen had the right to all the privileges of membership of the Established Church, even if he also belonged to some other religious body. The Church franchise is now limited to baptized members of the Church, and representation on its assemblies to those who are communicants. This definitely excludes as far as possible those who are members of other Churches taking any part in the government of the Church of England. One of the chief reasons advanced by Bishop Hensley Henson in opposition to the Enabling Bill was that it would reduce the Church from its position of the Church of the whole nation to that of a sect among other sects—a move for "sectarianising" the Church of England was one of the phrases he sometimes used to stigmatise the Life and Liberty Movement. But the Enabling Act was the legal recognition of what had long been a fact, that the Church of England is not inclusive, that it has its own rules of admission and of membership, and that no man is entitled to claim he is a member of the Church simply because he happens to be an English citizen.

Thirdly, experience has proved that this large Assembly is capable of doing valuable work. It was doubtful if the seven hundred members, many of them accustomed as clergymen or leading laymen to speak frequently in their own parishes, deaneries, and dioceses, would exercise sufficient restraint on their natural eloquence to enable practical work to be done within the very limited time which the Assembly has at its disposal. There are, of course, some who feel it is a duty to themselves and to the Assembly to speak on every possible occasion; towards these the Assembly shows praiseworthy patience, and most of its members refuse to follow their example of tedious garrulity. There is also in a predominantly middle-aged or elderly Assembly a fairly large group which views with considerable alarm all measures which involve changes from the accustomed ways, and is most happy when it is able to refer them to some committee for further consideration. There are also those who have a touching faith in the value of resolutions and declarations, and are always urging the Assembly to pass with inadequate knowledge sweeping resolutions on great subjects. But notwithstanding these difficulties, the Assembly has steadily settled down to its main work, namely, that of legislation. When it has made up its mind that the Measure before it is good, it goes steadily forward with it, listening very patiently to obstructive minorities, but voting them down by large majorities. It has sent up to Parliament a large number of useful reforms. It has also from time to time helped both to form and to express the mind of the Church on matters of public importance, such as the relationship between Church and State, peace, finance, education, and the staffing of parishes. It has dealt quickly and efficiently with its budgets. The rules of procedure are baffling to those unfamiliar with the Houses of Parliament, and a bishop suddenly asked to take the chair may easily find himself in difficulties, but the Assembly has been fortunate in having had as its Chairman four successive Archbishops of Canterbury who have guided the Assembly safely through shoals of amendments, and have proved themselves fully capable of dealing with difficult points of order. Quite apart from the debates in public, a very large amount of valuable work has been done by committees either preparing reports on which future legislation would be based, or in revising measures which have already received general approval.

Parliament has shown itself well disposed to the Assembly. Only four of the many Measures sent to it have been rejected. The first dealing with the City Churches had not been very tactfully introduced and met with great hostility from the City. The second containing a scheme for the division of the diocese of Lichfield was strongly opposed by Churchmen of the the diocese of Hereford. The third and fourth rejected Measures were of first-class importance—the revision of the Prayer Book. The earlier Measure was passed by the House of Lords, but both were rejected (1927, 1928) by the House of Commons. From the point of view of the relationships between Church and State it was almost impossible to exaggerate the importance of this. For fourteen years the Church had been engaged on the task of revision: the proposed book had been accepted by large majorities in the House of Bishops, the House of Clergy, and the House of Laity. After a debate of a few hours on the first occasion the work of years was undone by the House of Commons. On the second occasion the debate took two days and the result was the same. This was a dramatic expression of the supremacy of Parliament over the Church. No longer could it be claimed that it was the vote of the laity of the Church. Nonconformists, Presbyterians, and even a Parsee swelled the majority; they were fully entitled to vote; many of them would have felt that if they had abstained they would have been failing in their duty to their constituents. The Church has no right to complain that Scottish, Welsh and Northern Ireland Members took part in the division; as Members of Parliament they were doing their duty. But the fact is that the wish of the Church to revise its liturgy, expressed through its constitutional assemblies, was over-ridden by a majority which included many who were not members of the Church of England. When the Enabling Bill had been passed its promoters had expressly acknowledged that the supremacy of Parliament remained unchanged, though over-optimistically they had thought that it would have accepted all Measures sent to it by overwhelming majorities in the Church Assemblies.

The hostile vote was due to three causes[1]—division of opinion in the Church expressed by resolutions and personal letters to

[1] A further statement of the causes of the defeat of this Book is given in Chapter X.

members—the deep-rooted fear of Rome—and on the first occasion the opponents of the Measure had certainly the better of the debate. But whatever were the reasons it is impossible to escape from the hard fact that Parliament refused legal authority to the Church to worship God in the manner its bishops, clergy and laity thought most fitting. Months before, Archbishop Davidson had realised how grave the position would be if Parliament refused its assent to the Measure—at least two years before the revised Book went to Parliament he said to me, "If Parliament refuses to allow the Church to say its prayers in the way it thinks right, we shall be faced with a demand for disestablishment"; but a few days before the critical debate he told me he had reason to believe the Measure might be rejected, and asked me what I thought he ought then to do. I replied, "We should ask for disestablishment."[1] To this his answer was, "But what good will that do?" At that time the Church itself would have been hopelessly divided on this drastic step. Many would have opposed it to the last. Others would have felt that the bishops were asking for it in a fit of bad temper. Only a few voices were actually raised in favour of it. So a few months later the archbishop, in the name of the whole body of bishops, made the following statement to the Assembly, "It is a fundamental principle that the Church—that is the bishops together with the clergy and laity—must in the last resort, when its mind had been fully ascertained, retain its inalienable right in loyalty to Our Lord and Saviour Jesus Christ, to formulate its Faith in Him and to arrange the expression of that Holy Faith in the forms of worship." The statement and the Archbishop's speech making it were ordered to be entered on the minutes of the House. Later on a Commission was appointed to report on the present relationships between Church and State, and in subsequent chapters its recommendations will be discussed. But in the next two chapters we must consider the nature of the Establishment to-day, its privileges and its duties, and an answer must be given to Archbishop Davidson's challenge, "What good will disestablishment do?"

[1] An older and more experienced bishop than myself felt the same at the time of the rejection of the Measure. Bishop Strong of Oxford wrote: "I think the business has confirmed my opinion that Parliament is a wholly incompetent body in matters of this sort. Sooner or later—I hope sooner—we must cut ourselves adrift from Parliament unless we are to become the laughing stock of Christianity." (Harold Anson, "T. B. Strong," p. 64.)

VI

THE ESTABLISHMENT

At the close of the wedding of Princess Elizabeth in Westminster Abbey, Field Marshal Smuts turned to Mr. Churchill, who was sitting next to him, with the remark, " This has taken me back to the Middle Ages," and Mr. Churchill replied, " Not to the Middle Ages, but to all the Ages." And if this was true of the wedding, it would have been still more so of the Coronation. Then within the space of two hours the pageantry of the past history of Church and State was unrolled, and their ideal relationship in all the ages was made manifest. Rites only read of in Scripture or in the pages of the past were enacted and seen; the anointing of the king with oil, the ransoming of the sword, the crowning, the enthronisation, and the paying of feudal homage. The origin of some of them goes back far beyond our own history. A few years after the Coronation of George VI, I was in the cathedral at Moscow for a great service of prayer in connection with the war; I was invited to come from behind the screen to witness the vesting of the patriarch—wearing a long purple robe he took his place on a small platform in the midst of the nave; the robe was taken off and he stood clad only in a simple white vestment, and then splendid robes were put on; he was handed the insignia of his office, and finally the mitre, in the shape of a gold crown, was placed on his head. Dimly I was conscious I had seen this before, and then it dawned on me—it was at the Coronation I had witnessed it; both the coronation of a king and the vesting of a patriarch come from Byzantine rites, which in their turn incorporated some pre-Christian symbolism.

Our Coronation Order expresses in the most vivid way the ideal relationship between Church and State; the archbishop representing the Church, and the king the State; they are the two figures in the drama standing out from the many other subsidiary actors. It is the archbishop who presents to the people their king with the words, " Sirs, I here present unto you King George, your undoubted king: Wherefore all you are come this day to do your homage and service. Are you willing to do the same?" And the people signify their willingness and joy by loud and repeated acclamations. Then before the anointing and the crowning the king must take the oath to govern according to law and custom, to cause law and justice in mercy to be executed, and to "maintain and preserve inviolately the settlement of the Church of England, and the doctrine, worship, discipline and government thereof, as by law established in England," and to "preserve with the bishops and clergy of England, and to the churches there committed to their charge, all such rights and privileges as by law do or shall appertain to them, or any of them." And as the ceremonies are performed—the anointing, the vesting with the royal robe, the delivery of the sword, the orb, the ring, the sceptre, and finally the crowning and the presentation of the Bible, they are accompanied with prayers and blessings that the king may preserve the people commited to his charge in health, peace and godliness; that he may use the sword as "the minister of God, for the terror and punishment of evil doers, and for the protection and encouragement of those that do well." After the enthronisation the archbishop sums up the ideal relationship between Church and State: "Stand firm, and hold fast from henceforth the Seal and State of Royal and Imperial Dignity, which is this day delivered unto you, in the Name and by the authority of Almighty God, and by the hands of us the bishops and servants of God, though unworthy: And as you see us to approach nearer to God's Altar, so vouchsafe the more graciously to continue to use your Royal favour and protection." All through the ceremony the special duties of Church and State are brought out. The Church blesses the State, prays for its welfare, and helps its people on the way to life eternal. The State protects the Church, administers justice, cares for the weak, and preserves peace. The archbishops and bishops, as ministers of God first anoint, bless and crown the king, but presently as holding land from him they will pay him homage and promise to "do and truly acknowledge, the service of the Lands which I claim to hold of you, as in the right of the Church."

The Church and State each have their special functions in the nation; the Church cares for its spiritual and the State for its temporal welfare. But they are so closely connected that it is often hard to draw a clear limit between their respective spheres of influence. At best they work together in harmony for the spiritual and temporal welfare of the nation, at worst each regards the other as a rival to be feared or an enemy to be fought. The relationship between Church and State is far more complicated now than it was in the Middle Ages; for then every citizen was a member of the Church, while to-day only a minority of the citizens are practising members. Under these changed circumstances it is sometimes argued that an established Church is a meaningless anachronism, and that common sense and justice require disestablishment. But there are many who hold that the increased secularism of the day is an additional reason for the existence of a Church which witnesses to the necessity of religion in the life of a nation, and has been given a special responsibility to call the nation to obey the law of God. It is not easy to define Establishment; it is the more difficult as there never was a time when the State entered into a contract with a Church to perform certain duties on its behalf; still less a time when the State in return for duties performed conferred upon the Church certain privileges. Instead, therefore, of attempting a definition of what is meant by Establishment, it will be more convenient to describe the present position of the Church under three headings—its privileges recognised by the State; its obligations to the State and the nation; and the control exercised over it by the State.

The Privileges of the Church

(1) The Church, as Established, has an unique relationship with the Soveriegn. He must be a member of the Church of England, and he promises at his Coronation to protect its rights and privileges. He is crowned by the Archbishop of Canterbury. His chaplains in England are ordained ministers of the Established Church. One of the bishops acts as the Lord High Almoner, makes the accustomed offerings at the Epiphany, and represents him at the Maundy Service, when the king himself is not present. He has another bishop as Clerk of the Closet, who at one time acted as his theological adviser, and if tradition is true, sat near him during the time a sermon was preached, correcting any false teaching, or even dispersing boredom by whispering learned or witty comments to His Majesty. To-day the Clerk's duties are less important; he is present when a

newly-appointed bishop pays his homage; he advises on names suggested for vacant royal chaplaincies; he looks through religious books which their authors desire to give to the king, either recommending or refusing them for presentation; and usually once a year preaches at the Chapel Royal. The king has his own chapels at Windsor Castle and Buckingham Palace, and when he is in residence, attends them for the Sunday services.

(2) The two archbishops, the three senior bishops—London, Durham and Winchester—and twenty-one other bishops according to their seniority have seats in the House of Lords. One of them takes prayers at the opening of the daily sitting, though this is usually in the morning when the judges alone are in the House. In the past the two benches set aside for the bishops were usually crowded for the debates, but now few of them are able to be present regularly, and the vacant places are occupied by lay peers, who must move elsewhere if they wish to address the House. On one occasion this rule was forgotten by Lord Birkenhead (F. E. Smith), who, notwithstanding cries of "Order," made a brief speech from the second episcopal bench; when he sat down a note was sent to him by the Lord Chancellor congratulating the bishops' bench on its latest recruit! The bishops wear their white rochet and black chimere, though at State openings of Parliament with scarlet robes over them. The past record of the bishops in the Lords is unsatisfactory to a democratic age; for they were silent when they should have spoken, and spoke when it would have been better had they been silent; they failed to denounce injustice and defended social abuses; and their votes were usually cast on the side of reaction. But for at least fifty years they have broken away from this evil tradition. It is unjust to condemn the bishops of to-day for the political sins and errors of their predecessors, who shared the prejudices of their age and of the society in which they moved.

But quite apart from any contribution the bishops in the Lords may make on political or social problems, they have expert knowledge on matters which directly concern the work of the Church, and for which legislation is often required. It is often necessary that the established Church should ask Parliament to approve of many of the reforms and changes it requires. Most of these now come to Parliament in the shape of measures which have been passed by the Church Assembly; and if questions arise in connection with them the bishops possess special knowledge which enables them both to expound the proposed reform and to reply to criticism. This was true of the measures dealing with the creation of new dioceses, the suspension of benefices, changes in connection with clerical pensions, the reorganisation of the Ecclesiastical Commissioners and Queen Anne's Bounty, clergy discipline and a number of other similar measures : all of them required explanation, and in some cases unexpected points were raised which called for immediate answer. The bishops are qualified to present and defend measures for which they have asked and which they may have to administer in their dioceses ; they have a detailed knowledge of their subject matter, possessed by few of the lay peers. As long as the consent of Parliament is required for so many ecclesiastical reforms, it is only reasonable that there should be in one of the Houses those who are able to advocate them with first-hand knowledge.

If the House of Lords is ever reformed the number of bishops would be fewer than at present. The number left should be relative to the reduction in the representation of lay peers. The two archbishops, the three bishops of the senior sees, and possibly three or four others elected by the total number of diocesans should have seats. As it is doubtful if all the bishops so chosen would be able to attend as regularly as the lay peers, it is important that there should be a number large enough to ensure the attendance of at least two or three at the ordinary sittings of a reformed House, whose responsibilities would be greater than those of the House as at present constituted. But the day, long promised, for the reform of the composition of the House, still seems very remote, and no Government has yet shown itself ready to carry through a change which is generally regarded as overdue.

(3) The sentences of the Ecclesiastical Courts are enforced by the State, provided that they deal with matters under their jurisdiction, and that the cases have been heard with the correct procedure. " A very distinctive mark of establishment is that the State not only recognises and tolerates the Church Courts as *Courts*, but also enforces the sentences of the Church Courts by what is known as the process of significavit. By virtue of the process the State, if appealed to, arrests and imprisons a man who disobeys a sentence of an ecclesiastical court."[1] The sentence of the deprivation or deposition of a clerk in Holy

[1] Lewis Dibdin, " Establishment in England," p. 59.

Orders for some grave offence is accepted by the State without further trial, unless an appeal is made to the Royal Courts.

(4) Marriages are performed in a parish or licensed church by a clergyman of the Church of England without the presence of a registrar. At one time it was assumed that any citizen had the right to be married in church with the Church of England service, unless he was excommunicated. Now it is widely admitted that this is unsuitable when both the parties are unbaptized, for the service is clearly intended for those who belong to the family of the Church and accept its rules. The Church through its Convocations has also declared that the use of its marriage service should not be allowed in the case of anyone who has a former partner still living, and Parliament has made it legal for a clergyman to refuse to take such marriages or to lend his church for the purpose.

(5) The State recognises and protects the possession by the Church of a large amount of property. But this has not been given to the Church by the State. It is most difficult to remove the popular illusion that the Church has been endowed by the State, and that its clergy are paid out of the national revenue. After the Great Fire of London the State helped out of coal duties the rebuilding of certain churches in the city of London; between 1809 and 1820 it made grants of just over a million pounds to Queen Anne's Bounty; and in 1818 and 1824 it made grants amounting to a million and a half for the erection of churches in populous areas—but some of this went to the Presbyterian Church of Scotland.[1] In addition, the State pays the Service and prison chaplains of the Church of England as well as of the Roman Catholic and Free Churches. But with these exceptions the State has neither made grants nor endowments to the Church, nor has it ever paid its clergy.

The ancient endowments of the Church consist of gifts of tithe, land, and money made voluntarily by individuals for religious purposes. They were not given to the Church as such but to sees, cathedral chapters, and individual parishes. "People talk as if 'Church property' were the property of one vague corporation called 'The Church.' In truth it is simply the property of several local churches, the ecclesiastical corporations sole and aggregate, bishops, chapters, rectors, and vicars or any other. The Church of England as a single body has no

[1] Selborne, "A Defence of the Church," pp. 166–167.

property."[1] A large amount of Church property is now held by the Church Commissioners (a recent amalgamation of the Ecclesiastical Commissioners and Queen Anne's Bounty). The Ecclesiastical Commissioners not only administered Church properties for the purposes they were given, but so wisely and skilfully that their capital increased and the large additional value thus obtained has been used for the benefit of the whole Church. The original Commission was set up by the State, but all its lay members had to make a declaration that they belonged to the Church before they took their seats. Among them were the five principal Officers of State, two judges, two laymen appointed by the Crown, one of whom had to be a Member of Parliament to answer questions in the House of Commons. In this way "the constitution of the Commissioners recognises the link between Church and State which results from the establishment of the Church."[2]

Queen Anne's Bounty was not formed by a gift to the Church of revenues which belonged to the State. The Bounty consisted of the first year's income of benefices, and the tenth part of their income in subsequent years, originally paid by the incumbent to the Pope. At the Reformation this money was appropriated by the king. Queen Anne restored these payments to the Church; this was not a grant by the State to the Church out of national funds, but the restoration to the Church of money which was annually paid by its clergy.[3] The Bounty at one time used its revenue to augment the poorer benefices, but more recently it became the central authority for parsonage houses, and has made large grants towards the payment of dilapidations. The State as well as the Church was fully represented among the Governors of the Bounty; all Privy Councillors, judges, the Law Officers of the Crown, all King's Counsel, and the Speaker! On the new Church Commission representatives of the State have their place, though in smaller numbers than in the past.

[1] Professor Freeman, "Disestablishment and Disendowment" (1885), p. 16.

[2] J. R. Brown, "Number One Millbank," p. 11.

[3] Anne in a message to the House of Commons in 1704 after stating she had taken into consideration the poverty of the clergy, went on to say: "For an augmentation of their maintenance her Majesty is pleased to declare that she will make a grant of her whole revenues arising out of first-fruits and tenths, so far as it now is, or shall become, free from incumbrances, to be applied to this purpose." Much of the money had, however, "been settled by Charles II upon his mistresses and natural children." A. Tindal Hart, "The Life and Times of John Sharp," pp. 248, 249.

(6) But far more important than any of the privileges mentioned above is the recognition by the State that the Church of England is the national Church and has privileges and rights as such. This makes itself felt in innumerable ways both great and small. It is the clergy of the Established Church who take the lead in arranging both in town and country the services in connection with national days of prayer and praise, and it is to the parish church that the people instinctively go on such occasions. It is the parish priest who has a recognised position and who visits by right all the people within his parish. This duty is expected of him, and non-churchgoers, as well as churchgoers, criticise the parson who never visits. Frequently ex-Nonconformist ministers, who have been ordained in the Church of England, have told me how great is the difference which this makes to the way in which their visit is received; they find it is accepted that they now have a ministry not merely to the members of a congregation but to all who live within the parish. Behind the clergyman of the Church of England there is the authority which comes from past centuries in which his place in the community has been built up by custom. How long this position of spiritual authority would be retained if the Church were disestablished is an open question, but the Anglican clergy to-day have exceptional opportunities of spiritual and religious leadership. And this status given by the Church to its clergy at home often helps them in their relationship to both the unreformed and reformed Churches on the Continent and elsewhere. The fact that they represent an Established Church adds weight to an official visit made by any of our clergy to the Churches of the West or the East; though frequently their hosts over-estimate the political influence which an Anglican bishop possesses in his own country. I have no doubt that additional importance is attached both to his presence and his words as a representative of an Established Church which crowns the king, which has its bishops in Parliament, and which possesses famous cathedrals and churches.

The Obligations of an Established Church

If an Established Church has certain privileges, it also has definite duties to the State and nation. It must pray for them, provide them with religious ministration, and give them spiritual leadership.

(1) The Established Church has a special responsibility in praying for the State and the nation. This is focused in prayer for the king. In all its services there are repeated prayers for the king and the royal family. When the order set forth in the Prayer Book is strictly followed, there are prayers every morning and evening throughout the year for the king. In the Holy Communion prayers are offered for him twice, in a special prayer and in the prayer for the Church. There is a prayer for the Council; "and grant unto his whole Council, and to all that are put in authority under him, that they may truly and indifferently minister justice, to the punishment of wickedness and vice, and to the maintenance of true religion and virtue." There is a prayer also for the High Court of Parliament "that thou wouldest be pleased to direct and prosper all their consultations to the advancement of thy glory, the good of thy Church, the safety, honour and welfare of our Sovereign, and his dominions." In the Litany the needs of State and Nation are remembered, in its petitions for the king, the royal family, for the Council and all the nobility, for the magistrates, for all the people, for the prisoners and captives, and for all that are desolate and oppressed. There are special prayers for the nation in days of trouble and of thanksgiving for it in its hour of deliverance. In both Houses of Parliament the sittings are opened with prayer. At the Assizes the judges attend public worship, and prayer is offered for God's guidance. Other Churches also pray for both the king and the nation, but in an Established Church special stress is laid upon this duty. I doubt if in any other Church so many opportunities are given of prayer for the king. Our Church has never been ashamed of its loyalty. In many of our churches the royal arms are on the walls or over the chancel screen, though I have never seen them so profusely set up in an English church as in many of the cathedrals in Spain.

(2) The Church of England, as the national Church, must make spiritual provision for all who wish to take part in its worship and to share its ministrations. It is one of the glories of the Church that its clergy minister not only to a congregation, but to all who live within the parish. It is true that in these days when the clergy are few in number, and there are many who have no wish for their ministration, this ideal is far from realisation. But the door of the parish church is open to all who care to enter, its bells ring out to call all to worship, and

the sick, the suffering, the mourner, and the needy all have the right to turn to the parish priest for help and counsel. From the signing of a paper to the administration of a sacrament he must be ready to minister to all. He baptizes the children, prepares them for confirmation, gives them their first communion, marries them at the altar, and buries the dead. The clergy are to be found in remote country parishes and in crowded and poverty-stricken slums. Nearly fifty years ago Beatrice Webb entered in her diary that at that time any outside demand for disestablishment and disendowment was dead. "The town workman is now neither a Nonconformist nor a secularist; he is simply indifferent to the whole question of religion or metaphysics. On the other hand he is inclined to think the hard-working curate, who runs his club, looks after his children on Sundays and holidays, stirs up the sanitary inspector and is sympathetic because acquainted with the struggle for better conditions of employment, a good fellow. He sees the dissenting parson moving out to the suburbs, the rich congregation preferring a new and fine building there to the old meeting-place down town. But the priest of the Established Church remains in the old city parish, and is constantly about in the slums."[1] This is still true, though the assistant curate is not always to be found, for the Established Church recognises its obligation to minister to those who live in the worst slums as well as to the comfortably housed in the suburbs.

This duty of making spiritual provision for the whole nation does not mean that all within it have an equal right to the ministrations of the Church. As far as social rank, wealth or learning are concerned, all must be treated as equal—that is why the pew rent system is so objectionable, for it brings a money standard into the worship of the fellowship. But the Church lays down conditions which must be observed by those who wish to enjoy the greatest privileges it offers; for baptism there must be godparents who promise to see the child is brought up in the faith of the Church; confirmation is only for the baptized, and must be preceded by preparation; and the communicant must have been confirmed or desirous of confirmation, and must have repentance, faith, and charity. And according to the law of the Church it can only marry those who have no previous husband or wife still living. Provided the conditions

[1] "Our Partnership," p. 208.

laid down in the Prayer Book are observed, the ministrations of the Church are open to all, and its clergy are at the service of all.

This work of ministration is not confined to the parishes. The clergy of the Church are serving in large numbers in the armed forces, both at home and abroad, though here, too, the numbers of chaplains are insufficient to meet all the demands. In prisons, hospitals and different public institutions they are appointed, though often they share this work with ministers of other Churches. When there is no full time chaplain, the clergy of the locality always recognise it is their duty to arrange that some of their number are set apart, often without remuneration, for this work in institutions. When I was vicar of Portsea I was also chaplain to the local prison, to the hospital, to the hospital for infectious diseases, and to the cemetery, though the greater part of this work was done by my assistant curates.

The Church has a special responsibility in providing churches and clergy for the large housing estates which have come into existence in the last thirty years. It has built halls, missions and churches in districts which otherwise would have been without any kind of spiritual provision; often these churches were in full use before any community centre had been opened. "We had three visitors in our first week here," said a tenant of an L.C.C. estate in South London, "the curate, the bookie's tout, and the insurance agent, and the curate came first." Very large sums of money have been raised for the purpose, as well as for the payment of clergy and women workers in these areas. The financial resources of the Church have been strained to the utmost in carrying out this duty to the nation.

(3) An Established Church has the responsibility of arousing and educating the conscience of the State and the nation on matters of public policy and administration. It must show that Christianity has a message not only to the individual but to society. It must proclaim God's laws of justice, mercy, and love, and at the same time show their relevance to current politics. Though an Established Church has exceptional opportunities of doing this, its close connection with the State has sometimes made it blind to contemporary evils or so timid that it has chosen silence as the wiser policy. The industrial revolution was a period when the Church failed to see and to denounce

the appalling sufferings of the poor in the factories and mines. Only here and there did individuals raise their voices against the worship paid to Mammon.

An Established Church should be the keeper of the national conscience. It should uphold steadily and uncompromisingly the law of God as revealed in the Scriptures, and should boldly bear witness against political and social wrong doing. Far better that the Church should be blamed for speaking unwisely but boldly, than despised for cowardly silence. It must give the prophetic utterance instead of the balanced statement. It is not the duty of the Church to prepare schemes of its own for the solution of domestic problems or for the conduct of international affairs. It has neither the special knowledge nor the experience to entitle it to do this. Amateur excursions on the part of the Church into the field of legislation bring discredit on the Church and harm to the nation. But the Church should proclaim the Christian standards by which all public policy should be judged and condemn actions and conditions contrary to them. The Church through its leaders or its official assemblies should demand obedience to commands of God which are in danger either of being broken or ignored, and should protest vigorously against policy or acts which are plainly repugnant to His Word. Sometimes these protests will be made with the greatest possible publicity, but at other times privately to those primarily responsible. Archbishop Davidson was often looked upon as the timid and cautious ecclesiastical statesman, but his *Life* shows how outspoken he could be both in public and in private. In public he protested against the reprisals proposed in 1916 on German non-combatants; again later against the reprisals inflicted by the Black and Tans in Ireland; and on both occasions was attacked with great bitterness for his speech. Privately he wrote letters of protest or criticism to the Prime Minister and others in authority, when he had reason to believe action was contemplated or indeed had been decided upon which he felt was contrary to the Christian standard. In recent years in the House of Lords, in the Church Assembly, and in Convocation the Church has borne Christian witness by speech, resolution, and vote, on subjects so different as war, religious freedom, housing, the persecution of the Jews, displaced persons, German prisoners of war, the condition of defeated Germany.

It is not however the Church of England alone which upholds

the Christian standard on international, social and economic problems. The Roman Catholic and Free Churches have frequently spoken on these subjects. Previously to Italy's entry into the war the Pope made a series of impressive utterances on Christianity and world affairs; and at one time the "Nonconformist conscience" was a greater power for good in the cause of social morality than the Church. From time to time the different Churches have made united statements on great international or domestic issues; a notable illustration of this was when the two English Archbishops, Cardinal Hinsley, and the leaders of the Free Churches united in support of a declaration made by the Pope on the necessary conditions of world peace. But though many statements are now made jointly by the Churches, the Church of England as the national Church still has the special responsibility of calling upon the State to follow the ways of justice and mercy. This duty is admirably summed up by Canon Vidler: "It must therefore be said, in season and out of season, that a Church to be worthy of the name, however small a minority it may be in any given society, is charged with the responsibility of bearing testimony to God's sovereignty and God's will before kings and rulers and the whole people. It must declare man's civic duties as well as his ecclesiastical duties. . . . In particular it must be said that a national Church, such as the Church of England, may not relinquish the responsibility for and to the whole people with which God entrusted it in the past, and which in spite of its failures and the anomalies in its present relation to the State, God has not yet removed from it."[1]

State Control

In various ways the State exercises control over the Church. It is true that it has some control over all voluntary societies as well as over private individuals within the nation. It is often pointed out that Nonconformists as well as Churchmen must go to Parliament to obtain changes in the conditions on which they hold property in trust. But the control of the State over the Church is different both in kind and degree from that which it exercises over other religious bodies. The king as Supreme Governor has visitatorial powers over the Church, and historical circumstances have made it necessary for the

[1] "The Orb and the Cross," p. 133.

Church to ask Parliament to sanction changes, which in other religious societies could be carried out without an appeal either to the Crown or to Parliament. The Church of England has never been entirely free, with the possible exception of the earlier Anglo-Saxon period when the relations between Church and State were in a fluid condition, and communications with Rome were especially difficult. In the Norman and Medieval days the Church was controlled by both Pope and king. The Reformation transferred this dual control to the king. In the centuries which followed it passed from the king to his ministers and to Parliament.

Sir Lewis Dibdin in an important article on " The Christian Prince " argues that as the Christian Emperor once protected the Church, so now Parliament possessing the powers which once belonged to the Crown, continues to act as its protector. The Christian Prince need not be an individual, though Sir Lewis makes it plain that Parliament has no right to act as the Christian Prince unless it is Christian. He claims that Parliament opened by prayer and with a large number of Christian members in both Houses, can rightly be treated as a Christian Assembly; but since the article was written some twenty years ago the position has changed and many members, including some Ministers, now affirm instead of taking the oath on the New Testament. Assuming the State is Christian, he explains that the supremacy exercised by the State over the Church is not of initiation but of rule: " The supremacy is a supremacy of rule—of seeing that bishops, clergy and laity perform their various ecclesiastical functions properly. The special prerogative of the bishops and clergy is to minister the Word and Sacraments—that is to use the power of the Keys—with the exclusive power of ordination, confirmation, excommunication and administration of the Sacraments of Baptism (if possible) and of the Holy Communion." But he goes on to say " nothing substantial can be altered without the consent of the ruler. For if the society ruled and protected is at liberty to make changes of substance, that is, of its teaching, ritual and services, without the consent of the ruler, that ruler—that is, the Christian State—may be left in the absurd position of ruling and protecting under circumstances and for purposes which it neither contemplated nor desired."[1]

If a Church is allowed privileges by the State, it is reasonable

[1] Dibdin, " Establishment in England," pp. 76, 77.

that it should have some control over the doctrine the Church teaches and the manner in which it worships ; not indeed that the State should have any right either to initiate or to make changes in the doctrine, worship or discipline of the Church : its right is strictly confined to seeing that any changes made by the Church are in accordance with its accepted doctrine and practice. If substantial changes are made they must come from the Church, and not be imposed upon it from outside ; but at some stage, after the Church has decided upon them, it must inform the State and ask for its approval, if it wishes to retain its position as an Established Church. If the State refuses approval, and the Church insists on the proposed changes, then, unless a compromise is reached, disestablishment should follow. In four ways the State exercises its control over the Church :

(1) The Crown appoints all bishops and deans. This has always been regarded as the crucial point of State control. In previous chapters we have seen how the Crown gradually obtained possession of the right of appointment against both the Pope and the cathedral electoral bodies. At first the appointment of bishops was made by the Crown through arrangement with the Pope ; then solely by the Crown ; now by the Crown on the recommendation of the Prime Minister. But with some exceptions, such as when the Chapter was ignored by the high-handed action of Pope or king, or when for a very brief time the method of making the appointment by Letters Patent was adopted, the form of election by the Chapter has been preserved ; and always before the bishop-elect could consecrate or ordain, he had to be consecrated by other bishops. The Crown at the height of despotism might claim to appoint without consultation with the Chapters, but never at any time was there any serious claim by the Crown, its ministers or Parliament to *make* either the bishops or the priests of the Church. The Crown also appoints the deans of cathedrals, and to parishes when they become vacant through the incumbent's appointment to a diocesan bishopric ; through the nature of the case these are usually important parishes. In addition there are a large number of benefices in the patronage of the Crown, 160 in sole patronage, and 130 alternately with the diocesan bishop. The Lord Chancellor appoints to 558 parishes, as well as to another 41 alternatively with the bishop. Frequently also the appointment lapses to the Crown through the failure of the patron or the bishop to fill the vacancy. Through its appointments of

bishops and its very large benefice patronage, the State has in its power the means of imposing its views on the Church. By a series of appointments made in accordance with a pre-determined policy, the doctrinal emphasis and the political outlook of the Church might be changed within a comparatively short period. It is a long time however since ecclesiastical appointments have been made for political reasons; and even should one party adopt this method of strengthening its position and of rewarding its followers, a change would almost certainly be made when the opposition came into power.

(2) All bishops, incumbents, and curates must take an oath of allegiance to the king and his successors before they are consecrated, instituted, licensed or ordained. It is taken by deans and canons before they are installed. In addition a diocesan bishop must pay homage to the king.

(3) No changes can be made legally in the doctrine or the public worship of the Church without an Act of Parliament, or in the case of services or prayers on special occasions without an Order in Council. According to Lord Hardwicke: "Now the constant uniform practice ever since the Reformation (for there is no occasion to go further back) has been, that when any material ordinances or regulations have been made to bind the laity as well as clergy in matters ecclesiastical, they have been either enacted or confirmed by Parliament; of this proposition the several Acts of Uniformity are so many proofs, for by these the whole doctrine and worship, the very rites and ceremonies of the Church and the literal forms of public prayers are prescribed and established."[1] Sir Lewis Dibdin however points out that this judgement was not intended to deny the right of the Church to deal with doctrine and worship, but it must act with the concurrence and agreement of the State. Parliament's right to be consulted before changes in worship are made was recognised when the Church presented for its approval the revised Prayer Books; and the power of Parliament to refuse such approval was shown by its twofold rejection.

(4) The Convocations can only meet when summoned to do so by Royal Writ. They can only make canons with the royal licence, and these can only be promulgated with the authority of the Crown. With the dissolution of Parliament, Convocation automatically comes to an end, and an election is necessary to choose new proctors of the clergy for the Lower Houses.

[1] Quoted in Dibdin's "Establishment," p. 56.

(5) The final court of appeal in ecclesiastical matters is a secular court, consisting of laymen, members of the Privy Council who are holding or have held important judicial posts. Five bishops sit as assessors when the judicial committee of the Privy Council hears ecclesiastical cases, but they have no votes, and their opinions can be totally disregarded.

(6) The State exercises considerable control over the property and administration of the Church. It has its representatives on the Church Commission which also presents an annual Report to Parliament. The approval of Parliament is required for measures creating new sees. The union and re-arrangement of the boundaries of parishes and the creation of new parishes are effected by Orders in Council on the recommendation of the Commissioners; appeals also against the union of benefices are heard by the Privy Council. There are a large number of Statutes regulating the property of the Church; for while the State has the right to intervene when the property owned by a voluntary association is not used in accordance with the trust under which it is held, or when Parliament is asked to sanction some alteration in the trust, the case of property held by the Church of England is different; here "Parliament by public Acts has directed how the property of its corporations is to be held, sold, leased or otherwise disposed of, much in the same way as it has regulated the holding and disposal of property by the Crown and by the civil departments of the State; and accordingly such questions respecting Church property as come before the civil courts are determined not by reference to any declared trusts but to a body of public law."[1]

In these ways the State has very great powers over the Church. It could use them to bring the Church almost completely under its control. Its bishops could be chosen from men certain to support the party predominant in the State, and its Convocations could be suspended. Requests for Church reform could be refused. The whole life of the Church could be partly paralysed and gravely obstructed by a Government which was deliberately hostile to the Church. An American historian is quoted by Dr. Hensley Henson as describing the organisation of the Church of England in 1908 as follows: "The Church possesses organs so arranged and distributed as to imply a closely-knit, if not centralised, form of self-government; and yet these

[1] Sir Maurice Gwyer in evidence before Church and State Commission, Vol. II, p. 177.

organs have so little power, either legislative or administrative, and the units are so independent, that for practical purposes the Church resembles a profession rather than an organisation. It has an assembly which can exert no authority over its structure, doctrine, or ritual, and which cannot even discuss these matters, or offer advice upon them, without the consent of the Crown—a consent not given at all for the 120 years preceding the reign of Queen Victoria, and not given with entire freedom now. It has bishops and archbishops whom it does not select, whose right to give orders to the clergy is extremely small, and who cannot, as a rule, discipline, punish or remove a single parson, except by means of legal proceedings before lay judges, ending perchance in a Court of Appeal in the selection of whose members the Church has no voice."[1] The statement is open to considerable criticism in detail, and the subsequent granting of Enabling Powers to the Church Assembly should modify some of its strictures, but it is a fair picture of the legal position of the Church of England as seen by an outside observer.

Spiritual Freedom

If the above is accepted as a full account of the Church of England it would appear that it has little freedom, and that it is completely under the control of the State. And yet in actual fact the position is very different. The bishops, the clergy and the laity have freedom which is not found in any service or department of the State. From the moment he is ordained until his death a minister of the Established Church finds himself almost completely free from any State interference. After the bishop has been consecrated and paid his homage, the State makes no attempt to interfere with him either in his teaching or in the administration of his diocese. A member of one of the fighting forces or of the civil service is frequently reminded that he is a man under authority; he is sent here and there at the command of his superiors, and must obey their orders if he is to retain his post. But the minister of the Church of England, whether bishop or priest, is rarely made aware of the control of the State over and above what it exercises over all its subjects. Only now and again does the State make its control felt. This is not an altogether healthy position. Possibly

[1] Quoted in "Bishoprick Papers," p. 90, from Dr. Lawrence Lowell, "Government of England," Vol. II, p. 362.

it is often due to the bishops and clergy quietly ignoring the ecclesiastical supremacy of the Crown. Archbishop Temple said that the subjection of the Church of England to Parliament in respect to its worship " is a prolific source of evils ; but they are rather evils of lawlessness and insincerity than of undue servility to the State. What actually happens on a large scale is not that congregations find their mode of worship unduly controlled by the State, but that clergy square it with their conscience to break the law."[1] Not only has the State refrained from asserting its supremacy over bishops and clergy in their regular ministrations, but from time to time it has given help to the Church. The grant of Enabling Powers to the Church Assembly was a remarkable concession, and most of the Measures it has sent to Parliament have been approved without the slightest difficulty.

And yet when all this has been fully and gratefully acknowledged the fact remains that the rejection of the Prayer Book Measures of 1927 and 1928 " revealed in unmistakable fashion the subordination of the Church to a Parliament which might consist largely of non-Christians, and does consist largely of persons who are not members of the Church of England."[2] There were special reasons which made Parliament refuse the permission for which the Church asked, and many would regard the rejection of the two Prayer Books as isolated incidents unlikely to occur again. But there are three questions raised by the present position between Church and State which must be faced and answered. (1) The State is steadily moving in the direction of totalitarianism. Before many years are over a predominant party may determine to place every department of national life completely under the State. In such circumstances it is quite possible that an attempt may be made to turn the Established Church into a department of State, rigidly controlled by Government officials. A quarter of a century ago such a possibility would have seemed fantastic, but in view of what has taken place on the Continent no one would dare to dismiss this as inconceivable. If the State cared to use the power it possesses it could go far towards making use of the Church as an instrument for its own ends. Have we any right to allow the relationship between Church and State to remain as it is if there is any possibility of this happening ?

[1] " Citizen and Churchman," p. 67.
[2] " Church and State Report," p. 41.

(2) The Church may be confronted with an even graver danger within the next few years. We may be very near a world-wide catastrophe through another war, and an economic collapse. There is little hope that the State as we know it would survive this crashing down of Western civilisation. The Church would suffer with the rest of the nation and would be greatly weakened materially, but if legally it is closely bound up with the State, it would be unable swiftly to adapt its organisation and administration to meet the needs of an age of revolution. The Church of the first centuries survived when all else was falling into ruin, for it was detached from the world and ready to meet catastrophe. Can we assume that the Church under the present conditions of Establishment would have the freedom for swift action essential for a time of crisis?

(3) If it should be felt that these two questions deal with a situation so unlikely to arise that they can be dismissed as prompted by an unreasonable pessimism, there remains still a third question. However satisfactory in practice the position may be between Church and State, is it possible to reconcile with Christian principles a Church whose chief ministers may be nominated by a non-Christian; whose public worship can only be changed by the permission of an assembly which need not be Christian; whose sacred synods can only meet and make rules for its own members by the leave of the State; and whose doctrine in the last resort is interpreted by laymen who need be neither Churchmen nor Anglicans?

When I ask myself these questions I feel profound disquiet of soul. I find it impossible to regard the present relationship between Church and State without grave heart-searching and discomfort.[1] I dread the results which might follow from it in the years of stress and storm before us. In loyalty to Our Lord Churchmen must look for some considerable change in the connection between Church and State. There are three lines of action—the drastic surgery of disestablishment; a new relationship on the model of the Established Church of Scotland; or the acceptance by Parliament of reforms which will still preserve an Established Church, but which will give it greater freedom for its spiritual work. These three possible lines of action will be considered in the next chapter.

[1] "The essence of the matter is that a system well adapted to the needs of a community which, in the eyes of the law at least, consisted entirely of Anglicans, is fantastic in a society in which practising Churchmen have become a minority." "The Economist," April 23rd, 1949.

VII

DISESTABLISHMENT OR REFORM?

THERE are many who would regret the raising of the issue between Church and State at this time. They fear that it might lead to an unprofitable controversy and distract the Church from its primary duty of evangelism. They argue that with the one exception of the rejection of the Prayer Book the relationship between Church and State in this country has on the whole been smooth and happy; sometime changes will have to be made, but they doubt if it wise to demand them at the present time. Those who take this position fail to recognise the vitally important differences between the State of 1949 and that of 1900. In two directions the contrast is startling.

Fifty years ago it was generally assumed that the less the State interfered with individuals, industries and cultural associations, the better it would be for all concerned. To-day State interference with every department of life has grown to an extent which would have been quite incredible to our forefathers. No one can predict with confidence what future developments may be. It looks sometimes as if the State might become totalitarian in spirit and in claims. This dangerous tendency will only be checked if within the nation there are a sufficient number of free societies and associations to set up a successful resistance. The Church should be in England, as the Churches have so often been on the Continent, in the vanguard of the fight for freedom. But if the State should ever decide to use its power of control over the Church it would be gravely handicapped; for a thorough-going totalitarian State would not only repress any action the Church might take in the cause of freedom, but through its appointments to sees, deaneries and parishes it would gradually use the Church as an instrument for propagating the views of the party in power. The Church would oppose such attempts, many of its clergy and laity would form the hard core of resistance to totalitarianism, but it would from the outset be crippled and hampered in the fight by the many legal ties which bind it to the State.

The other change compared with fifty years ago is of greater importance. Then the Church had a large majority among the members of the two Houses of Parliament. A quarter of a century later it could be claimed that even if the majority of the members were not Churchmen, yet most of them were Christians. It would be wrong to deny the term "Christian" to the two Houses to-day; they still open with prayer; many of their members are practising Christians, and many more are under the influence of Christian moral teaching. But a large number of them dislike institutional religion, and certainly would not commit themselves to the definite acceptance of the Christian faith. In a few years' time the whole temper both of the nation and of the House of Commons may possibly be secularist and even aggressively anti-Christian. The Church, then, if it wanted reform would have to appeal to an assembly which had neither knowledge of nor sympathy with the Christian faith. Some may think that such a position is improbable, but if it is even possible, and not the most optimistic would deny this, the Church should now, while it still has the chance, attempt to secure greater freedom from the State. Churchmen would be both unfaithful and short-sighted unless they strengthen their Church against storms which may arise suddenly and endanger both it and the State.

Before we consider how the relationship between Church and State should be readjusted, there is an important point to keep in mind. No individual or voluntary society can escape from all State control. A subject must obey the law, and a voluntary association if it has property must submit to a certain degree of State supervision. The use of its property is defined by trusts; any change in the nature of the trust must be legally sanctioned; any departure from it can be checked by legal process. To this extent all non-established Churches are subject to the State, and when a Church is disestablished it will still find this is the case, though it will be free from the special controls which are due to its position as an Established Church.

Disestablishment

Disestablishment seems at first sight the quickest and surest way of gaining spiritual freedom. By it the Church would be placed in the same relationship to the State as any other Church in England. The king would neither necessarily be a member of it, nor crowned by the Archbishop of Canterbury; the Coronation might be performed without any religious ceremony; the bishops would no longer be appointed by the king, nor would they pay homage to him; the bishops and clergy would not be required to take the Oath of Allegiance; the bishops would lose their seats in the House of Lords, and it is doubtful if the sittings of either House would be opened with prayer. The Church of England and its ministers would no longer possess any authority or precedence which an Established Church carries with it. The decisions of its Courts would not be enforced by the State, and it is unlikely that the facilities for legislation now granted to the Church Assembly would continue after disestablishment.

But to Archbishop Davidson's question "What good would disestablishment do?" there are three answers. First, the Church would have the right to appoint its own bishops and deans; it would choose its bishops either by unfettered election on the part of the cathedral Chapter, or by some other electoral method which would give both the clergy and the laity the responsibility of choosing their father-in-God. Secondly, the Church would be self-governing; its convocations would not require permission from the Crown either to meet or to enact canons; it would be able to formulate its faith or revise its worship without reference to Parliament; it could order its own discipline and control its own affairs without appealing to an external body; neither Acts nor Measures would be required for changes in its organisation and administration. Through this independence it would acquire a sense of responsibility which has sometimes been lost through undue reliance on the State. Thirdly, the Church would have its own spiritual courts to which appeal could be made on disputed matters of doctrine, worship and discipline; these courts would be spiritual in their origin and in their authority, and their decisions would be binding on the consciences of the clergy and the laity.

Disestablishment should mean a free Church in a free State. The Church would no longer be open to the reproach that it was controlled by a secular State; that its bishops were chosen by a Prime Minister who might be opposed or indifferent to all religion; that it could make no change in its worship without the approval of Parliament; and that its final court of appeal was a judicial committee appointed by the State. The Church would have gained freedom to develop its own life as a spiritual society independent either of the Pope or Parliament.

These would be valuable gains if they were certain to follow disestablishment; but there is no guarantee that it would bring this freedom, while on the other hand there are objections which must be carefully weighed and considered before the Church asks for it.

(1) It must be remembered that the State would not allow the Church to retain considerable property unless the constitution and doctrine of the Church as the owner were carefully defined. "One inevitable condition of disestablishment is that the State would have either to define, or to accept a definition of, the constitution and distinguishing formularies of the Church as the owner of its property, and to prescribe or provide for the methods by which that constitution and those formularies could subsequently be varied to meet future needs. If it were willing, as it possibly would be, to accept what the Church itself desired with regard to these matters, there might be no objection to this. But it would be disastrous if the Church were put into the position of having its constitution and basic articles determined for it by any secular authority."[1] If the State itself did not draft a constitution and articles for the Church, it would scrutinise them with jealous eyes if they had been prepared by the Church. Moreover they might have been drawn up by the Church under the influence of one of the parties within it, and this might result in the exclusion of those who had different views. The controversy over an attempt to frame a statement on faith and worship might cause dangerous tension within the Church. Even if general agreement were reached a written constitution endorsed by Parliament might arrest future growth and development. This is no imaginary danger; twice at least in recent years a non-Established Church has had State courts attempting to interpret its doctrines and the laws of its worship. The most famous case was when the Free Church of Scotland, which for over half a century had been a non-Established Church, united with another branch of Scottish presbytery under the title of "The United Free Church of Scotland." This was challenged on doctrinal grounds by a small body of ministers and laymen commonly known as "the Wee Frees"; they won their case and gained the whole of the property of the larger Church. Very soon an Act of Parliament set right what was

[1] "Report on Church and State," Vol. I, p. 50.

generally regarded as morally unjust. But the case and the verdict show how questions of property even in connection with non-Established Churches are dealt with by the civil courts. Recently in the Australian courts a successful action was brought against one of the bishops on the ground that directions in worship he had given did not conform with those in the Book of Common Prayer. It is, therefore, unwise to take it for granted that disestablishment will necessarily give the Church complete freedom from State control. It may even narrow its boundaries and take away from it liberty which at present it enjoys. This seems to have been the case in the Church of Ireland since disestablishment. Dr. Gregg, at the time Archbishop of Dublin, made the following statement to the Archbishops' Commission on Church and State: with disestablishment "a written constitution immediately became necessary, and with the process of making explicit the many details which forthwith required statutory authorisation an inevitable process of crystallisation set in. . . . With every new step in legislation there is a loss of flexibility. Flexibility has been hitherto the privilege, if the danger, of an Established Church; loss of flexibility is the penalty of disestablishment. To make one's own laws may be the sign of freedom, but those laws once made tend to be fetters upon freedom. And under our written constitution the individual tends to be submerged beneath the committee; the exercise of personal or local discretion is reduced within narrow limits, or hedged about with checks and counter-checks which both breed delay and weaken sense of responsibility."[1] At present the Church has great freedom in practice, but little in theory; we must be careful not to gain unlimited freedom in the abstract, but very little in the concrete. Against the freedom which might be secured there must be set the danger of loss of freedom in doctrine and worship through over-rigid definitions or declarations drawn up at the time of disestablishment, which would bind the Church for all time. Moreover in a free Church it is possible that individual members, both clerical and lay, might lose much of the freedom they now enjoy. Non-Established Churches frequently gain cohesion at the cost of freedom. They are "Catholic" or "Protestant" and find no room for diversity. There is greater freedom within the Established Church of England than within the disestablished

[1] Ibid., Vol. II, p. 215.

Church of Ireland or the non-Established Episcopal Church of Scotland, though both have freedom which we do not possess in relation to the State, and happily escape the irregularities in worship and the controversies on matters of faith which often injure our Church.

(2) There is little doubt that if the Church of England were disestablished at the present time, the world would interpret this as the national repudiation of Christianity. In saying that I am not forgetting the warning in G. K. Chesterton's poem on Mr. F. E. Smith's statement that the Welsh disestablishment Bill has "shocked the conscience of every Christian community in Europe."

"Are they clinging to their crosses,
F. E. Smith?
Where the Breton boat fleet tosses,
Are they Smith?
Do they fasting, trembling, bleeding
Wait the news from this our city?
Groaning 'That's the Second Reading!'
Hissing 'There is still Committee!'
If the voice of Cecil falters
If McKenna's point has pith,
Do they tremble for their altars?
Do they, Smith?"

The news of the disestablishment of the Church of England would not cause through the world a cry of indignation or a wave of sympathy. But where religion is actively hated it would be welcomed as another victory; and where the Church is attacked by militant atheism Christians would feel a sense of discouragement. In all probability the reasons which led to disestablishment in England would not be anti-Christian; for many are genuinely convinced that Christianity would gain in strength through the severance of the connection between Church and State. But at a time when millions are under the sway of ideologies which regard the Christian Church as their most dangerous foe, and when in many Moslem lands Christianity is hard pressed in the fight for survival, disestablishment would be widely misinterpreted as the national rejection of religion. Probably disestablishment would be followed by the disuse of prayer on many national and civic occasions. It is doubtful if the Coronation would be solemnised with its ancient religious rites. Those who live in countries where there is no Established Church often regret the frequent absence of prayer at the laying of foundation stones, the opening of civic halls, and on other public occasions; the reason usually given is the difficulty of deciding which of the ministers of the different Churches should be asked to conduct the service. This problem is rarely present in England, where the official position of the bishop or vicar is recognised. It would not be possible to break away from the tradition of 1500 years and more in which the Church and State have been united without giving rise to a widespread impression that the State was divorcing itself from the Christian religion. For the Church to take the initiative in asking for disestablishment would be a grave responsibility only justifiable if it had become plain that there was no other road to spiritual freedom.

(3) Disestablishment would mean loss both to the State and the Church. Through its special relationship with the Church the State bears witness that religion is necessary for the life of a nation. The Church on its side teaches that the authority of the State is from God, that it is divinely ordained to protect the weak and to administer justice, and therefore it has the right to obedience and reverence. The Church thus looks upon the State as more than a mere political association. It calls upon its subjects to honour it as divinely appointed to preserve order and to promote righteousness. But if the Church only did this, it might encourage the deification of the State and the rendering to it of the honour and worship due to God alone; so the Church also has the duty of calling upon the State to obey the laws of God, and of condemning and rebuking it when it breaks or ignores them. Frederick Denison Maurice gives a noble description of the duty of a national Church to the State: "A national Church should mean a Church which exists to purify and elevate the mind of a nation; to give those who make and administer and obey its laws, a sense of the grandeur of law and of the source whence it proceeds, to tell the rulers of the nation, that all false ways are ruinous ways, that truth is the only stability of our time or of any time."[1] The Church if disestablished would still continue this witness to the divine commission of the State, but it would no longer have behind it the same authority which laid on it this special responsibility.

The Church also would lose by disestablishment. Doors of

[1] Quoted by Alec R. Vidler in "Witness to the Light," p. 191.

usefulness and opportunity would be closed to it. The incumbent of a parish either in the town or the country now has a right and duty to go to all those who live within the borders of his cure; he visits them not only as a priest of the historic Church of the land, but also as commissioned by the Established Church. He has behind him the weight and authority of centuries. There are many who think that with disestablishment he would lose his long-recognised place as the "parson" and the spiritual leader of the community in which he is working. This might not be so, but it would be rash to attempt to foretell the results which would follow from the withdrawal of the recognition of religion by the State.

(4) In all probability disendowment would go with disestablishment. There is no logical reason why it should, but in fact the two have usually gone together. Both in Ireland and in Wales the Church was disendowed as well as disestablished. The case against disendowment is twofold: that the possessions were given to the Church by private benefactors, and not by the State, and therefore the State has no moral right to them; and that the Church is making the best possible use of its property for religious, spiritual and moral purposes. Against this the supporters of disendowment argue that as long as the Church was recognised as the national Church and served the whole community, it had the right to its endowments, but that now it is a minority Church, one among other Churches, it has no right to property given to it at a time when it alone made spiritual provision for the nation. But the arguments for and against disendowment are largely academic, for almost certainly it will come with disestablishment, and the only problem to decide will be the amount of property which will be taken from or left to the Church. It is often said that the Church in Wales suffered no material losses and is now better off than before disestablishment; I doubt if this would be the opinion of those now responsible for the finances of the Church in Wales, though it is true that disestablishment has not had the crippling effect anticipated. This has been partly due to Parliament at that time, immediately after the end of the war, wishing to make a generous settlement; and even more to the large help given by the Ecclesiastical Commission from its funds. With the Church of England the property involved would be very much larger; there is no guarantee that an impoverished State would be able to act generously; and certainly there would be no

outside source to which the Church could look for help. At the best the Church would lose several millions in its annual income if disendowment followed earlier precedents.

Whether disendowment were on a large or small scale it would most certainly gravely injure the work of the Church for many years to come. As it is the Church has insufficient funds to pay adequately either its clerical or lay workers. The increased cost of living, high taxation and often excessively large parsonage houses have made the financial position of many of the clergy very precarious. Recently it has lost large sums through the Tithe Act, the Coal Act, the redemption of local loans and the nationalisation of the railways. The immediate effect of disendowment would be a financial crisis in the Church. Much existing work would have to be abandoned, as well as many plans for Church extension. Attempts to raise the incomes of underpaid clergy would be made more difficult than ever. Money now generously given to various charitable associations would in the future be required by the Church for its own purposes. To meet the financial difficulties many more parishes than now contemplated by the most ardent reformers would have to be grouped together and worked by one clergyman. The poorest parishes would be the greatest sufferers. On a long term view disendowment might prove a benefit, for it would bring more of the laity to recognise their responsibility for the stipends of their clergy, instead of depending so largely upon the generosity of their forefathers. It is widely experienced that the members of Churches which have no ancient endowments give more largely and systematically towards the ministry and worship of their Church. But the immediate effect of disendowment would be to cause widespread dislocation of long-established work, and for many years an undue concentration on the gigantic task of raising money to replace that which had been lost.

It is also possible that by disendowment the Church might lost some of its ancient buildings, notably its cathedrals. If they should be taken from the Church it would be on the grounds that as national monuments they belonged to the whole nation, and that a disendowed Church could not afford to keep them in proper repair. No attempt was made in the cases either of Ireland or Wales to transfer the ownership of the churches. But this has been done elsewhere. On the Continent there are some famous cathedrals and churches labelled as " National

Monuments." They are owned by the State and can be visited on the payment of a small fee; but life seems to have gone from them; they are splendid and cold; noble specimens of architecture, but their atmosphere is as different as possible from the church which is used day by day for worship. They are treated as museum pieces. A cultured Communist, the wife of a foreign diplomat, was once visiting an English cathedral city; there was an hour or so to spare before it was necessary to go to the station; her hostess suggested they might visit an institution associated with one of the Churches, but this was negatived on the ground that it was religious in character—then after a pause she said she would like to see the cathedral. Her hostess, very perplexed, said, "But that also is religious." "No, it is not," came the uncompromising reply, "it is a national monument!" Any attempt to take from the Church its ancient churches and convert them into national monuments would be resisted to the last. The Church to-day makes the fullest possible use of them; most of our cathedrals and old churches would long ago have crumbled into ruin if the members of the Church had not raised very large sums of money for their repair and preservation. The total amount spent on the upkeep and restoration of these churches must far exceed the sums they originally cost in building. It is not probable that the State would propose to take from the Church its old churches, but this is a possibility which must not be altogether overlooked when disestablishment is discussed.

Sometimes it is said that the Church objects to Disestablishment lest it should carry with it the loss of loaves and fishes. This is an unworthy charge. We should be false to our trust if we lightly gave up endowments bestowed by our forefathers for purposes of religion. We claim that they have been faithfully used. But we also shrink from disendowment, because we know that the poverty of the clergy would be increased, that in many of the poorest parishes it would be impossible to have a resident clergyman, that Church extension in new districts would be held up, that offerings for work overseas would be curtailed, and that more than ever clergy and laity would have to turn from spiritual work to the raising of money. These are reasons which should make us hesitate before we embark on a course which might lead to disendowment.

The dangers which might come with disestablishment are so great that the Church ought not to take the responsibility of asking for it, unless it is clear that it can gain freedom in no other way. If, however, the nation should decide that the connection between Church and State should be brought to an end, then the Church should be ready to help the State in carrying through disestablishment without bitterness or injustice. It is much to be hoped that the days will never return when platforms were surrounded with banners denouncing " spoliation " and when Churchmen made a political issue of this question. The day may come when the State with an advanced Left-Wing Government will take the initiative in ending the connection of the State with the Church. It would do so on the ground that an Established Church is an anachronism, that it represents only a minority of the people, that better use can be made of its endowments, and that on various matters the law of the Church is different from the law of the State. A demand for disestablishment may be precipitated by an unpopular stand taken by the Church against policy or legislation which it regards as against the law of God. But when Parliament has made it plain, if it ever should do so, that the Establishment should be ended, the Church should accept the decision with dignity and restraint. Three demands, however, it must uncompromisingly make—first that any declaration which set out the constitution and doctrines of the Church must be drawn up by the Church and not imposed on it from without. This is of vital importance. It would be fatal to the spiritual influence of the Church if the State gave authority for its institutions, doctrine and worship. Far better to remain as we are than to become a State-created Church; then the last condition would be far worse than the first! Secondly, the Church must make clear in any declaration it makes affirming its constitution and doctrines, that it is a living body which has inherent powers of self-development: " the essential minimum of any claim we make for the Church must depend on its recognition as a social union with an inherent power of self-development acting as a person with a mind and a will of its own "[1] And thirdly, though this is on a different plane of importance, the Church must claim its right to the continued possession and use of its cathedrals and ancient churches.

It is possible that the Church itself might in the last resort be compelled to ask for Disestablishment. It ought only to do so if it became plain that the State would never relax its

[1] J. N. Figgis, " Churches in the Modern State," p. 99.

present control over the Church. Before, however, the Church decided to take this step, it should press the State to grant it greater freedom in managing its own affairs. In Scotland there is an Established Church which is free, though it is unlikely that the Church of England will be able to obtain the freedom enjoyed by the Church of Scotland.

The Church of Scotland

The Church of Scotland is the outstanding example of a Church which is Established and yet is Free. It is free both in principle and in practice. From the earliest days of the Reformation in Scotland the reformers had insisted uncompromisingly on the freedom of the Church from the State. John Knox was the protagonist in the fight for the spiritual freedom of the Church against the interference of the Crown in spiritual matters. Mary Stuart told him that the people have been commanded by God to obey their princes. "Religion," replied Knox, "comes not from princes, but from the eternal God alone." She objected to the General Assembly meeting without the royal permission: "Take from us," was the reply, "the freedom of assemblies and you take from us the gospel."[1] The Confession of Faith of 1560, and again the Confession of Faith drawn up at Westminster in 1643, proclaimed the independence of the Church with Jesus Christ as its only head. When in the middle of the last century a series of judicial decisions asserted that the kirk derived its powers from Parliament and must submit to it, two-fifths of the ministers of the Church of Scotland in 1843 surrendered their stipends and manses and formed "the Church of Scotland Free"—a great and noble act of sacrifice for the sake of spiritual freedom. "Within four years of the disruption, the seceders had raised £1,254,000 and built 654 churches. No other religious body within the dominions of the Crown showed such energy and self-sacrifice during the Victorian age."[2]

When a hundred years later overtures were made by the Church of Scotland for the healing of the breach, it was essential that the Free Church should be assured that in any scheme

[1] Carnegie Simpson, "The Church and the State," p. 144.

[2] E. L. Woodward, "The Age of Reform," p. 509.

of union the religious freedom for which it had sacrificed so much should be unconditionally recognised. Articles declaratory of the constitution of the Church of Scotland were therefore drawn up and approved by the two Churches. Then Parliament in 1921 was asked to pass an Act declaring the lawfulness of these articles. The articles were prepared by the two Churches and were not discussed by Parliament. They are thus completely spiritual in their origin. No other Church has a constitution which asserts so strongly its complete freedom from the State. In the Act the declaratory articles are contained in its schedule. The Fourth states the freedom of the Church: "This Church, as part of the Universal Church wherever the Lord Jesus Christ has appointed a government in the hands of Church office-bearers, receives from Him, its Divine King and Head, and from Him alone, the right and power subject to no civil authority to legislate, and to adjudicate finally, in all matters of doctrine, worship, government and discipline in the Church, including the right to determine all questions concerning membership of its Courts, and the mode of election of its office-bearers, and to define the boundaries of the spheres of labour of its ministers and other office-bearers. Recognition by civil authority of the separate and independent government and jurisdiction of this Church in matters spiritual, in whatever manner such recognition be expressed, does not in any way affect the character of this government and jurisdiction as derived from the Divine Head of the Church alone, or give to the civil authority any right of interference with the proceedings or judgements of the Church within the sphere of its spiritual government and jurisdiction." The eighth article sets out the provisions by which the Church can modify or add to the articles. Any such proposal by the General Assembly must be transmitted as an overture to the Presbyteries in at least two immediately successive years. If this overture is accepted by two-thirds of the Presbyteries, the Assembly may receive the overture in the light of suggestions received from the Presbyteries. The overture so revised must again be sent to the Presbyteries, and if they consent again by not less than two-thirds of the total number of Presbyteries the General Assembly may, if it thinks fit, add to or modify the overture; a somewhat cumbrous process, but one which gives the Church full opportunities of making up its mind on a proposed change and is a safeguard against undue haste.

The Church of Scotland Act, 1921, with the schedule containing the Articles Declaratory made it plain that the Church of Scotland, while Established, is nevertheless completely Free in all spiritual matters. A Presbyterian divine is not overstating the position when, with legitimate pride, he claims that there is in existence in Scotland a Church "which, to a degree which no other Church in reformed Christendom can claim, is united, national and free."[1] Many of us in the Church of England look in admiration at the Church of Scotland, not only for its freedom but also for the high standards of scholarship in its ministers, and for the way in which so many of its laity are ready at any moment to launch with intelligence into the deep waters of theological controversy. It is therefore natural that some of our Church reformers should ask that the relationship between Church and State in Scotland should be taken as a precedent for England.

But there are serious difficulties in the way. In Scotland the freedom of the Church has been for centuries recognised. The approval by Parliament of the Declaratory Articles was only the formal sealing and ratifying of what had for long been accepted. In England, on the other hand, there have been long periods when the Church made no attempt to assert its spiritual freedom, and when the majority of the laity looked upon it as the religious department of the Government, under State control and authority as much as the navy, the army or the civil service. In England, therefore, it would be almost impossible to persuade a Parliament of laymen to give the Established Church on this side of the Tweed complete religious freedom. Scotland has both religious unity and uniformity to a degree not known in England. For not only are there various schools of thought within the Church, but in addition there are many other communions in England which have always been opposed on principle to Establishment and which are unlikely to agree to reforms which would give the Anglican Church the freedom enjoyed by the Church of Scotland. In Scotland, too, the laity have always had a much more assured position in the government and administration of their Church than has been the case in England both before and after the Reformation.

I see no hope of persuading Parliament to give our Church the freedom which is possessed by the Church of Scotland.

[1] Carnegie Simpson, "The Church and the State," p. 206.

We must therefore ask for various reforms which will lead to an easing of the present position, and which will give to the Church greater freedom than it now enjoys.

Church Reforms

In four directions we must ask for considerable changes in the existing relation between Church and State, and in addition we must also ask the State to allow the Church larger powers than it has already been given to enable it to deal with some practical problems of administration. In later chapters these reforms will be discussed and explained in detail; here they are only given in brief summary. The four essential freedoms concern the appointment of the chief officers of the Church, the right to revise worship, a new code of canons, and Church courts. The less important demand is for the increase and strengthening of the powers which the Church already possesses for the reorganisation of its parochial system.

First, the Church must ask for some voice in the choice of its bishops. In the past king, Pope and Parliament regarded the right of appointment as essential for the control of the Church. To-day a great body of clergy and some of the laity are profoundly dissatisfied with the present method by which bishops are chosen. Reforms which would give the bishops greater discretion are opposed and criticised for this reason. As long as the Church is established the final word in the appointment of diocesan bishops must rest with the Crown, but some plan should be accepted by which the Church is consulted as a matter, not of favour, but of right.

Secondly, the fate of the revised Prayer Book in 1927 and 1928 makes it necessary to reach some arrangement by which the Church could revise its worship without a debate in Parliament. Any plan to secure this would have to be approved by Parliament, and it would require to be satisfied that subsequent changes in worship were agreed upon by the great mass of Church people, and that the laity as well as the clergy had been fully consulted. It is clearly unsuitable that a Parliament in which Churchmen are in a minority should debate and decide on the manner in which the Church should worship God and administer the Sacraments. "There are features of the present 'Establishment' in England which seem to me to be in the proper sense intolerable. The Church, as a fellowship of worshippers, ought to have absolute freedom to order its own worship without any restriction from persons and representatives of persons who may or may not be members of that fellowship."[1]

Thirdly, the existing canon law is admittedly obsolete. In accordance with the recommendation of the Report on Canon Law the Convocations are now both revising the old canons and preparing new. All of these canons must receive the licence of the Crown before they are promulgated, and as some of them alter or modify ecclesiastical Statutes passed by Parliament, it will be necessary to ask for the approval of both Houses for the proposed changes; in several cases this will mean that an Act of Parliament will be required.

Fourthly, the ecclesiastical courts have always been a subject of controversy. In the past it was the laity who objected to coming under the jurisdiction of an ecclesiastical court, but to-day it is the clergy supported by a large body of laity, who are conscientiously opposed to accepting a lay court—the Judicial Committee of the Privy Council—as the final court of appeal in matters spiritual. At present it is impossible to enforce obedience to its decisions. For many years it has been recognised that some change in the nature of the final court is necessary. If the new canons and a new law of public worship are to be obeyed, sanctions to punish deliberate and grave disobedience must be possessed by courts which are accepted and trusted both by Church and State.

The fifth freedom required is different in character; it is not concerned with the relationship between Church and State; it is the demand for greater freedom in reorganising the parochial system which is to a considerable extent unsuitable and unworkable under modern conditions. Already Parliament has approved of various Measures giving the Church wide powers—for instance, the Union of Benefices Measure and the Pastoral Reorganisation Measure—but further powers may be still required. It is not likely that any difficulty will be made by the State when it is asked for these additional powers for a strictly practical purpose.

If these reforms affecting the constitutional relationship between Church and State are to be secured, three preliminary conditions are necessary.

[1] Temple, "Citizen and Churchman," p. 67.

There must be agreement in the Church. The Church must make up its mind what it wants. A seriously divided Church cannot expect Parliament to help it. There will always be a minority which will never be convinced, and which will threaten secession whenever a reform is carried with which it disagrees. It will be useless to wait for unanimity; if this is done all progress will be impossible. The Church should, however, be prepared to wait until the great majority of its members are agreed on the reforms required. Their views should be expressed not only through Convocation and the Church Assembly, but also through the Diocesan Conferences. A united Church should go to Parliament with the demands on which, by overwhelming majorities, it has agreed.

Secondly, the laity must be fully consulted. Parliament will never accept reforms, however good they may be, which have the support only of the clergy. Both Houses of Parliament suspect the bishops and the clergy, and will have to be convinced that the laity also are giving whole-hearted support. Nearly fifty years ago when an Education Bill was in its committee stage in the Commons, my vicar, a keen educationalist, asked Randall Davidson, then Bishop of Winchester, if he should send up a clerical petition in support of certain amendments. "For heaven's sake, don't do it," was the reply; "the Committee is in the mood to vote against anything which they think the clergy want!" This was at a time when Churchmen and Conservatives had a majority in the House of Commons! The more active and vocal the laity, the more likely are we to obtain the necessary reforms.

And thirdly, if these freedoms should be deliberately and decisively refused by Parliament, then the Church would be compelled to ask for disestablishment, with the full knowledge that some disendowment will accompany it. It must be ready for the sake of spiritual freedom to make the same sacrifices as were made by the ministers of the Free Church of Scotland when they gave up their manses and their incomes. We shall never convince the world that we are in earnest unless we are ready, if need be, to purchase our freedom at a great price. To the last we shall hope that Parliament will give us the help we require. We shall go to Parliament asking for its help and anxious to persuade it of the justice of our case. We shall approach it as a friend and not as a foe. We shall be encouraged by the fact that it gave enabling powers to the Church Assembly.

Only if we fail, only if it is plain that all other roads are closed, must we reluctantly but firmly take the road to freedom through disestablishment and disendowment.

Our immediate duty, however, is to decide on the reforms we regard as the minimum necessary for spiritual freedom and then to press forward with them. I know there are some who hold this is sheer waste of time, and that it would be more realistic to ask at once for disestablishment; they are afraid that Convocation and the Church Assembly will first delay, and then Parliament reject, the necessary reforms. I am not so pessimistic, though I fully realise the possibilities of both obstruction and defeat. Encouragement can be found in successful earlier movements of reform. The lessons to be learnt both from the success and failure of reform in the past will give us both hope and guidance. Some of these we shall describe in the next chapter, before we go on to consider the four reforms which appear to be necessary if the Church is to carry out under modern conditions its work for its Lord and for the good of the nation.

VIII

CHURCH REFORM IN THE PAST

A LIVING Church must always be a reforming Church, either because it is penitent for its sins and failures, or because it sees the necessity of adapting its organisation and work to new needs and conditions. When the Church is most alive it is most conscious of the need of reform. Usually the movement for reform comes in the first place from the prophetic insight of a few; their warnings and exhortations may be disregarded during their lives, but they are the sowers of the seed which later brings forth its harvest in the acceptance of reforms which they had urged in vain.

Reform in the Tenth Century

During the first half of the tenth century the need of reform in the Anglo-Saxon Church was great. It had suffered severely from the Viking invasions. Many of its cathedrals and churches had been pillaged and destroyed. The monastic life once so strong in England had come almost to an end. Where the buildings had survived they were more frequently used as shelters for the clergy than as the homes of men vowed to live together under a common discipline. The movement for reform came in this case from the enthusiasm and statesmanship of one man—Dunstan of Glastonbury. He had been banished from the Royal Court, but when the king was in danger of death through a horse out of control bringing him to the edge of a precipice, he suddenly remembered the wrong he had done to Dunstan and resolved that if his life were spared he would make amends. In 943 he made him Abbot of Glastonbury, and seventeen years later Dunstan became Archbishop of Canterbury. His real greatness has been partly hidden by the mass of legends which have grown round his name, and to many he is only known as a half-comic figure who seized the devil's nose with hot tongs. His place is among the greatest of English Churchmen. On one side of his nature he was a mystic and a dreamer; on the other a practical mechanic, a capable administrator, a far-seeing statesman and a fearless man of God. He reformed and revived the monastic life. In this he was helped by Ethelwold and Oswald, abbots of Abingdon and Westbury. When Ethelwold became Bishop of Winchester, he found at the cathedral *canonici* who were neither monks nor parish priests; they were under no strict rules and apparently did not observe scrupulously the lax rule they accepted. When he decided to expel them the king sent one of his officers to assist with an armed force. When they were waiting outside the cathedral for the mass to be finished they heard the singing of the words, " Serve the Lord with fear, and rejoice unto Him with trembling: get you discipline lest you perish from the right way"; they took this as a good omen, and entering ordered the *canonici* either to depart at once or to accept the stricter monastic rule. Powerless and indignant they left the building, though afterwards three of them returned to join the new community. Later at Winchester a meeting was held at which a Rule (*Regularis Concordia*) was accepted by all the heads of the communities in England; this Rule was not in substance new; it was based on the customs observed by most of the Continental monasteries, with however some special modifications to suit the colder climate of England: " thus a fire is allowed in a special room in winter, and the monks may work in shelter instead of in the cloister when the weather is cold . . . especially peculiar to the *Concordia* is the exhortation to daily communion," and what is of special interest is the place given to the king and queen as ex-officio patrons and guardians of the monasteries: " this," writes Dom Knowles in his book on " The Monastic Orders in England," " has no exact parallel in medieval monastic history, and the special prayers for Edgar and his consort said after every portion of the Office save Prime, together with the offering of the Matin Mass for the same intention are quite peculiar to England and must have given to the intercessory prayers of all the monks and nuns a strongly national sentiment."[1]

The revival had great influence for good on the parochial clergy. They came under bishops who were monks and who demanded from them a higher standard of life and conduct than that to which they had been accustomed. Synods were once again held and diocesan visitations made by the bishops.

[1] Pp. 44-45.

The parish priests were ordered to preach every Sunday, and collections of homilies were issued to help them in this. Dunstan and Ethelwold also encouraged ecclesiastical art and literature. Cathedrals and parish churches were enriched by the handiwork of skilled craftsmen. Ethelwold's organ in Winchester cathedral must have produced awe-inspiring sounds—its bellows were worked by seventy strong men, "so swells the sound that as you hear you must clap your hands to your ears to enable you as you draw near to abide the brazen bellowing. All through the city the melody can be heard." In Winchester, too, there was produced at this time the richly decorated Benedictional of St. Ethelwold. With the spiritual and artistic revival there came a flowering of English literature. "There can in fact be no question that the Benedictine Reformation of the tenth century brought fresh vitality to the whole English Church. But its significance is misunderstood if it is dismissed as one of the many movements which have merely influenced a generation and then passed into history. It opened a new phase of English culture which survived the political catastrophe of the Norman Conquest, and contributed to the distinctive quality of medieval English civilisation. The outstanding feature of the phase was the development of a new religious literature in the English language."[1]

The reform movement spread also to the laity. It was a vicious drunken age. One of Ethelwold's monks tells without any hint of censure that once when the king and his nobles were visiting a monastery he called for mead and ordered all doors to be shut, so that no man might escape from his share in drinking. They continued drinking until evening, when the nobles were as "drunk as hogs," for the chronicle stated that through a miracle the mead in the barrel never shrank more than the breadth of a hand! Edgar's canons dealt with the laity as well as with the clergy: concubinage was forbidden; and at church wakes there were to be prayers but no drinking. Dunstan is said to have ordered that drinking cups should be fitted with pegs so that those who used them might know how much they were drinking.[2]

The results of most of these reforms quickly passed away. Between the death of Dunstan and the Norman Conquest there came days of trouble both to Church and State. The Danish

[1] Stenton, "Anglo-Saxon England," p. 45.

[2] Hunt, "A History of the English Church, 597–1066," p. 359.

raids increased in number, confusion and alarm spread. The Crown was too weak to assert control, and its prestige was weakened by the murder of King Edmund at Corfe Castle. Signs of exhaustion appeared. The Church was affected by the general deterioration in national morale, though, as most of the evidence for this comes from post-Conquest writers, there is probably some prejudice in their statements. The standard of life and work of the parochial clergy had become low; this was partly due to the bishops deserting their dioceses for offices at the King's Court, and abandoning their synods and visitations. The more important monasteries appeared to have escaped the general decadence: "We may say then, that the monasteries of England, on the day when King Edward was 'alive and dead' were as a body living and powerful. There is no trace of serious moral decadence, nor of that lay encroachment which in previous centuries had had such disastrous consequences both in England and abroad. At the majority of the important houses the liturgical and cultural life inaugurated a century before was still in being if somewhat less intense."[1] The Church had become intensely insular, for the Danish invasion had broken its connection with the Continent. By the middle of the eleventh century the Church clearly needed another period of reform if it was not to become demoralised and powerless. From within the nation there were no signs of a new movement of reform, Church and State alike were suffering from the losses caused by the invasions and from internal strife. The revival it needed came from the shock given by the Norman Conquest, which brought new ideals and practical vigour from the Continent.

The Norman Reformation

While the initiative for the tenth-century Reformation came from an ecclesiastic, Archbishop Dunstan, in the eleventh century it came from a layman—William the Conqueror, assisted by Archbishop Lanfranc. William was familiar with the reform movements taking place on the Continent, and was impressed by the lethargy and weakness of the English Church as contrasted with the vigour and order of the Church he had left in Normandy. In an earlier chapter some account has been given

[1] Knowles, "The Monastic Order in England," p. 81.

of the changes he effected in the relationship between Church and State, but there were other reforms of equal importance.

Unity or one-ness was the keynote of much in medieval thought and administration. William aimed at complete unity both in Church and nation. If this was to be attained in the Church it was necessary that the supremacy of Canterbury should be asserted; without this, centralised Church government would be impossible. As long as William was king, Lanfranc was certain to have his complete support in upholding his authority. The Archbishop of York reluctantly made his submission, and later the cruel ravaging of the north intimidated both the clergy and laity who might have been tempted to resist ecclesiastical reforms. Very rapidly the sees vacant either by death or by deprivation were filled with Normans bound by feudal allegiance to the king as the overlord from whom they held their lands. The new bishops were ordered to hold synods twice a year in their dioceses. Many of them launched out on great schemes of building. They despised as unworthy the small cathedrals and churches they found in England, and were ambitious to replace them by buildings as massive as those with which they had been familiar in Normandy. Most of these plans were only partially executed in the lifetime of the bishop who had started them. Some, however, acted with such energy that they were able to watch the uprising of great and splendid houses of God. The new cathedral at Canterbury was built in seven years: at Winchester the Norman transepts show how magnificent the cathedral would have been if it had been left as Walkelin planned it, within the stonework of William of Wykeham's perpendicular nave there are still hidden the earlier Norman pillars. It is said that Walkelin asked the king to give him the timber required for the cathedral roof. Very grudgingly the king agreed to allow him to take as much as he could cut and carry from one of his woods within three days. The bishop thereupon collected a multitude of helpers and cleared the wood within the time he had been given. Great was William's fury when he found the wood had vanished, though afterwards he forgave the bishop saying it had been the case of too generous a giver and too grasping a taker. All over the country new churches were rapidly built: York, Rochester, Worcester and other cities were given new cathedrals; and their splendour was rivalled by the great monastic churches built by the Norman abbots.

Lanfranc was greatly concerned over the monasteries : looking at them from the standpoint of a Continental monk, English discipline seemed lax and, in some of the communities, the rules imposed by Dunstan were ignored. At the time of the Conquest there were twenty-five self-governing monasteries ![1] They had considerable wealth, and their social and political influence in the nation was great. Not more than half a dozen of the abbots fled the country, but these vacancies and others which soon came through death were filled by Crown nominees who brought to England the stricter discipline followed on the Continent. Most of the new abbots were good and capable, intellectually and devotionally above those whose places they filled. Occasionally, however, serious mistakes were made in the appointment of men who had neither understanding nor sympathy with the native monks over whom they had been placed. Possibly Thurstan of Caen is the worst example of an unimaginative foreigner as the head of an English community. He ordered the monks of Glastonbury to change their music for unfamiliar chants ; many a modern incumbent has learnt by bitter experience how choir and congregation dislike new tunes and can be persuaded to acccept them only by patience and tact ; but Thurstan had neither of these qualities, and called his men-of-war to enforce his orders. The monks fled to the choir and defended its entrance with benches and candlesticks, while the archers shot down on them from one of the galleries of the transepts, and armed men with spears attacked them on the floor ; the riot only ended with the death of some of the resisting monks and the wounding of others. The abbot was sent back to Caen in disgrace. As the monasteries were placed under Norman control discipline was tightened, and the monks compelled to keep the rules ; if married they had either to separate from their wives or depart from the monastery. But the Normans do not seem to have introduced new rules, but rather to have insisted on the strict observance of those already in existence. Monastic reform took " the shape of a return to what had been the norm a century before in such matters as regular silence, regular food, and the strict observance of property."[2] Walkelin proposed to take drastic steps at Winchester and had forty canons ready to take the place of the laxer

[1] Knowles, " The Monastic Order in England," p. 100.

[2] Knowles. Ibid., p. 121.

monks, but Lanfranc refused to allow this, and forty disappointed canons had to withdraw.

Lanfranc made an attempt to enforce celibacy upon the parochial clergy. He discovered very quickly that it would be impossible to apply indiscriminately the rule then accepted on the Continent; the resistance would be too great, and his authority would be weakened by failure to enforce a regulation so generally unpopular. The most he could do was to insist that no married man should be ordained either to the diaconate or priesthood; but those in Orders who were already married were not required to put away their wives. But Lanfranc was anxious to protect as well as to discipline the clergy. He ordered that no parish priest should be called upon to render any service to the patron for his benefice over and above what he had been liable for in the reign of Edward the Confessor. This strengthened the position of the clergy against a patron who was also Lord of the Manor and as such might demand some share of the income. Other regulations were laid down to help the parish priest resist the encroachments of wandering monks and unattached clergy who forced themselves upon a parish to the loss and annoyance of the rightful incumbent.

The Norman Conquest thus brought new life to the English Church. The replacement of Anglo-Saxon bishops and abbots by Normans who were ignorant of the language of the people to whom they were to minister was a severe trial to those accustomed to the past, and this was often the more so through the lack of sympathy the new rulers showed to English customs, even to the extent of wishing to excise from the Kalendar the names of many national saints. But the Normans brought new ideals of Church life and order; they gave to an insular Church a deeper sense of its place in Christendom, as well as the discipline, experience and culture of the Continent. They gave it not only a splendid architecture, but also learning, which had become weak in England in the troubled times of the Viking attacks, and they established libraries in their cathedrals and created new centres of education.

Frustration in Reform

The fourteenth century in England was a time of disturbance both in Church and State. It was the century of the Black

Death which swept away the whole population from villages and decimated the towns; it was followed by the rising of the peasants under Wat Tyler and the murder of an archbishop. All through the reigns of Edward III and Richard II the call for reform is heard both in Church and State. Both the clergy and laity protest angrily against repeated Papal exactions, especially as they suspected that some of the taxes raised for the Pope went into the coffers of the French king with whom England was at war. Papal taxation, the provision of bishoprics and benefices for the Pope's friends, and appeals to the Papal Courts were ever recurring subjects of complaint. At the beginning of the century the Parliament of Lincoln protested against "the marvellous and unheard of" pretension of the Pope in claiming Scotland as a fief of the Apostolic see. But attacks were made not only on a distant Pope, but also on the clergy at home. The bishops were accused of neglecting their dioceses and spending their time as royal officials of the king's court, and were blamed for silence when they should have spoken against social wrongdoing: "Shame on the bishops that they are dumb and raise no warning cry." So vigorously at one time did the laity criticise the employment of ecclesiastics in State offices that a clerical ministry, which included William of Wykeham, was dismissed and replaced by laymen, who, however, soon proved themselves so incompetent that they had to yield their posts again to bishops! The monasteries were also frequent targets for the attacks of reformers; they were accused of possessing great wealth and of using it wrongfully; the monks were charged with neglecting their prayers and the claims of the poor for the work of administering their great estates. Some of the abbeys were attacked by angry mobs and, when possible, the title deeds of their lands were seized and burnt. The growing movement for reforms found expression in the teaching of Wyclif who, taking the Bible as the sole standard of faith and life, denounced the Pope as the "head vicar of the fiend," the cardinals as "incarnate devils," and the bishops, archdeacons and rural deans for making in "their diabolical malice" money out of "the sins of lust." Most vehement of all were his attacks on the monks "with red and fat cheeks and great bellies" and the friars.[1] He considered all endowments as harmful to the Church, and as the source

[1] W. Capes, "A History of the English Church in the Fourteenth and Fifteenth Centuries," pp. 113–124.

of worldliness and covetousness. Through the translation of the Bible into English and through the sending out of poor priests to teach and preach he increased discontent with existing conditions, and prepared the way for the Reformation.

The popular opinion of the ecclesiastics of that time is best seen in Langland's "Piers Plowman."[1] In it we find a realistic account of what ordinary men thought of their spiritual leaders in the fourteenth century. He tells of friars who "preached to the people for the profit of their bellies"; of parsons and parish priests who petitioned their bishops

> ". . . for a license to leave and live in London,
> And sing there for simony, for silver in sweet."

of bishops who stay in London "counting coins in the king's chambers"; of the abbess "who would sooner swoon and die than suffer discomfort"; of the parson who knows neither the scales, nor the saints' legends, but "can find an hare afield or frighten him from his furrow"; of cardinals who make the parish clergy give them money for their furs and feed their horses and their followers, and of whom the people say "the country is the more cursed when cardinals come into it, and where they lie the longest lechery is greatest"; and of the Pope

> ". . . who pillages Holy Church
> Who claims that before the king he is the keeper of Christians
> Who counts it nothing that Christians are killed and beaten
> Who leads the people to battle and spills the blood of Christians."

But the poem is far from being a mere diatribe against abuses; for again and again it sets forth the vision of what the Church should be with holy ministers working for the salvation of the people and the realm.

Various attempts at reform were made. Statutes were passed against appeals to Rome, against papal provisions for foreigners, against incumbents holding several benefices. But the reforms failed. The statutes of mediæval days were usually the statement of ideals rather than legislation to be enforced. Both Pope and king either ignored them or used them for their own advantage. The Pope, for example, ordered the clergy to resign all but one of the benefices they held, and then appropriated for his nominees the parishes which thus had become vacant.

[1] Rendered into modern English by Henry W. Wells, pp. 4, 5, 68, 269, 270.

Appeals were still sent to Rome as if no statute had been passed forbidding this practice. The king himself set at nought the statute against papal provisions by asking the Pope to appoint to vacant sees ministers who had been useful to him. "The statutes of provisors and *præmunire* were as little executed as were the statutes of labourers or as some elaborate sumptuary legislation passed by the Parliament of 1363. The catalogue of acts of papal interference in English ecclesiastical and temporal affairs is as long after the passing of these laws as before."[1] Fear of the social teaching of Wyclif and his followers caused a reaction on the part of both clergy and laity against reform. If reform meant the sweeping away of all endowments and the substitution of the Scriptures for Church doctrine, then it seemed safer to offer to all suggestions of reform an uncompromising resistance. For a century and a half the clergy hid themselves behind the ramparts of extreme conservatism. Not content with attacking Lollardism by reasoned argument and by the spiritual weapons of excommunication, they persuaded the State to burn those who had been condemned by the Church for heresy. The University of Oxford was compelled by the king and the Archbishop of Canterbury to expel all supporters of Wyclif; by this step religious learning suffered and theological originality was penalised. By the end of the century all hope of reform had gone. Dr. G. M. Trevelyan thus explains the failure of reform: "Whereas Parliamentary institutions and servile emancipation were developing apace, religious reform was impossible. The Church in England had no power to reform itself, because she had no autonomy. She was part of a cosmopolitan organisation centred abroad, of enormous prestige and power, knowing nothing of English needs and of set purpose to resist change. If in England the Church had retired step by step before the rising tide of lay emancipation, there would have been no violent overturn in Tudor times. But pent waters gather force."[2] In the tenth century reform had been carried through by a great and vigorous churchman, Archbishop Dunstan; in the eleventh, king and archbishop had worked side by side for reform; but in the fourteenth century neither kings nor archbishops were strong or disinterested enough to force through reforms in face of the opposition of the Papacy and of the fear and suspicion of the clergy.

[1] T. F. Tout, "The Political History of England, 1216–1377," p. 378.
[2] "History of England," p. 244.

It was not until the fifteenth century that the determination of a king supported by the laity in Parliament carried reforms which were long overdue.

The Reformation

The reforms made in the sixteenth century were of such importance that they have always been known as "the Reformation." They can be divided into two great groups. Those which asserted the supremacy of the laity over the clergy, and those which were due to an appeal to sound learning. It is unnecessary to say anything further about the reforms in the first group; they have already been discussed in an earlier chapter. They led to the complete repudiation of the jurisdiction of the Pope, and in the submission of the clergy to the Crown. In future the king appointed the bishops, and without his previous approval the Convocations could neither meet nor make new canons. But some of the results of the appeal to sound learning must be briefly described, for though in England the Reformation started as a political movement, presently it became both religious and intellectual.

Its appeal to sound learning was an appeal to the Bible, the early councils, and the early fathers for truth in doctrine. The translation by Tyndale and Coverdale was revised, and the Great Bible was set up in all parish churches so that those who could do so might read it. To the test of the Scriptures were brought many medieval doctrines, notably the doctrine of transubstantiation, and rejected as false. The Bible was taken as the standard by which all teaching as necessary for salvation was to be judged. The forty-two articles, afterwards reduced to thirty-nine, were intended as a test of the orthodoxy of preachers and teachers.

The worship of the Church was drawn up in accordance with sound learning; it was to be Scriptural and purged of medieval legends and superstitions; it was to be in the vulgar tongue, and the prayers read audibly so that the congregation might both follow the service and take part in it. No longer was the priest to say mass silently in an unknown tongue at an altar separated from the people by chancel and screen, but at a Table moved to the midst of the chancel. In the future Morning and Evening Prayer were normally to be said by the minister from a desk either at the upper end of the nave, or in the case of large churches, some way down it. The object was so that the people could easily hear and follow the prayers. Archbishop Grindal in his Injunctions ordered the clergy, " in your church or chapel at convenient hours reverently and distinctly say or sing the Common Prayers appointed by the laws of this Realm both in the forenoon and afternoon, standing in a pulpit or seat appointed for that purpose and turning your face towards the people so that they may best hear the same." In the presentations at Visitations there were frequent complaints of the inaudibility of the clergy, and there is at least one case when a vicar had to do public penance for this ; standing in the pulpit after reading the Gospel, he said, " Whereas I good people have many times in saying of divine service mumbled up the same in such sort that few or none of my parishioners being then and there assembled to hear divine service could understand the same . . . by God His assistance I will endeavour myself from henceforth to read sing and say divine service distinctly and plainly so that you may understand the same."[1] The removal of the Holy Table to the chancel for the Celebration, and the placing of a desk in the nave instead of behind the screen were for the purpose of securing that the services could be read and followed either by the communicants in the choir or by the congregation in the nave. " The process by which medieval churches were adapted for Prayer Book worship might be summed up as one of taking the communicants into the chancel for the Eucharist, so that they can be within sight and hearing of the priest at the altar ; and of bringing down the priest from the chancel into the nave so that he could be amongst his people for Morning and Evening Prayer."[2]

The Reformers had as their ideal an instructed laity ministered to and taught by an educated priesthood. Immediately before the Reformation the standard of education among the clergy was deplorably low. In the middle of the sixteenth century Bishop Hooper found in his diocese of Gloucester a hundred and seventy clergy unable to say the Ten Commandments, and twenty-seven ignorant as to who was the author of the Lord's Prayer. During the Marian reaction the position became worse,

[1] J. S. Purvis, " Tudor Parish Documents of the Diocese of York," p. 127.
[2] G. W. O. Addleshaw and Frederick Etchells, " The Architectural Setting of Anglican Worship," p. 45.

as many were apparently ordained without any intellectual qualifications. In Elizabeth's reign Church and State both took great pains to improve this. In the first year of her reign she issued Injunctions which repeated and amplified similar Injunctions by her brother Edward VI. Two of them stress respectively the importance of an educated clergy and laity. In the 43rd article of the Injunction it is ordered that "Forasmuch in these latter days, many have been made Priests, being children and utterly unlearned so that they could not read to say Mattins and Mass: the Ordinaries shall not admit any such to any cure or spiritual function." And in the 44th article, "Every Parson, Vicar and Curate shall upon every holy-day, and every second Sunday in the year, hear and instruct all the youth of the Parish for half an hour at the least before Evening Prayer, in the Ten Commandments, the Articles of the Belief, and in the Lord's Prayer, and diligently examine them, and teach the Catechism set forth in the Book of Common Prayer." The Archbishop of York used his domestic chaplains to examine and try the clergy; schoolmasters were examined before they were allowed to teach; and the clergy were forbidden to admit to the Holy Communion any above twenty-four years of age who could not say by heart the Commandments, the articles of the faith, and the Lord's Prayer; while those under twenty-four years were required to say by heart the Catechism. In addition the clergy were forbidden to marry any persons unless they could say the Catechism by heart "and will recite the same to you before the asking of the banns," or to accept any as godparents unless they "have before received the Holy Communion and can say by heart the articles of the Christian faith in English, and will recite the same before you at the time of the ministration of baptism"; or if they be "young folks, except he she or they can say by heart the whole catechism."[1] Dr. Purvis in his book on "Tudor Parish Documents of the Diocese of York," writes, "Special attention should be given to the fact that the Catechism was not only a standard body of instruction to be given to the young; it was also regularly and extensively used as a test of religious knowledge and even of religious conformity; it was used to guard the Sacraments of the Church against unqualified persons. Both clergy and laity, according to their respective duties, were

[1] Archbishop Grindal's "Injunctions for the Clergy," quoted by J. S. Purvis in "Tudor Parish Documents," pp. 129, 130.

subjected to a constant and scrupulous examination in their knowledge and use of the Catechism."[1]

The clergy were ordered to use the pulpit for instruction, but only the limited number who were licensed were allowed to preach their own sermons. The unlicensed incumbent had either to secure a licensed preacher for a sermon once a quarter, or if this was not possible, to read one of the authorised homilies. There are many complaints that the quarterly sermon was not preached. The strict regulation of preaching was necessary if the pulpit was not to be used for controversial purposes. In November, 1577, Ambrose Shawe, Minister of the Parish Church of Penrith, has to confess that in a sermon "I forgetting my duty to Almighty God and falling into great oversight did inveigh against the right reverend Father in God Richard now Bishop of Durham and lately Bishop of this see of Carlisle and did utter of and against his Lordship (although I do not at all know him or of my own knowledge understand any fault in him) diverse false untrue and slanderous words speeches and sentences and called his honour unreverent uncharitable and unseemly names especially in this manner. That is to say I called him a cub, a tyrant, a wolf, a satan, and a money master."[2]

Sufficient credit is not usually given to the archbishops and bishops of Elizabeth's reign for the strenuous and repeated efforts they made to create an educated clergy and laity. Nowhere else did the Reformers insist so strongly on the importance of sound learning for a Church which had to withstand the assaults both of Roman Catholics and Puritans. It was a great ideal, though only partially realised. The nature of the Reformation in England cannot be understood unless it is seen that through all changes in doctrine and in worship there runs this appeal to sound learning, and above all to an intelligent understanding of the Scriptures.

"*The Second Reformation*"

For twenty churchmen who could give some account of "the Reformation," there is hardly one who has any knowledge of what Dr. Williams, the Bishop of Durham, has recently

[1] Ibid., p. 128.

[2] Ibid., p. 135. I have transcribed this and other quotations into modern spelling. I recommend this book for a series of interesting quotations throwing light on parish life in Elizabethan days.

described as "the Second Reformation."[1] This consisted of a series of ecclesiastical reforms promoted by Sir Robert Peel in the first half of the nineteenth century. It is difficult to exaggerate their importance. Canon Charles Smyth writes: "As far as any human power did save the Church of England it was saved not by Mr. Keble, but by Sir Robert Peel."[2] At the beginning of the nineteenth century the necessity of reform was plain to all outside the Church, and to many of its laity, though only a few of the bishops and clergy seemed aware of the threatening storms. The agitation for the Reform Bill had made the nation critical of existing institutions both in Church and State. A fierce light was poured on the weak places in the administration and finance of the Church by those who bitterly resented the opposition the bishops had shown to Parliamentary Reform. An anonymous publication was circulated entitled "The Extraordinary Black Book." It was unfair and prejudiced, but it contained a number of facts and figures which stirred public opinion. It accused the bishops of being political nominees in the possession of huge incomes—Canterbury with £32,000 per annum, and Winchester with the still larger amount of £50,000 (in the Middle Ages it was said that Canterbury had the higher throne, but Winchester the deeper manger). These large episcopal incomes were contrasted with the miserable pittances received by so many of the clergy. The anonymous author declared that there was no Church discipline; clergy of all degrees went their own way, with no check on their sloth and neglect of their duties. He attacked abuses which had been tolerated for generations: patronage was sold and bought; many of the clergy were pluralists who drew large incomes from the benefices they held, but left them to the care of underpaid curates; many of the incumbents lived far away from their cures, visiting them rarely or never; it was alleged that the proportion of non-resident to resident clergy was three to two.

So great was the stir caused by these and other attacks upon the clergy that in 1835 Sir Robert Peel appointed a commission to enquire into Church reform. It drew up its report very quickly, and most of its recommendations were soon carried into law. The excessive incomes of some of the dioceses were reduced: Canterbury to £15,000, York and London to £10,000,

[1] A. T. P. Williams, "The Anglican Tradition in the Life of England," p. 83.

[2] Rawlinson and Smyth, "The Genius of the Church of England," p. 37.

and Winchester £8,000; and part of the surplus thus saved was used to raise the incomes of the poorer sees. Two new dioceses were created in the north—Ripon and Manchester, and the boundaries of others altered, thus reducing the size of some of the larger dioceses which had sprawled over several counties. Drastic as these changes were, they did not go far enough in the opinion of some; one of the critics in the House of Commons complaining that the revenues left to the Archbishop of Canterbury were sufficient to provide a decent income for three hundred poor clergymen trying to live on 2s. 8d. a day. The capitular bodies were also dealt with, and the endowments of suppressed sinecures and rectories were invested with the commissioners who were now established as a permanent body with the title of the Ecclesiastical Commissioners and given the responsibility of administering Church property and of preparing schemes to carry into effect the recommendations of their report. It is impossible to speak too highly of the work of the Commissioners; they not only have acted with great wisdom as the trustees of large endowments and funds belonging to the Church, but they have frequently initiated schemes for the improvement of the position of the clergy.

Another reform dealt with the payment of tithe to the clergy. This had been paid in kind, the tenth of the produce of the year both of the earth and of live-stock, and had been a frequent cause of controversy and irritation between the incumbent and his parishioners. The large and picturesque tithe barns seen in many parts of the country were built to store the corn and other produce due from the farmer to the parson. There were the greater tithes paid to the rector, not necessarily a clergyman or even an individual, but sometimes a layman or a college, whose only legal obligation to the parish was to keep the chancel of the church in good order; the lesser tithe was paid to the vicar. It was difficult to decide on the amount of tithe payable each year; the tithe proprietor took an over-cheerful view of the harvest, but the farmer who had to pay the tithe gave a more depressing account of the crops he had gathered. Until recently it was said that the farmer never spoke as if the harvest had been satisfactory; probably this was an almost instinctive defence against possible demands by the owner of the tithe! Disputes inevitably arose between the owner and the payer as to the amount of the tithe that was due, and at the best it was vexatious to collect and store it. The Act of 1836 abolished payment in kind, and substituted a money payment assessed on a seven-year average.

The accumulative effects of these reforms were great. They removed long-standing abuses and placed the Church in a more favourable position to meet the new demands made upon its resources through the growth of the industrial towns. "It may fairly be said that in a decade or two, by means of these reforms, by the establishment of new sees and by the re-arrangement of diocesan boundaries, by the creation of new parishes, and by measures for the building of new parsonage houses and towards the equalising of benefice incomes, the legislature and the Commissioners had removed a mass of hampering obstructions and had paved the way for a continuing adaptation of resources to needs. Much remained and still remains to be done. But a decisive and effective beginning had been made."[1] Though these reforms were actively supported by the Archbishop of Canterbury and by some of the bishops, the initiative came from the State, and it was the resolution of successive Prime Ministers which secured the necessary legislation.

Twentieth-Century Reforms

But if the Church reforms of the nineteenth century were mainly due to State action, the reforms of the twentieth century are due to the Church. In insisting to-day on the need of Church reform, it must not be forgotten that within a short period a large number of reforms have been effected, either by the Church alone, or by the Church with the help of the State. Two great reforms have been carried through without any help from the State. The first is in connection with candidates for Ordination. For a long period their preparation had been inadequate, and they were drawn from a very limited field. At one time a knowledge of Greek and a university degree were regarded by many bishops as sufficient. An ordinand at the end of the eighteenth century described how before his examination by the bishop he consulted the domestic chaplain who told him the passages from the Greek Testament which the bishop would probably ask him to translate; all went well until in his nervousness he dropped the Testament, and picking

[1] A. T. Williams, "The Anglican Tradition," p. 84–85.

it up the wrong way up still continued to translate; the bishop noticing this rejected him saying: "Next time you must come better prepared." With the establishment of theological colleges in the nineteenth century the standard of preparation was raised. In the twentieth century, especially since the last war, great advance has been made both in the selection of candidates and in the thoroughness of their subsequent training. At no time in the history of our Church have its clergy been more thoroughly and carefully trained than at present. The field from which they are chosen has been enlarged; they are no longer drawn only from the classes which can afford to pay for their time at one of the universities. Kelham and Mirfield were pioneers in opening colleges for those unable to afford residence in one of the older universities. Since then the Church has raised large sums of money to help its ordinands, and still larger sums will be required in the future.

The Church has also revolutionised its finance. At the beginning of the century each parish was responsible for its own finances, making voluntary contributions towards diocesan and missionary funds. The system was simple, and it gave to parishes an independence in raising and spending their funds which they do not now possess. But this method suffered from two serious defects: central Church funds were always uncertain of their income, and the Church had not the means to undertake the financing of central schemes which were urgently required. In the diocese all was well with the wealthier and stronger parishes, they could meet all their needs and give support elsewhere at their discretion, but the poorer parishes were engaged in a perpetual struggle to make both ends meet. A system has now been built up by which each parish according to its means pays an annual quota to the diocesan fund, which is thus able to help the poorer parishes; and each diocese makes a fixed contribution to the Central Board of Finance, and so enables it to become responsible for plans which concern the whole Church, such as the provision of grants for ordinands and the support of the Church Training Colleges. The new methods of finance are a great improvement on the old haphazard methods of raising money, especially when through Free Will Offering schemes individual churchmen are taught the duty of systematic giving. On the other hand there are very real dangers that too much thought and time may be given to finance, that undue burdens may be placed upon the clergy by repeated demands that the quota should be paid in full, and that excessive centralisation in London may weaken the independence of the diocese. Though both legally and theoretically the quota is a voluntary offering, the moral compulsion used to secure its payment is very great, and the incumbent is blamed if the parish fails to contribute the amount allotted to it. The same kind of pressure is brought on the dioceses if they do not annually send to London the sum for which they have been assessed.

Since the Enabling Act a large number of Measures of reform, both great and small, have been sent by the Church Assembly to Parliament, and only four of these have been rejected. The most important of the Measures can be grouped under three heads.

First, there are various administrative reforms. Very soon after the Assembly received Enabling Powers it passed Measures providing for the creation of several new dioceses: the most important of these was the division of the ancient diocese of Winchester into three. The creation of smaller dioceses made corporate life within them more possible; for in the large dioceses it had proved impossible for either the bishop to know his clergy or for the clergy to know one another. But some of these schemes were carried through with undue haste, and the lines of division have not always proved satisfactory. An important reform was effected by the Cathedrals Measure of 1931; under it obsolete Statutes of cathedrals were revised, the greater Chapter made a reality, and capitular finance overhauled. A number of useful Measures were passed dealing with parishes—by the Union of Benefices Measures, 1923–1936, the union of parishes was simplified and the Pluralities Measure, 1930, made it possible for parishes to be held together temporarily when a permanent union was inadvisable.[1] By the Benefices (Suspension of Presentation) Measure, 1946, the bishop can suspend an appointment to a vacancy for five years, without the patron losing his right to appoint. The Pastoral Reorganisation Measure of 1949 gives wide powers for the reorganisation of

[1] Under the Pluralities Act of 1838 the holding of more than two benefices with the cure of souls was prohibited and for the holding of more than one with the cure of souls a dispensation from the Archbishop of Canterbury was required. By the 1930 Measure two or more benefices may be held together if this is recommended by a Commission of enquiry and approved by the bishop, the patron and the Ecclesiastical Commissioners; but the Archbishop's dispensation was still required. By the Pastoral Reorganisation Measure, 1949, the bishop of the diocese will issue the order for plurality.

the parishes of a diocese. Various Measures were passed to meet the emergencies caused in parochal life by the dislocation of war and for the reorganisation of districts which had been affected either by bombing or by the movement of population. The most important of administrative reforms was one which recently has received the Royal Assent: this united the Ecclesiastical Commission and Queen Anne's Bounty under the title of the Church Commissioners. This will avoid overlapping, will make for economy, and for greater speed and efficiency. The Church Commissioners will have undivided responsibility for preparing and administering schemes for the payment of the clergy, the union or creation of parishes, and the sale or improvement of parsonage houses.

Secondly there were Measures which affected the status of the clergy. The Church Councils have been given a voice in the choice of a new incumbent. Reforms concerning the payment of dilapidations on the parsonage houses have done something to relieve the incumbent of a great anxiety and burden. Pensions Measures will, when they are in full effect, remove from an incumbent the payment of part of his income to a predecessor, while he will have the right to draw a pension of £200 if he decides to resign at the age of 70: though this is a pitiably small sum in relation to the rise in the cost of living.[1] The Church Assembly has also taken some part in the raising of the incomes of all incumbents to a figure more in accordance with modern conditions.

Thirdly, some long-standing abuses have at last been removed. The scandal of simony is now almost at an end. A Measure was passed in 1933 which forbade the sale of a benefice after the next two vacancies. In close connection with this was another Measure which gave parishes the right to repurchase the patronage of their parishes which had without their knowledge been bought on behalf of an extreme party trust. After long discussion and much opposition Measures were approved which would enable a bishop to remove an incumbent who through prolonged illness, mental infirmity, or the weakness of old age was unable to perform his duties, or when, by his conduct or neglect, he caused scandal in the parish.

This list of reforms is encouraging. The Church has shown itself alive to the necessity for reform, and Parliament has been

[1] Where the total income of the pension is less than £250 the Pensions Board and the diocese will endeavour to increase the pension to this sum.

ready to co-operate. But since the passing of the Enabling Act no Measure has been carried which has modified the relationship between Church and State. Moreover the most important of the reforms proposed by the Church, the revision of the Prayer Book, was rejected by Parliament. The State still has the power it possessed over the Church at the time when the whole nation belonged to the Church and when every Member of Parliament was a Churchman. The Crown still appoints its chief officers; Convocation cannot meet and canons cannot be made without the approval and licence of the Crown; the public worship of the Church cannot be legally altered without the approval of Parliament; the final Court to interpret Church doctrine is appointed by the Crown; and a large number of administrative reforms are still impossible unless they are agreed to by Parliament. The Church must now decide on the changes necessary for its spiritual freedom. It must ask the State for larger spiritual freedom than it has possessed in the past. There is good reason to hope that the State may regard with sympathy and understanding the reasons which have led to this request. But the days have gone when the State took the initiative in Church reform; this must now come from the Church, and unless Churchmen agree on what they regard as essential the present precarious position will continue until a crisis arises which, whether they like it or not, will compel a revolutionary change in the relationship between Church and State.

IX

THE APPOINTMENT OF BISHOPS

READERS of " Barchester Towers " will remember the opening chapter in which Archdeacon Grantly is seen by the deathbed of his father, the old Bishop of Barchester. The archdeacon is deeply troubled in mind: he was a loyal and dutiful son devoted to his father, but he hoped to succeed him; hints of his appointment had been discreetly held out, but while the bishop was slowly dying, the ministry was tottering. It was a race between the death of his father and the fall of the ministry. " No probable British Prime Minister but he who was now in, he who was so soon to be out, would think of making a bishop of Dr. Grantly." But a few minutes after the death of the bishop the news arrives of the fall of the ministry. " Thus terminated our unfortunate friend's chance of possessing the glories of a bishopric." This is an unduly simple account of the making of bishops in the Church of England, but behind the exaggeration there is a long and interesting history leading up to the nomination to the Crown by the Prime Minister of those he chooses to be elected, confirmed and consecrated as bishops of the Church of God.

The Early Church

In the early Church the bishop was chosen by election. Only after he had been freely chosen by the Church which he was to serve could he be consecrated. Election and consecration were both regarded as essential: " A bishop had first to be lawfully chosen by a particular community to occupy the vacant *cathedra* of its church, and secondly to be lawfully entrusted with the *charisma* of the episcopate by the ministry of those already recognised as possessing it. When the neighbouring bishops met to bestow on the bishop-elect the laying on of their hands, they in fact ratified with the sanction of the

Church at large the choice of the individual community."[1] It is impossible to overstate the importance attached to the free election of the bishop, this was regarded as almost as important as the actual laying on of hands. The election took various forms: sometimes it was made by the local Church; sometimes by the neighbouring bishops, with the assent of the clergy; frequently the laity were asked to show their approval —which was signified by their applause, rather than by direct voting, much in the same way as at the Coronation assent is given by the cries of the congregation when the king is presented to them by the archbishop. For several centuries the Churches clung "to this right of choosing their own bishop with great tenacity, despite constant attempts at interference both by the emperors and by synods of bishops." At the end of the fourth century the bishops "were virtually the only *elected* representatives of the cities who had survived the flood of officialdom."[2]

A bishop duly elected and consecrated was bound for the rest of his life to the diocese which had chosen him. He was the centre of its unity, of its ministry, of its charity, and of all its spiritual activities. He was as inseparable from it as husband and wife. Translation from see to see was denounced by Church Councils and sometimes spoken of as adultery. This is in striking contrast to our own time when translations are frequent, and often are for the good both of the diocese and the bishop. But the bishop who remains for a long period of years in the same diocese has opportunities of knowing his people, both clergy and laity, which are not possible if he is with them only for a short time. The ideal case against translation is well stated by Bishop Hensley Henson, after it was made plain that he would not be translated to York, an event expected by some of his friends, but not by himself: "It was not without cause that the ancient Church looked with disapproval on 'translation.' There is such a thing as fidelity to one's own diocese, and this is not easily consistent with a desire to leave it, or the expectation of doing so. Single-mindedness is not easily consistent with a double objective, and a man's energies are not assisted by divided interests. Probably also the effect of definite and apparent assignation to a specific pastorate is considerable in the diocese itself. The people can no longer suspect

[1] "Essays on the Early History of the Church and the Ministry," edited by H. B. Swete, p. 107.

[2] "The Apostolic Ministry," edited by K. E. Kirk, p. 278.

their bishop of the squalid fault known as 'seeking preferment.' His health may arouse hopes or fears as the case may be, but his motives are no longer suspect. He may, and probably does, become less interesting, but he may possibly gain influence."[1]

The free election of their bishop by the clergy and laity of the diocese concerned was gradually curtailed. The right of the laity was at first limited to a few of the leading nobles and later abolished altogether. In the East the clergy soon lost their share in the election, which was made in future by the synod of the bishops of the Province. In the West the laity retained their right to take part in an election for several centuries after it had been abolished in the East. The right of the clergy as a body to elect passed into the hands of the cathedral Chapters, and by the thirteenth century it is established by law that they have the sole privilege of choosing the new bishop, though a canon of the Lateran Council of 1139 states that they are not to exclude *religiosissimi* from the election. There is uncertainty over the interpretation of "*religiosissimi*"; it might mean some of the diocesan clergy, but more probably it was intended to allow neighbouring bishops to take part in the election.

The Claims of Kings and Popes

While in theory the cathedral Chapters had the right to elect the bishop, the practice, as in so many other matters in the Middle Ages, was very different. When the laity were excluded from taking part in the election of a bishop, there was one momentous exception. As the general body of the laity lost their right to be consulted, the influence of one layman steadily increased, namely that of the king. At first kings and nobles were uninterested in the choice of those called to the spiritual leadership of a small and insignificant group of their subjects. But it was different when the Empire was converted and Christians multiplied in numbers. The bishops of the Church were no longer men who might pay for their dignity by outlawry and even death, but the occupants of an office of dignity and influence which carried with it increasing wealth and power. Under these new conditions it was a matter of importance to the king that the chief sees should be held by those upon whose loyalty he could rely, while the nobility coveted bishoprics for their sons and dependants as posts of

[1] H. Hensley Henson, "Retrospect of an Unimportant Life," Vol. II., p. 210.

honour and wealth. In the East the Emperor claimed the right to control all episcopal appointments; the college of bishops might elect, but the Emperor could refuse to accept its choice, and substitute a nominee of his own. Even Gregory the Great had to wait several months for his consecration until the Emperor had ratified his election—"the Emperor by the fourteenth century was acknowledged to possess a decisive and controlling part in episcopal appointments. All elections by the college of bishops had to be submitted to him for confirmation, and he might, if he chose, substitute a nominee of his own."[1]

In the West we can see in France of the sixth century the royal invasion of the right of the Church to choose its own bishops. The clergy and people still met under the presidency of the Metropolitan for the election, but after they had made their choice, it was necessary to obtain the approval of the king; he might refuse to ratify it and order the electors to make another choice, or he might himself make the nomination. Large bribes were often necessary, and the appointment went to the highest bidder. The king might choose some favourite or courtier, who was still a layman.[2] "The sees of France were filled by roystering captains, whose knowledge of religion and the duties of their new station was in inverse proportion to their knowledge of horses and dogs."[3] Gregory of Tours gives an example of the high-handed action of the king. The Bishop of Bordeaux, with other bishops, expelled from his see a certain Emerius who had been consecrated under a mandate from King Lothar and without the consent of the Metropolitan. In his place they chose Heractius, a priest of Bordeaux, and sent him to King Charibert (who had succeeded his father, Lothar), with the document announcing his choice. The king, after hearing his statement (which appears to have been made in a somewhat tactless manner), "falling into a fury, ordered him to be dragged from his sight, placed on a wagon filled with thorns, and driven into exile." The Bishop of Bordeaux was fined a thousand pieces of gold, and the other bishops punished "as far as their circumstances allowed."[4]

[1] R. C. Mortimer in "Thy Household," p. 55.

[2] As late as 1606 the king of France nominated Richelieu, the future Cardinal, then a layman aged twenty-one, to the see of Luçon, and he was consecrated in the following year in Rome. The see and its revenues had been given to the Richelieu family by a previous king.

[3] O. M. Dalton, "The History of the Franks," by Gregory of Tours, Vol. I., p. 291.

[4] Ibid., Vol. II., p. 136.

In Spain the right of nomination to bishoprics belonged to the king. In the seventh century the twelfth Council of Toledo enacted a canon which declared that the archbishop should prefer and appoint to bishoprics those selected by the king, provided they were found worthy. For many centuries the king sent to the Pope the names of those he desired to fill vacant sees, and the Pope accepted these nominations. It is said that even now the dictator Franco continues this long-standing custom and that his requests are granted by the Pope.

But the kings were not alone in overruling the right of election by a Chapter. The Pope frequently claimed the right to make the appointment. At first this was only in the case of an election when an appeal was made to Rome by one of the defeated candidates; but as there were frequent disputes this often gave the Pope the opportunity of overruling the decision of the Chapters; if the appeal was successful he might either appoint the appellant, or some candidate of his own choice. When a bishop died at Rome (then a most unhealthy city) while waiting for the Papal confirmation of his election, the Pope claimed the right to fill the vacancy so caused. In the case of translations which could only be made by Papal dispensation, the Pope filled the empty see on the excuse that as he had caused the vacancy, it was his duty to remedy it. And later he claimed the right to make provision himself for the vacancies which might occur in the future in certain sees. In this way he was able to fill with his favourites or "yes" men large numbers of dioceses.[1] The election by Chapters under the encroachments of both king and Pope became a mere formality. Eventually the Pope made good the claim that no bishop could be consecrated, whether elected by Chapter or chosen by the king, until the Pope had given his approval. To-day the appointment of all bishops in the Roman Catholic Church is made by the Pope, though it is usual for the Chapter of the diocese to send three names for his consideration; these may be, and sometimes are, passed over in favour of a candidate hitherto unknown; it is generally understood that twice at least in recent years the Pope has appointed to important sees in England men whose names had not been suggested either by the diocese concerned or by the Roman Catholic bishops.

[1] Though sometimes he appointed good and learned men.

Appointment of Bishops in England in the Middle Ages

In England in pre-Reformation days the king, the clergy and the Pope had unequal shares in the appointment of bishops. Before the Norman Conquest the king seems to have appointed at least to the more important sees, though sometimes with the advice or approval of the bishops and nobles assembled in the Witan, and there is also reason to think that occasionally the election was made directly by the Chapters of the cathedral. During the three centuries previous to the reign of Edward the Confessor the Pope had little influence over the appointment of English bishops: " between 669 and 1050 there were consecrated in England three hundred and seventy-six bishops, but during the whole of that period there was not one single case in which the Pope had any share either in the appointment or in the consecration."[1] With the Norman Conquest there was a great increase in Papal intervention; this was inevitable, as the invasion had been blessed by the Pope as a crusade against a schismatic nation. The Norman bishops were familiar with the struggle on the Continent against lay investiture, which consisted in the giving by the king of the pastoral staff and ring to the newly-elected bishop. The dispute with Henry I ended with the compromise that the king gave up the claim to invest with staff and ring, but the bishop must pay homage to the king for the temporalities or possessions in land. Although this controversy seemed to turn round a mere question of ceremonial detail, beneath it there was a deep division of opinion on a matter of fundamental principle, namely whether the appointment of bishops should be made by the temporal or the spiritual authority; by the king or by the Pope. Possibly an even greater issue was involved—not unlike that raised by totalitarian states to-day—the claim of a king or a state to be the source and ruler of all man's rights, both material and spiritual. When one of Becket's murderers was disputing with him, he asked from whom he had the archbishopric. Becket replied, " The spirituals I have from God and the Pope; the temporals and possessions from the king." " Do you not hold both from the king? " " No," retorted the Archbishop; " we have to render to the king the things that are the king's, and to God the things that are God's." Neither the spiritual nor

[1] Quoted by Professor Jenkins in " Episcopacy Ancient and Modern," p. 77.

temporal powers were ready to accept any limitation to their claims, and the European dispute between Pope and Emperor was reproduced on a smaller scale in the frequent controversies between the king and the cathedral over the appointment of bishops. King John granted a charter which "may be regarded as the fullest and final recognition of the canonical right"[1] of the Chapter to elect. The election was to take place in the Chapter House instead of in the royal chapel under the direct supervision of the king; the king's wishes were to be signified by letter, and his assent had to be given to the election; the election was then examined and confirmed by the archbishop of the Province, who subsequently consecrated and received a profession of obedience from the bishop; and before or after the consecration the bishop made his homage to the king, and received in return the temporalities of his see.

On paper this looked as if the Chapters had freedom to elect. But the influence of the king was exerted both through the letter containing the name of his candidate which he sent to the Chapter with his permission to elect, and by the necessity of informing him of the result of the election, before the archbishop could proceed to confirm and consecrate. When the Chapter refused to act upon the royal recommendation, strong pressure was brought either to persuade the Chapter to reverse their decision, or the Pope to overrule it on the ground of irregularities. Henry III was anxious that his half-brother Ethelmar should be elected to the see of Winchester. As he was in every way a thoroughly unsuitable candidate, and under twenty-three years of age, the Chapter informed the king they could not elect him. The king was furious, offering bodily violence to some of the monks. He summoned them to listen to a sermon preached by himself, and took as his text, "Mercy and truth are met together; righteousness and peace have kissed each other." He denounced the monks, and hinted what might come upon them if they persisted in their opposition, and as the result of his eloquence or threats they elected Ethelmar.

In the thirteenth century the Pope intervened actively in the appointment to English dioceses; already by the gift of the pallium he had some part in the choice of the two archbishops; now through the opportunity given by appeals in disputed elections, through translations, and by the use of the method of provisions he was able to appoint to a large number of dioceses.

[1] Stubbs, "Constitutional History," Vol. III., p. 304.

This led to frequent disputes with the king who was supported by the nation, as foreign bishops were very unpopular with it. Eventually an arrangement was reached by which the Pope agreed to accept the nominations of the king. Both parties were satisfied; the king had the substance and the Pope had the shadow. The king asked the Pope to appoint his candidate, and the Pope by a bull of provision accepted and ratified the nomination as if it were his own. Sometimes the Pope refused to accept the king's nomination and then there was hard bargaining, and probably a compromise was reached. But when the Pope had unwillingly to agree to a candidate, he could always show his displeasure and cause inconvenience all round by long delays before he issued the necessary bull. By the end of the fifteenth century the majority of the appointments to vacant sees were in actual fact made by the king. The forms were carefully observed; outward respect was paid to the Pope, but the Papal consent was so completely taken for granted that the Crown bestowed "the temporalities upon its candidate without waiting for his confirmation or translation."[1]

But this arrangement between Pope and king led to the loss of the rights of the Chapter to elect, and of the right of the Metropolitan to confirm. The Chapter still received the royal *Congé d'élire*, and met for the election; but the result was always the same, the candidate mentioned by the king was duly elected. Confirmation and examination by the Metropolitan were no longer necessary, for they were now superseded by Papal action. The Pope claimed complete jurisdiction over the whole of Christendom, and thus completely overshadowed the Metropolitans. Papal approval of the royal candidate was sufficient without any reference to the archbishops; it was only left to them to carry out by consecration the bidding of Pope and king.

The Reformation and After

The Reformation made a considerable external alteration in the manner of appointing bishops, but in substance the change was unimportant. The king made the appointment as he had for centuries past, but the Pope's formal consent and approval were no longer required. The procedure to be followed was

[1] A. Hamilton Thompson, "The English Clergy and Their Organisation in the Later Middle Ages," p. 30.

laid down by a Statute in 1534. The Crown sent the Chapter a licence to elect, and with it a Letter Missive containing the name of the person to be elected. If the Chapter failed to elect within twelve days, the king nominated by Letters Patent. The name of the person must be sent to the king, who then informed the archbishop of the Province in which the vacant diocese was situated, and directed him to confirm the election and to consecrate. If the Chapter refused to elect, and the archbishop to consecrate, they were liable to the penalties of *præmunire*, by which the offenders were put out of the king's protection and their lands and goods forfeited. The forms of capitular election and of confirmation by the Metropolitan were restored, but the actual appointment was with the king. No longer was it necessary to keep up the pretence that the Pope had made it. The election by the Chapter, and the confirmation by the archbishop thinly camouflaged the practice which had been followed for many centuries, namely, that the king appointed the bishops. There was nothing new in this. "What was a novelty in this was not the recognition of the King's rights, or the system of the *congé d'élire*, accompanied by the Letter Missive, which practically gave the Crown the right of appointment, but the coercive methods to be employed if necessary, subjecting a recalcitrant Chapter or archbishop to the penalties of *præmunire*, and providing by statute for a method of filling a vacant see should the Chapter fail to elect a nominee of the Crown."[1]

The appointments at first were made personally by the king, though no doubt he would consult with others. There is evidence that even during the reign of Henry VIII names were submitted to him by the Secretary of State.[2] In the following reign, as the king was a minor, the appointments were made on the recommendation of the Council. Elizabeth was advised by Cecil, who in turn had before him names sent by Archbishop Parker. Charles I was advised by Laud, but the final responsibility for an appointment rested with the Sovereign, and if he wished to do so he could make it without consultation with any of his Ministers. Under Charles II a commission of six was appointed, consisting of the Archbishop of Canterbury, the Bishop of London, and four laymen, to be consulted by the Secretaries of State before presenting any names to the

[1] Report of "Joint Committee on Crown Nominations to Ecclesiastical Offices" (1920), p. 4.

[2] Ibid., p. 13.

Crown. But it is doubtful if this Commission was of any value. The precedent was followed on the death of Mary, for her husband William knew nothing of the Church of England. The new Commission appointed in 1695 consisted of the two archbishops and five bishops who were to " recommend persons for ecclesiastical preferment to the end that the names of such persons may be presented to the Crown by one of our principal Secretaries of State that the royal pleasure may be further known therein." The Commission was reappointed in 1699 " for recommending to his Majesty persons to succeed to any bishoprick in England or any other ecclesiastical preferment in England above the value of £20 in His Majesty's Books." But the king was not bound to accept the recommendations of the Commission and it was soon found that " preferment was too valuable a royal asset for it to be controlled by other than the king and his ministers."[1] Queen Anne did not renew the Commission, and usually acted on the advice of her ministers, though occasionally she appointed to bishoprics without reference to them. In 1707 the sees of Chester and Exeter were vacant; and there was great anxiety among the Whig Ministers as to who would be selected for them; Archibishop Tenison was asked to find the Queen's views, but he was unsuccessful. " My discourse was short, it being said to me on my entrance that the thing was already determined, though the person was not declared."[2] The Queen made the appointments to the annoyance of her Ministers; writing afterwards to Marlborough, she said: " I do assure you that these men were my own choice. They were certainly very fit for the station I design them; and indeed I think myself obliged to fill the bishop's bench with those who will be a credit to it and the Church."[3] But the protests made by the Whigs were effective, and the Queen promised that in future she would consult her Ministers.

With the Hanoverian kings the responsibility for making the appointments passed to the Prime Minister. Now and again, however, the king overruled him. The best known case, perhaps, is of George III who hearing of the death of the archbishop rode at once over to Windsor and made the offer of the primacy to his old tutor, Manners Sutton. Pitt was most indignant, as he had already written to the king suggesting the

[1] E. Carpenter, " Thomas Tenison," pp. 171, 176.

[2] Quoted in Winston Churchill's " Marlborough and His Times," Vol. III, p. 315.

[3] Quoted in Report of Joint Committee, p. 14.

Bishop of Lincoln—he protested strongly against the king's "apparent disregard of his nomination of the Bishop of Lincoln to succeed to the Archbishopric of Canterbury. He entreats your Majesty humbly to reflect that such a recommendation appears uniformly to have been graciously accepted for a long course of time in every instance."[1] In the reign of his successor it was made plain by Lord Liverpool that the will of the Prime Minister must prevail if he insisted. The king had made a nomination and the Prime Minister disapproved. The king at Lady Conyngham's request had appointed her son's tutor, Mr. Sumner, to a canonry at Windsor. As soon as Lord Liverpool was informed of this "he got into his carriage and went down to the king to state unless he was allowed to have the distribution of this patronage without any interference, he could not carry on the Government and would resign his office if Sumner was appointed. The man was only a curate, and had never held a living at all."[2] To-day there is no doubt that the nomination to a bishopric rests with the Prime Minister, and that by the threat of resignation he can always enforce his wishes upon the Crown, for it is not easy to imagine a dissolution and general election over a disputed appointment to a see! We have now reached the position which justified Archdeacon Grantly looking to the Prime Minister to secure for him the vacant see of Barchester!

This does not, however, mean that the Crown has no voice in the choice of bishops. Queen Victoria had strong views on episcopal appointments, and sometimes succeeded in making them prevail against the original intention of the Prime Minister. Bishop Wilberforce, while at Oxford, made the following entry in his diary of a conversation he had with Dean Wellesley: "Disraeli recommended . . . for Canterbury! ! !—the Queen would not have him; then Disraeli agreed most reluctantly and with passion to Tait. Disraeli then proposed Wordsworth for London. The Queen objected strongly; no experience; passing over bishops, etc.; then she suggested Jackson, and two others, not you, because of Disraeli's expressed hostility, and Disraeli chose Jackson."[3] The Queen's "Letters" show how great was her interest and influence in making good appointments. In 1860 she writes to Lord Palmerston urging him not

[1] Ibid., p. 17.
[2] "The Greville Diary," Vol. I, p. 111: May 2nd, 1821.
[3] "Life of Samuel Wilberforce, D.D.," Vol. III, p. 269.

to confine his nominations to "respectable parish priests, but to bear in mind that the Bench of Bishops should not be left devoid of some university men of acknowledged standing and theological learning."[1] In 1890 she has a lively correspondence with Lord Salisbury. She persuades him, though reluctantly, to accept Westcott for Durham; she fails to obtain Winchester for Davidson, and agrees to the appointment of Thorold of Rochester, though she describes him as "an old frail man of no particular talent," but adds, "she cannot help reminding Lord Salisbury that when the question of naming a bishop for the diocese in which Hatfield is situated arose, the Queen, out of consideration to Lord Salisbury and to what might be agreeable to him, made no objection to what was proposed whatever, though Canon Liddon was one mentioned. But in the case of Winchester, which borders on Windsor and includes Osborne, the Queen's personal wishes and conveniences are overlooked."[2] Lord Salisbury in his reply reminds the Queen that already that year she had declined two nominations he had made! Later in the year when the Archbishopric of York became vacant, the Queen suggested in a tentative fashion the names, first of Bishop Westcott and then of the Bishops of Lichfield, Wakefield and Manchester. But Lord Salisbury nominated Magee, the Bishop of Peterborough. The correspondence proves that though the Queen had great influence in the choice of bishops, the Prime Minister always had his way when he had really made up his mind. The Queen's views on the principles on which appointments should be made were sound and interesting: "the men to be chosen *must* not be taken with reference to satisfying one or the other party in the Church, or with reference to any political party, but for their *real worth*; we want people who can be firm, and yet conciliatory, else the Church cannot be maintained."[3] She did not, however, feel that elevation to the episcopate usually led to a heightening of gifts of leadership, for writing to her Dean, Dr. Davidson, on his appointment to Rochester, she says that with one exception she "never found people promoted to the Episcopate remain what they were before. . . . The whole atmosphere of a Cathedral and its surroundings, the very dignity

[1] "Letters of Queen Victoria," Vol. III (First Series), p. 416.

[2] "The Letters of Queen Victoria" (Third Series), Vol. III, p. 640.

[3] Ibid., p. 554.

itself which accompanied a bishopric, seem to hamper their freedom of speech."[1]

The Making of a Bishop To-day

There are five steps in the making of a diocesan bishop to-day which concern both the Church and the State: the nomination by the Prime Minister and approval by the Crown; the election by the Chapter; the Confirmation by the Archbishop; the Consecration; and the Homage.

The Prime Minister decides on the names to submit to the Crown. It is obvious that a Prime Minister overwhelmed by many duties cannot know, without seeking advice, which of the clergy are the most suitable for nomination. Sometimes the accident of personal acquaintance may assist him in his choice; or as a Churchman he may be familiar both with the needs of the vacant diocese, and with men whom he could nominate to it with complete confidence. But the statesman who has spent all his life in the political field may know few of the clergy by name, and if he is not a Churchman probably he has no personal knowledge which will help him. Mr. Lloyd George quite frankly admitted that he had neither the time nor the knowledge for ecclesiastical appointments. The Prime Minister, if he is to make wise nominations, must make inquiries from those who have this knowledge. Foremost among these are the two archbishops. When Mr. Lloyd George was asked that the two archbishops should be consulted by the Prime Minister before the submission of names to the Crown for a diocesan bishopric, he replied to the Archbishop of Canterbury: "It has been my invariable practice, since I became Prime Minister, to invite your counsel, which you have at all times been kind enough to give me, upon all important appointments in the Church. Certainly in this case of Diocesan Bishoprics my recommendations to His Majesty have only been made after careful and anxious consultation with yourself, and in the case of sees in the Northern Province with the Archbishop of York also. It is also within your knowledge that I have in regard to all higher appointments taken the further step of seeking the opinion of a number of prominent churchmen representing all shades of opinion."[2] Of the method in which the Archbishop

[1] Ibid., p. 649.
[2] G. K. Bell, "Randall Davidson," Vol. II, p. 1246.

of Canterbury gave this advice, Dr. Bell writes, when a vacancy occurred he "would, without loss of time, either speak or write to the Prime Minister about the particular bishopric. . . . As a rule he would discuss both the diocese and the possible successors in conversation with the Prime Minister, as well as in correspondence. And, in all but quite exceptional cases, he would furnish the Prime Minister with some three or more names of people to be considered—only very rarely concentrating the whole of his strength on a single person."[1] This method of consultation has been followed by recent Prime Ministers. The archbishops have been either invited to suggest suitable names, or to comment on names which already the Prime Minister has before him. It should be emphasised that the Prime Minister always has his own sources of information independent of the archbishops, and receives from responsible and irresponsible persons both suggestions and advice over the filling of a vacant see. The information at his disposal is comprehensive and detailed. When I was offered nomination to the see of Winchester by Mr. Ramsay Macdonald I had a long conversation with him, and I was surprised to find how much he knew about many of the bishops, their opinions, their work, and in one case even the nickname! Mr. Macdonald was not naturally interested in bishops, but evidently he had a mass of accurate information about them, with a record of their less discreet as well as their wiser public utterances! He had been well served by his secretariat. There is every reason to believe that subsequent Prime Ministers have been equally well informed. It can be said without any breach of confidence that the archbishops still have full opportunities of expressing their views to the Prime Minister either by writing, or in the case of the more important dioceses by interview; secondly, that the greatest possible trouble and care are taken over these nominations; and thirdly, that the final decision for the choice is always made by the Prime Minister who takes complete responsibility in making the nomination to the Crown. It may be assumed that this again is no mere formality, that the Crown is fully consulted, and is aware of all the reasons for the nomination, before the offer is actually made. But it can never be taken for granted that the offer will be accepted. It is a popular delusion that a bishopric is always joyfully accepted. "Nolo episcopari" is not a mere convention; there are men who, though attracted

[1] Ibid., p. 1238.

by the offer of a see, have refused it for the sake of work which they felt they ought not to leave.

When the offer has been accepted, the Crown sends to the Dean and Chapter permission to elect and a letter containing the name of the man they are to choose. If they refuse to elect him, either by delay or by a negative vote, they are subject to the savage penalties of *præmunire*, and the Crown then appoints by Letters Patent. The permission to elect is a farce, and the result is a foregone conclusion. The name of the man sent to the Chapter has already been announced and discussed in the Press; he has received letters of congratulation and welcome; he has probably already ordered his episcopal gaiters, and speculation is rife as to who will be his successor. Now and again a Chapter has threatened resistance. In 1847 the Dean of Hereford wrote to Lord Russell saying he would not vote for Dr. Hampden's election as bishop, and received the following reply from the Prime Minister: "I have had the honour to receive your letter of 22nd inst., in which you intimate to me your intention of violating the law." The Dean and one canon alone voted against his election. Since then there have been cases when the election was disputed, but there never has been a failure to elect the nominee of the Crown. It is often said that the Chapter votes after invoking the Holy Spirit for guidance; before the Reformation prayers were offered for guidance in making a right choice, but as far as I know they are no longer used, and the *Veni Creator* is neither said nor sung. The election by the Chapter is only of interest on account of its ancient history, and of value because it gives the Chapter the opportunity of making a futile but dramatic protest against the unworthy choice of an unsuitable bishop; but these advantages at present are more than outweighed by the unreality which marks the whole procedure. If, however, the suggestions which are made later on are accepted, the ancient method of election might be used to give the diocese a real part in the choice of its future bishop.

When the election is complete the Crown then orders the archbishop of the Province to confirm and consecrate. The Confirmation is usually taken by the Vicar General, though in the case of an archbishop by a commission of bishops of which the other archbishop is chairman. Originally the purpose of the Confirmation was to enable the archbishop, and other bishops, to discover if the person had been duly elected and was suitable for consecration. But now, while many of the old forms and some of the old language are preserved, the reality of Confirmation has passed away. When Dr. Gore was appointed to Birmingham objections were raised at his Confirmation on the grounds of doctrine. The Vicar-General ruled that these could not be entertained, and an appeal to King's Bench upheld the ruling. If doctrinal objection to a bishop-elect could be heard, it was feared it might give the archbishop the right to overrule the king's nomination. By these decisions it appears that the only valid objections would be those alleging that the technicalities at the election by the Chapter had been irregular, or that the bishop-elect appearing at the Confirmation was not the man chosen by the king. The Confirmation is thus a mere form, expensive to the bishop, meaningless to the public, and an opportunity for self-advertising objectors to make a noisy protest. The Confirmation should be made a reality or abolished. Its legal effect is, however, important. By it the bishop-elect receives jurisdiction over his diocese. He can appoint to benefices, license, and institute. He can exercise discipline. He can undertake all the duties of a bishop except the three most important—assisting in the consecration of bishops, the ordination of priests and deacons, and the laying of hands on the unconfirmed. These functions he cannot perform until he has been consecrated by the archbishop and other bishops, according to the rites and ceremonies of the Church of England.

It is unnecessary to say anything about the consecration of a bishop. For here, with the exception of the reading of the Royal Mandate, and the administering of the Oath of Allegiance, the State falls into the background. The State can nominate and appoint, but it cannot make a bishop; this can only be done by those who already have been duly consecrated as bishops of the Church of God. The Preface to the Ordinal declares: "No man shall be accounted or taken to be a lawful Bishop, Priest, or Deacon in the Church of England, or suffered to execute any of the said Functions, except he be called, tried, examined, and admitted thereunto, according to the Form hereafter following, or hath had formerly Episcopal Consecration or Ordination."

Nor is it necessary to say anything about enthronement. This in recent years has become increasingly magnifical. In the past the bishop in many dioceses did not trouble to attend it, but was represented by proxy. It has no legal significance, but it is the ceremonial and public entry of the new bishop into his cathedral and diocese ; it affords him an opportunity of speaking to his flock ; it enables them to welcome him, and the Chapter secures from him the promise to protect their rights and privileges.

At some period after his consecration, usually, though not invariably, before his enthronement, the bishop must pay his homage to the king ; until he has done this he cannot possess the temporalities of the see. The ceremony is very simple ; when clerk of the Closet I often took part in it. The new bishop enters into the Royal Presence with the clerk by his side, bearing an open Bible on a cushion. The king is alone in the room with the Home Secretary ; the bishop kneels before the king placing his hands between those of the king, and repeats the homage sentence by sentence after the Home Secretary ; the clerk then presents the Bible for the bishop to kiss. Usually the king has some talk afterwards with the new bishop, and then the bishop departs, in full possession of his temporalities and spiritualities.

The terms of the homage at first reading is somewhat alarming : " I do hereby declare that Your Majesty is the only Supreme Governor of this your realm in spiritual and ecclesiastical things, as well as in temporal, and that no foreign prelate or potentate has any jurisdiction within this realm ; and I acknowledge that I hold the said Bishopric, as well the spiritualities as the temporalities thereof, only of your Majesty. And for the same temporalities I do my homage presently to your Majesty." My predecessor in the clerkship told me that an Erastian Home Secretary used to place tremendous emphasis on the word " spiritualities " until he was told that it only referred to ecclesiastical revenue from other sources than land ![1] This is clear from Cavendish's " Life of Wolsey," when he describes the Cardinal's fear of poverty after his disgrace, and reports him as expressing the hope that the king would leave him the spiritualities he drew from the see of Winchester even if he took from him the temporalities.

This survey of the manner in which Church and State make a bishop shows that the State takes the initiative in his choice, and then step by step carries it through by missives, mandates,

[1] Stubbs gives the following definition : " The ecclesiastical revenue arising from other sources than land ; which spiritualities he acquires together with the temporalities on doing homage."—" Constitutional History," Vol. III, p. 302.

and threats, until the Church has accomplished its bidding and its nominee is duly confirmed and consecrated. The Prime Minister is the effective agent acting for the State; he may consult with others; he may even defer to their advice, but his will can always prevail. There are only two limitations the Church can set to his discretion. He can only choose from those who have been freely ordained by the Church; and in the last resort the archbishops could refuse to consecrate.

Advantages

It must be allowed that there are certain advantages in the method by which English diocesan bishops are appointed. Appointment by the king has behind it a long history, and at the time of the Reformation it had been for centuries in practice the custom in this country. Until quite recently the bishops in Austria were nominated by the Emperor, and in Spain by the king. It is said that even to-day the President of Haiti nominates to the Pope, and his nominations are accepted. The King of England appointed bishops both as Supreme Governor of the realm, and also in the eyes of many as the Lord's Anointed, possessing by his unction at the Coronation a semi-priestly nature. "Dr. Grantly," we are told, "if he admits the Queen's supremacy in things spiritual, only admits it as being due to the quasi-priesthood conveyed in the consecrating qualities of her Coronation." There is nothing unusual in the appointment of a bishop by a Christian king; and in the last resort the archbishops could, and would, refuse to consecrate a man whose opinions or character rendered him unsuitable to be made a bishop.

In this manner of appointment there are various practical advantages. The Prime Minister has a larger field of choice than that possible for a cathedral Chapter of a diocese, and he can often take a more detailed and less partisan view of the kind of bishop required at any special period in the history of the Church. The appointment by an elective body results occasionally in unseemly wire-pulling on behalf of certain candidates; or an open struggle between ecclesiastical parties, each pressing its nominee; or a division of opinion between the clerical and lay electors. The electing body may fail to reach a decision by a clear majority; then a compromise must be arranged, and a third-rate candidate is accepted by general agreement; at other times an appeal has to be made to the Archbishop of Canterbury, or a small group of home bishops, to make the appointment. Often those who have had experience of the Church overseas speak of the disadvantages of the elective method of choosing bishops, and envy the traditional procedure followed in this country. All of this must be carefully weighed and considered before the present plan for the making of diocesan bishops is jettisoned.

Disadvantages

On the other hand, the disadvantages and dangers are great. In the past the appointment was made by the king, now, as we have seen, it is made to all intents and purposes by the Prime Minister. Once the Prime Minister was always a Churchman, and behind him there was a Parliament of Churchmen. To-day the Prime Minister need not be a Christian, and yet he has the responsibility of appointing the spiritual masters and pastors of a spiritual community. If he should happen to be a Churchman, he has to consider in a democratic age the opinions of a Parliament in which Churchmen are often now in a minority. The bishops of the Eastern Church are elected by colleges of bishops, the bishops of the Roman Catholic Church are appointed by the Pope, the bishops of the Provinces of the Anglican Communion are in various ways elected, but for the Church of England they are chosen by a Prime Minister who need not be a member of the Church or even a believer in God. He may discharge his responsibility most faithfully and conscientiously, and non-Church Prime Ministers have already proved this can be done, but in principle it is wrong that the chief officers of a spiritual society should be chosen by a layman who need neither belong to it nor be sympathetic towards it.

The practical dangers are also great. As the State extends its powers, it reaches out into every department of national life. It controls education, soon it will control industry, presently it may attempt to control religion in its own interests. It has an unrivalled opportunity of doing this when it appoints to a Church its chief administrators and teachers. Through these appointments it can control the Church, especially if they are made on a definite policy over a considerable period of years. In the eighteenth century the Whigs consistently used their power to fill vacant sees with men of their own views, and thus used the Church for political purposes. Political influence has made itself felt occasionally in episcopal appointments even in the last hundred years. Bishop Wilberforce's biographer says that it was on account of his political views that he was not appointed to London: "it was not on any personal grounds that Mr. Disraeli did not name the Bishop for London. Mr. Disraeli was before all things a politician. The General Election on which his Ministry depended was in progress: Bishop Wilberforce was represented to him by one who knew better as an extreme High Churchman, whose appointment to London would estrange many votes from the Conservative party."[1] This fear of losing votes by nominating High Churchmen to sees is shown in a letter from Lord Beaconsfield to the Queen on January 27th, 1879. He is urging the importance of showing some mark of respect and recognition to those "who, tho' High Churchmen firmly resist or hitherto have resisted the deleterious designs of Canon Lyddon, and the Dean of St. Paul's [Liddon and Church !] who wish to terminate the connection between the Crown and the Church, and ultimately unite with the Greek Church. The Church Union is entirely under their control, and now at every election, that Union systematically votes against your Majesty's Government . . . these dangerous malcontents who would support any candidate, even Bradlaugh, against your Majesty's Government."[2] Many years later Lord Salisbury refused the Queen's suggestion that Dr. Westcott should be translated to London on the objection "not only of his recent promotion, but a much more serious one arising from the Socialist tendencies of the speeches he has made since he became a bishop."[3] Dr. Bell states that Mr. Macdonald when Prime Minister found that "some of his colleagues in the Labour Party were at first perturbed because he did not appoint clergy who had served the Labour Party in their parishes; but he soon made it plain that service to the Labour Party was an insufficient qualification for the office of a bishop." Conservative Prime Ministers appointed Dr. Gore to Worcester and William Temple to Canterbury, and no political bias can be discerned in the recent appointments by a Labour Prime Minister.

[1] Life of Bishop Wilberforce," Vol. III, p. 268.
[2] Buckle, "Life of Benjamin Disraeli," Vol. VI, p. 407.
[3] "Letters of Queen Victoria" (Third Series), p. 666.

There is another danger which may arise when all the bishoprics are filled by the nominations of a Prime Minister who is overburdened with work, and who may have little or no interest in the Church. It is conceivable that in the future he might regard appointment to vacant sees as a troublesome and unimportant duty which might well be carried out to all intents and purposes by a junior colleague or even by a capable secretary. The appointment to a bishopric is no longer as important to the State as once was the case. A hundred years ago there were fewer dioceses, and in the days when the Church had a larger membership than at present the bishop had considerable social and political influence. Possible appointments were widely canvassed beforehand, and when the appointment was made a prominent place was given to its announcement in *The Times*. To-day the dioceses have almost doubled in number; appointments to them pass almost unnoticed in the secular world; the bishop has comparatively little influence except among the faithful of his flock; and when he speaks he is probably unreported unless he has made some remark either controversial, sensational, or absurd. This is not true of the archbishoprics and some of the senior sees; importance is still attached to them, and there are bishops who will always make their influence felt whatever see they occupy. With the decreased importance of bishoprics, less care may be taken in appointing to them by Prime Ministers who have no real interest in the Church of England. It is said that at a critical period of the war a British Minister told Stalin that the support of the Pope to the allied cause might be important. "But how many divisions has he at his disposal?" was the reply. So in the future a cynical and overworked Prime Minister of a hard-pressed Government may feel that nominations to bishoprics are of little importance unless they result in favourable votes!

Reforms

The defects and possible abuses of the present method of appointment outweigh its advantages. While many would claim that the practical results are good and that the English bishops stand out in the Anglican Communion, large numbers of the clergy are highly critical of "the bishops" as a body, though usually very kind to their own bishop! They are suspicious of their opinions and of their work; they assert that they are out of touch with, and unrepresentative of, the mass of clergy. Most of these criticisms are unjust, but they come partly from the dissatisfaction which so many of the clergy feel over the manner in which their bishops are appointed; for they complain that they have no voice or share in the choice of their father-in-God, and that he is imposed upon them from without. For this reason they are suspicious of schemes of reform which seem to place more power in the hands of the bishop. It is possible, though by no means certain, that if the clergy were given some part in the choice of their chief pastors, some of the tension between them would disappear.

In looking for some reform which may remove some of the objections to the present method of appointment, it is necessary to take it for granted that as long as the Church is Established the appointment of its diocesans must rest with the Crown. Any other system would mean a breach with the past, and the surrender by the Crown of its most effective means of influence on the Church. To ask for the transfer of the right of appointment from the Crown to a college of bishops or to the diocese, acting either by the Chapter or by some other electoral assembly, would in effect be a demand for disestablishment. All through this book I am attempting to indicate a policy of reform which can be carried through without disestablishment, though the position may arise when, for the sake of freedom, the Church might be compelled to ask for separation from the State, with the loss of privileges and endowments. But it would be wrong for the Church to take the initiative in asking for disestablishment until all reform within the State connection has been found to be impossible. The suggestions which follow are not therefore drastic; they will not, if accepted, give to the Church complete freedom in the choice of its bishops, but they will enable it to have some real part in their choice.

It may be taken for granted that the present consultations with the archbishops will continue. These are of great value. A fuller interchange of opinion is possible in this confidential way than through an official committee elected for the purpose. If the archbishops felt that they needed a committee to help them in compiling a list of suitable names, there would be no difficulty over this. This committee would have no standing with the Prime Minister, but it would privately provide the archbishops with suitable names which they could use or not as they thought advisable.

There are four reforms which are highly desirable, and which could be carried through without destroying the present framework in which bishops are now chosen.

First, the penalties of *præmunire* should not threaten those who have been given the right to elect. It is highly improbable they would ever be enforced, but it is an insult to give a body the right to elect, and at the same time to make it liable to severe penalties unless it elected the person who had already been chosen. By the abolition of this threat the State would show the Chapter that it has the right to express freely its opinion on the man whose name had been sent to it. It could elect him at once; or it could ask from the Prime Minister reassurance on definite points; or it could express its misgivings before it actually voted; or in the last resort could refuse to accept the responsibility of electing him.

Secondly, at an earlier stage, before the *congé délire* is received, the Chapter should petition for the right to elect—this is the custom already with many Chapters—and at the same time it should send to the Prime Minister three names which it would like him to consider for nomination. The names would be sent in secrecy, and the Prime Minister need not choose any one of them for nomination: if he thought fit he could refuse even to consider the names, but he would have the opportunity of knowing the opinion of the diocese as to who would appear to be most acceptable to it. The Chapter which would send the names would not be the small Chapter of the dean and three or four residential canons, but the Great Chapter, including honorary canons.

Thirdly, the name approved by the king should be sent to the Chapter in confidence, before any public announcement is made. This would enable the Chapter to discuss it freely and to express with frankness their opinion to the Prime Minister. A strongly hostile opinion would give the Prime Minister the opportunity of reconsidering the proposed appointment.

Lastly, the archbishops should be given the right at the Confirmation to hear objections on the ground of heresy, and they should be free from all penalties if they should refuse to confirm.

The effect of these reforms would be to give the diocese a recognised right to be consulted in the choice of a new bishop, and would change the Confirmation from an archaic formality into a useful safeguard. There would be no interference with the Royal Prerogative ; the Prime Minister would still nominate and the Crown appoint, but the Chapter would without fear of any penalties be able to express its views, and if need be dissent altogether from the proposed appointment, thus compelling the Crown to act by Letters Patent. The archbishops would be able to hear bona fide charges of doctrinal heresy, and by refusal to confirm would invite the Crown to reconsider its choice. By this procedure the Church would be assured that the Prime Minister had received advice from those competent to give it, while if the Chapter refused to elect, or the archbishop to confirm, time would be secured for reconsideration before a diocese had thrust upon it a bishop regarded as either unsound in doctrine or unsuitable for the diocese in question. But nothing in these proposals would take away either the right of the Prime Minister to nominate or the right of the Crown to appoint. Revision on these lines of the procedure for the choice of a bishop would be of benefit to the Church without injury to the Royal Prerogative.

X

THE REVISION OF THE PRAYER BOOK

THE rejection of the revised Prayer Book by the House of Commons in 1927 and 1928 was a dramatic illustration of the legal right of Parliament to control the worship of the Church. The many years spent by the Church on revision, and the summary rejection of its complete work after a few hours' debate revealed the sharpness of the conflict which might rise at any time between Church and State. The problem of Prayer Book revision remains unsolved, and bishops and clergy alike are open to the charge of illegality in sanctioning or using rites and ceremonies which are not found within the 1662 Book of Common Prayer.

The Necessity of Revision

The Prayer Book was intended to provide the only services for use in the Provinces of Canterbury and York. It took the place of the older service books, though it incorporated much that was within them. It aimed at providing public worship in the common language which all could understand, and in such a simple and intelligible form that all could take part in it. It was to be the common prayer for all, for every church and chapel throughout the land. Its purpose was to secure uniformity of worship. This was made plain by the preface to the 1549 Book, repeated in the 1662 Book, under the title "Concerning the Service of the Church": "So that here you have an Order for Prayer, and for the reading of the holy Scripture, much agreeable to the mind and purpose of the old Fathers, and a great deal more profitable and commodious, than that which of late was used . . . and that in such a language and order as is most easy and plain for the understanding both of the readers and hearers. . . . And whereas heretofore there hath been great diversity in saying and singing in Churches within this Realm; some following Salisbury use, some Hereford use, and some the use of Bangor, some of York, some of Lincoln; now from henceforth all the whole Realm shall have but one use." It is very doubtful if the earlier Books of Common Prayer had the authority of Convocation, but the 1662 Book has the full spiritual sanction of the Church, as well as the authority of Parliament, for it was freely passed by the Convocations before it was given legal authority by Parliament. Strict obedience to it was to be enforced, however, by an Act of Uniformity which ordered the revised Book to be used in all churches and chapels from St. Bartholomew's Day, 1662: and that all ministers should be deprived who did not use the Book. By a declaration inserted in the Canons of 1603, and now used in an amended form, the clergy promised to "use the form in the said Book prescribed in public Prayer and Administration of the Sacraments, and none other."

This attempt at uniformity in Public Worship was largely successful. For over two hundred years, from 1662 to the middle of the nineteenth century, in every church, the same prayers, the same order, and the same ceremonial were followed. Where there were variations they were slight and unimportant. Even up to sixty years ago the visitor to most churches would probably have found the same services with which he was familiar in his own parish at home. In the church of which my father was vicar the Prayer Book service was strictly followed at Morning and Evening Prayer; we had the full Dearly Beloved, the Psalms and Lessons as set, all the State Prayers; and in the morning either the Litany or the Ante-Communion. In the afternoon, for the service was held then and not in the evening, baptism was administered when required. Twice on Sunday there was a fifteen minutes' sermon, before which my father had the queer custom of going to the vestry during the hymn before he went to the pulpit, a relic of the day when he changed into the black gown. There were some abbreviations —we rarely had Mattins, Litany and Ante-Communion all on the same morning; and the late service of the Holy Communion, "the second service," commenced at the Invitation. The services were said, not intoned. I remember an old parishioner remarking to me, "As long as your father says aymen, and not ahmen, he won't go to Rome"! The psalms and canticles were sung. My father wore a scarf until, to his secret consternation, he was presented with a white stole. On great festivals we had a procession with a banner. At the Creed the choir turned to the east; as a child I was impressed with the solemnity of its recitation through my grandmother, who, on account of age and infirmity had to sit for the rest of the service, then rising and standing. But the ceremonial was of the simplest; the celebrant stood at the north end of the Holy Table, which had a cross and flowers, and candles lit only in the winter afternoons. The same type of service was found in most of the parish churches; and even if the parishioners thought it long and dull, they came regularly, at least once on the Sunday, and the more devout twice. And when we went away for the annual visit to the seaside, we were certain to find the same service, unless, greatly daring, we paid a visit to a "very High" Church.

In most of the churches to-day the services are still recognisably Prayer Book, and usually the variations from it are of minor importance, but in some churches the departures are considerable. There is uncertainty as to whether the psalms will be for the day or chosen for their brevity, whether the Lessons will be taken from the Calendar or from an anthology of the vicar's favourite passages of Scripture. There is un-uncertainty even as to where the services will start—at the "Dearly Beloved," or "O Lord open thou our lips"; but there is tolerable certainty that the second half of the service will not consist of the prayers in the Prayer Book: in the Holy Communion changes are sometimes made for which apparently there is no lawful authority, and the chance visitor may either find part of the service is inaudible, or if he hears he may wonder what has happened to the commandments, or to the invitation, confession and absolution, and even to the Prayer of Consecration. Still greater is the variety in ceremonial, in the vestments of the minister, in the gestures of minister and worshippers, and in the ornaments of the church.

The causes for these departures from the strict observance of the Prayer Book are mainly three.

The revival of the sense of beauty and the appreciation of it as seen in nature and in art resulted in a movement for greater beauty in our churches and in their worship. There are many who are content with a service without any beauty or colour, and are helped most by austere simplicity in public worship. But there will always be some who long to find in their worship the beauty and mystery which they enjoy in nature and in art; for they respond to deep-rooted instincts and give them an exaltation and satisfaction which otherwise would be absent. They feel it only right to offer to Almighty God in worship some of the beauty of colour and form which gives them joy in daily life. All beauty comes from God and should be returned to Him in worship. "High Church" worship impressed me greatly when as a boy I first encountered it. Its beauty and mystery deeply moved me. It seemed to give a glimpse of the heavenly places. The blaze of many lights, the vestments, and the incense changed reverence into adoration. It was then customary to attach symbolic meanings to all that was used in worship, every sacred object and ceremony was supposed to convey some teaching, and this was held to be their justification. I never felt very satisfied with what often seemed far-fetched explanations, and it was a great relief when as a freshman at Oxford I heard the vicar of St. Mary's—afterwards Archbishop Lang—preach on beauty in worship, and assert that all that was beautiful should be used in the service of God, irrespective of any teaching it might convey. The attraction which ceremonial had for me then was æsthetic; it gave me no teaching, but it helped me to worship. My own feelings must have been very much those which Walter Pater ascribed to Marius the Epicurean when he first attended Christian worship in pagan Rome. I am certain that my experience has been shared by many, and it helps to explain the attraction which so many find in the worship of an Anglo-Catholic Church. Not all this ceremonial was a departure from the Prayer Book, much of it could be justified as a loyal following of its directions, though some of it went beyond anything ever contemplated by its compilers. Many of the clergy who were looking for greater richness and colour in worship naturally borrowed from what they had seen in churches on the Continent. Rites and ornaments were introduced under the impression that they were Catholic and not merely Roman Catholic. No guidance was given to them by their own Church, a policy of repression was adopted by those who should have helped them, and they were left to their own resources or to inaccurate handbooks on "Catholic Ceremonial."

It would, however, be wrong to conclude that the introduction of ceremonial into Anglican worship was chiefly due to æstheticism. There was a much deeper reason, vestments were worn and pre-Reformation ceremonial restored as witnessing to the claim of the Church of England to be a living part of the Catholic Church both of the past and present. The Oxford

Movement reminded the Church of its forgotten, but never lost, heritage in the universal Church. Those who were most conscious of this were naturally anxious to express it outwardly. They wore vestments not because they were beautiful—to be quite frank often they were ugly—nor because they conveyed some special symbolic meaning, but because they had been worn long before the Reformation and witnessed to the continuity of the Church of to-day with the Church of all ages. The rites and ceremonies they introduced were not out of the love of novelty, but because they belonged to the Church of past centuries. Innumerable mistakes were made, and sometimes absurdities were perpetrated through lack of knowledge, but in the minds of most of those responsible for the revival of these rites and ceremonies there was no thought of disloyalty to their own Church.

Many changes were also made for practical and pastoral purposes. In the ordinary parish church it was found almost impossible to obey all the directions of the Prayer Book. The service was too long if Mattins, Litany and Ante-Communion were all said at the same time. The exhortations in the Holy Communion overweighted the service. It was found impracticable to demand that all intending communicants should "signify their names to the curate, at least sometime the day before." With the increase in the number of communicants and the growing desire for communion it was found necessary in many parishes to administer the Sacrament to the sick with the reserved Elements. The baptismal service was found too long and was unintelligible to many. The need was felt for additional prayers for subjects which could not have been in the mind of the compilers of the Prayer Book. Services more evangelistic than those officially provided were required. Mission priests, like Father Dolling, saw the teaching and attractive value of symbolism and colour in the drab slums in which they were working. To meet these needs the Prayer Book services were changed and altered without authority and often without liturgical knowledge. And this was by no means the practice of one party alone, both Anglo-Catholics and Evangelicals made in different directions the changes they thought desirable, while the great mass of central Churchmen amended, abbreviated and added to the regular services as expediency and edification seemed to demand.

Admirable and defensible as were many of these changes and praiseworthy as were the motives which prompted them, grave results followed. First, there was increasing disorder. The law of public worship was brought into contempt. Every ordinand, every priest about to be licensed or instituted, has to make the solemn promise that he "will use the form in the said book prescribed, and none other, except so far as shall be ordered by lawful authority." And yet all of us—bishops, priests, and deacons, High, Broad, Low, or unlabelled English Churchmen—frequently depart from the form which we have promised faithfully to use. It is useless to plead before the law that many of the departures are insignificant. According to a judicial decision given in the highest court: "It is not open to a Minister of the Church to draw a distinction in acts which are a departure from or violation of the Rubric, between those which are important and those which appear to be trivial. . . . The rule upon this subject has been already laid down by the Judicial Committee in Westerton *v.* Liddell, and their Lordships are disposed entirely to adhere to it: 'In the performance of the services, rites, and ceremonies ordered by the Prayer Book the directions contained in it must be strictly observed; no omission and no addition can be permitted.'"[1] It is possible that an appeal to the Courts made eighty years later might lead to a different judgement, for it is difficult to believe that "lawful authority" does not permit dispensation from the rigour of a rule now impossible to observe, and it seems absurd to hold that there is no distinction in gravity between omitting the "Dearly Beloved" and substituting a new Prayer of Consecration for that given in the Prayer Book. But until it is reversed this judgement declares the law of public worship. On it the Commission on Church and State (1935) thus comments: "We hold that the consequences of adopting this rigid rule have been very harmful. No one obeys the law so construed. Not the clergy, since there is scarcely one of them who makes no change in the authorised forms of service. Not the bishops, who are charged to see that this impossible law is carried out. Worse still, by the Declaration, as interpreted by the Courts, every priest solemnly undertakes to do that which in fact none of them performs. No wonder discipline has suffered. No wonder the laity are uneasy. It is difficult to find temperate words to apply to such a state of things. The situation can only be described as deeply insincere."[2] Severe criticism is often directed against the bishops for not compelling the clergy

[1] Martin *v.* Maconochie (1886).
[2] Vol. I, p. 85.

to obey the law, usually this means to obey that part of the law which the critic happens to regard as important. The bishops have incurred as much unpopularity by attempting to enforce the law of worship as by failing to do so. If they tried to enforce it as interpreted above, they would meet with universal opposition; if they tried to forbid additional services, while acquiescing in the omission of the saying of daily Morning and Evening Prayer in the parish church or chapel as ordered by the Prayer Book, they would rightly be accused of unfairness.

This variety of use and the departures from the Prayer Book have had a second serious result. They have alienated and angered many of the laity. The older members of a congregation have felt deep resentment when a new incumbent introduced practices and prayers not in the Prayer Book, and for which they could find no justification. The laity, accustomed in their own parish church to Prayer Book services, are indignant and shocked if they find in churches they go to on their holidays services which depart from it to such an extent that they are unintelligible to them. The law-abiding Englishman is irritated when he finds the clergy disobeying what appears to him to be plain and authoritative directions of the Prayer Book. This indignation was shown in prosecutions and riots in the last century, and in the imprisonment of some hard-working parish priests. The vociferous and hysterical complaints of party societies can be largely ignored, for the imprisonments due to their action discredited them beyond recovery. Ignorant and uncharitable denunciations have little effect on the general public. But there is legitimate grievance on the part of loyal Churchmen who find the manner of worship to which they have been accustomed arbitrarily changed at the will of their vicar. Sometimes I have heard incumbents admit that by these changes they have lost some of their congregation, but they add in justification: "My successor will reap the benefit." I have been long enough a bishop to see successors come and go and to know that all they reap is an empty church and suspicious parishioners. The indignation of the laity found a champion and spokesman in Sir William Harcourt, described by Bishop Creighton as "the colossal figure of a new Elijah denouncing judgement—the only wise and good man—but denouncing judgement and at the same time clamouring that somebody else (of course the bishop) should take off his hands the trouble of slaying prophets of Baal." Dissatisfaction with continued disorder steadily increased, and in 1904 a Royal Commission on Ecclesiastical Discipline was appointed.

At first it had been proposed that a Select Committee of the House of Commons should be asked to report on ecclesiastical disorders. But Archbishop Davidson after some hesitation pressed strongly for a commission on the ground that neither bishops nor clergy would be ready to give evidence before a committee appointed by Parliament. The Prime Minister, Mr. Balfour, favoured a committee and showed considerable annoyance at clerical objections to this course, saying on one occasion: "It is now clear to me that all the clergy, of whatever school, are equally stupid. I had thought the range of stupidity more limited."[1] But the Archbishop's contention eventually prevailed that "The Royal Supremacy is exercised by a Royal Commission much more truly, or at all events much more obviously, than by a Parliamentary Committee."[2] The Commission was appointed, and its Report was signed in June, 1906. It reached two main conclusions: First, "the law of public worship is too narrow for the religious life of the present generation. It needlessly condemns much which a great section of Church people, including many of her most devoted members, value; and modern thought and feeling are characterised by a care for ceremonial, a sense of dignity in worship, and an appreciation of the continuity of the Church, which were not similarly felt at the time when the law took its present shape. . . . Secondly, the machinery for discipline has broken down."[3] Its most important recommendation concerned the revision of the Prayer Book, and is so important it must be quoted in full: "Letters of Business should be issued to the Convocations with instructions (*a*) to consider the preparation of a new rubric regulating the ornaments (that is to say, the vesture) of the ministers of the Church, at the times of their ministrations, with a view to its enactment by Parliament; and (*b*) to frame, with a view to their enactment by Parliament, such modifications in the existing law relating to the conduct of Divine Service and to the ornaments and fittings of churches as may tend to secure the greater elasticity which a reasonable recognition of the comprehensiveness of the Church of England and of its present needs seem to demand."[4]

[1] G. K. A. Bell, "Randall Davidson," Vol. I, p. 459.
[2] Ibid., p. 461.
[3] Report, p. 75.
[4] Report, p. 77.

It was from this recommendation that the process of the revision of the Prayer Book started. It was thus the deliberate and unanimous conclusion of a strong and representative Commission that greater elasticity was required than that allowed by the existing laws; and, therefore, Prayer Book reform was an urgent necessity.

The Revised Prayer Book

It is not necessary here to describe the long, slow and cumbrous procedure which resulted from the issue of Letters of Business. The dilatoriness of the Convocations became a scandal. The war and three General Elections partly account for the slow progress which was made. But the critical outsider felt he was watching a revival of the Circumlocution Office, for when the Convocations finished their work in 1920 the newly-constituted Church Assembly had to be consulted. General approval was given, and then the Houses of Clergy and Laity sat separately for the work of revision. Their reports were next considered by the House of Bishops who spent between forty and fifty full days on them, and "not only went through the amendments of the other two Houses, but also made such a substantial remodelling that the result not unfairly produced the impression that they were addressing themselves to the improvement of the Prayer Book for the first time."[1] Eventually the new Book was approved by the Convocations of the two Provinces, and by the Church Assembly, with very large majorities, and at last it was ready for presentation to Parliament. The old Prayer Book was to remain unchanged, but various alterations and additions which were optional and not compulsory were to be allowed. Most of them were of minor importance: archaic terms and words were modified, some of the services, notably Baptism and the Burial of the Dead, were simplified, a number of additional prayers were included, and Eucharistic vestments allowed. None of these would by themselves have caused much controversy; this raged (and the word is chosen deliberately) round the proposal to allow the consecrated elements to be reserved for the communion of the sick, and the new Order of the Holy Communion. Both were fiercely attacked; the Evangelicals feared that Reservation would lead to superstition and to services of adoration usual in the Roman Catholic Church; the extreme

[1] G. K. A. Bell, "Randall Davidson," Vol. II, p. 1330.

Anglo-Catholics were afraid that they would be hindered in the devotional use they desire to make of the reserved Sacrament. The Evangelicals objected to the proposed Order of Communion as doctrinally unsound, while Anglo-Catholics and many who could not be described as extreme criticised it as Eastern rather than Western. A violent agitation was worked up against the proposed Book. It was denounced as a betrayal, in the interests of Rome, of the principles of the Reformation. The opposition was widespread, vociferous and vigorous. Much of it was conducted in a reasonable and Christian spirit; but this could not be said of all who took part in it. What Bishop Hensley Henson described as an "underworld" was let loose; the book was misrepresented, and the bishops unscrupulously attacked as Romanists and traitors. From one parish I was about to visit in my diocese I had a letter telling me that the people were praying that I might be converted from my secret allegiance to Rome, before I polluted their pulpit with my presence! A highly respected Evangelical layman once announced to a horrified audience that he had received a rude letter from a supporter of the proposed Book; there was hardly a bishop who could not have said he had received scores, if not hundreds, of letters from fervent opponents in addition to many reasoned protests. The pressure was concentrated on members of Parliament; resolutions and letters poured upon them from their constituents threatening them with the loss of support if they dared vote for the Prayer Book Measure.[1] It eventually came before the two Houses, and was approved by a large majority in the Lords, where the bishops were able to answer criticisms and remove misunderstandings; but in the House of Commons, after a debate of a few hours in which passion and emotion reached great heights, the Measure was defeated by thirty-three votes. Its critics were undoubtedly superior both in eloquence and argument, while its defenders were strangely ineffective; they seemed to be surprised and taken aback at the vehemence and strength of the opposition. When the result was announced many of the majority cheered wildly, waving their Order papers triumphantly at the old archbishop sitting in the Gallery. Rarely in all my life have I felt a deeper sense of humiliation for the Church than I did that night. Years of long and difficult

[1] It is only fair to add that the supporters of the revised Book also appealed to members of both Houses of Parliament.

work destroyed in a few hours! Many of us, who had prayed and worked for the Book, felt the iron enter our souls.

At once the question arose as to what should be the next step. It was impossible for the bishops to discipline the clergy who had adopted practices included in a Book which had been approved by the Convocations, by the Church Assembly, and by the House of Lords. One proposal was to ask immediately for disestablishment and freedom, but this would not have been supported by the main body of clergy and laity. Another suggestion was that the bishops should authorise the book and leave Parliament to take the next step. But the majority of the bishops resolved "to reintroduce the Measure into the Church Assembly as soon as possible with such changes, and such changes only, as may tend to remove misapprehensions and to make clearer and more explicit its intentions and limitations." I warmly supported this policy, but events proved it to have been mistaken. The two archbishops with their long experience of public affairs were very doubtful, but the majority of the bishops had been urged to adopt the course by many leading members of both Houses, as well as by other public men usually considered to have sound judgement. They felt that the adverse vote had been given under misapprehensions which might easily be removed. There were misunderstandings about the Prayers for the Royal Family, and ambiguities about the regulations to govern Reservation. It was thought that the wave of emotionalism which had swept the House would have ebbed in a few months' time; it might even have ebbed if the vote had been postponed until the next day: the Prime Minister, Mr. Baldwin, told the archbishop he regretted that he had not moved the adjournment. Many of us found it difficult to believe that the House of Commons had deliberately destroyed the work of twenty years. We, therefore, set ourselves to make various changes which might satisfy the more reasonable members of the opposition. But the majority of the bishops had no intention of going back on their original decisions about Reservation or the Order of Communion. The Archbishop of Canterbury was ready to make considerable changes about the regulations which should govern Reservation, and the Archbishop of York was in favour of abandoning the new Prayer of Consecration; but the bishops stood firm, and only minor changes were made. Most of us felt very strongly that at the bidding of Parliament it would be wrong for us to withdraw what we had decided was right for the celebration and administration of the Sacrament. But though some modifications were made, they failed in their purpose, for they reduced the majorities by which the Measure had been approved in the Convocations and in the Church Assembly, while they did not succeed in winning over any of its opponents in Parliament. The Measure then went again to the House of Commons; on this occasion all the argument was in favour of its passing. It was introduced with an excellent speech by Sir Boyd Merriman, then Solicitor-General, and supported by the Prime Minister and Mr. Winston Churchill; but debate by that time was unavailing—the majority of the House had already made up its mind, and the *coup de grâce* was given by Sir Thomas Inskip, a loyal Churchman and a good evangelical, who in winding up for the opposition stated that "with the concurrence of the Home Secretary and the present Lord Chancellor, I went to the Archbishop of Canterbury and told him that, with whatever influence we had, we were prepared to assent to a Measure passing through this House provided it did not include this perpetual Reservation, which is the keystone of the system. In his wisdom the Archbishop of Canterbury perhaps thought that offer unworthy of further consideration." As a matter of fact the archbishop had not so understood Sir Thomas, nor had the bishops known anything of this offer, but in any case its acceptance would not have been possible. This disclosure at the last moment, when no reply could be made, was fatal to the weak chance which still remained that the Measure might survive. It was defeated by a somewhat larger majority than on the previous occasion, and the closing comment was that of a Labour Member, who shouted: "The working man is not interested in the Prayer Book, but in the Rent Book." The Archbishop was very unwell and suffering much pain; as I walked away with him through the crowded corridors of excited members, he said, "These fellows don't know what harm they have done, though I am sure they didn't mean it."

The revised Prayer Book was rejected, not because of unfair propaganda against it—though that indeed had some weight—but for much deeper reasons. There were three.

First, the Church itself was divided. Quite apart from the more extreme Low Churchmen there was a solid body of steady, faithful Evangelical clergy and laity who were resolutely opposed to any Book which authorised perpetual Reservation and which contained the new Canon. They were prepared to acquiesce in much that the Book contained, but here were matters of principle on which they could not conscientiously yield. On the other hand there were the extreme Anglo-Catholics who were equally determined not to accept any restriction on Reservation; according to Dr. Darwell Stone there were some seven hundred Anglo-Catholic priests who were uncompromising in their resistance. In addition many of the laity who belonged to no party were, to say the least, lukewarm over the proposed Book, through their dislike of any change in the manner of worship to which they were accustomed. It is easy to understand that Members of Parliament unfamiliar with the subject, fastened quite legitimately on the fact that there was undoubtedly a serious division of opinion in the Church, and therefore decided to vote against the Book.

Secondly, there was deep dislike and suspicion of Anglo-Catholicism. Almost every Member had heard of congregations alienated by changes thrust upon them against their wishes. The eccentricities of individual Anglo-Catholics were exaggerated as they were repeated. Their defiance of authority increased the prejudice against them. And in the background there was the uneasy suspicion that they were attempting from within the Church to win England for Rome, and this by itself was sufficient to incite prejudice against them. Anger, too, was felt at the bishops, who perhaps since the rejection of the Reform Bill early in the previous century had never been so unpopular; they were accused of weakness in allowing the Anglo-Catholics much freedom, and it was doubted with reason if the bishops would be able to enforce obedience to the Book even if it were passed.

And thirdly, Dr. Bell was right in saying: "The deepest reason for the failure was that the whole method was from the very beginning wrong. The revision of Church services and the enforcement or ecclesiastical discipline are different things. A revision of worship, of common prayer, which is intended from the start to be used as an instrument for stopping disobedience is at any rate not likely to produce the happiest results in the realm of worship! And side by side with this, the recommendation of the Royal Commission to consider the preparation of a new Ornaments Rubric 'with a view to its enactment by Parliament,' and to frame modifications in Church services 'with a view to their enactment by Parliament,' started all on a false track."[1] Several of the bishops on their appointment found

[1] Ibid., Vol. II, p. 1357.

that the Church had already been on this track for many years—in my own case fourteen years; we had our misgivings, but it was too late to change the track and we hoped that Parliament would follow the precedent of 1662 and accept the Book without detailed discussion. But many of us would have refused to continue on this track if we had realised that it would end in a debate on the floor of the House on the doctrines and worship of the Church.

The rejection of the Measures made it plain that the Church does not possess full spiritual freedom, though the reasons just given mitigate the seriousness of Parliament's action. At one time it could have been argued that the House of Commons represented the laity of the Church of England; but the position now is very different. It has changed even since the rejection of the Book, probably then there was a majority of churchmen in the House, but this is no longer the case. Churchmen are now in a minority.

The bishops had to decide on their line of action in view of a defeat which had destroyed at one blow their policy; their authority had received a serious shock, and the Church had been subjected to open humiliation. There were some of the clergy and laity who saw in disestablishment the only remedy. Alone among the bishops Hensley Henson took this view; writing later he said, "I could no longer acquiesce in the anomalous conditions of the legal Establishment, since it had been made clear that they involved for the Church of England a subordination to the State which was plainly inconsistent with its spiritual independence, destructive of its public credit, and paralysing to its disciplinary action."[1] But the bishops were opposed to disestablishment; and if they had asked for it they would not have had the support of the clergy and laity. Some thought that William Temple would take the lead in demanding disestablishment, for in the early days of the Life and Liberty Movement he had insisted that unless the Church gained spiritual freedom it must ask for complete separation between Church and State. Privately he had told his friends that if the House again rejected the Measure some form of disestablishment would be inevitable, but when the time for decision came he hesitated about paying the price. After the rejection of the revised Prayer Book, he spoke in the Church Assembly in support of a new Commission on Church and State, and referring to the Life and

[1] Hensley Henson, "Retrospect of an Unimportant Life," Vol. II, p. 239.

Liberty days, declared, "I wish to add that I have seen more reason since, than I saw then, for valuing what is called the Establishment. While I still consider that spiritual independence is so essential that the price of disestablishment would not be too great to pay if it really appears that there is no other means of securing that independence, yet we must search long and carefully before we decide that that price has to be paid."[1] His biographer says: "In his later years he became more and more convinced of the advantages to be gained by the State from its connexion with the Church, and this dominated his thinking to the end."[2] Both the archbishops and practically all the bishops were anxious to avoid directly challenging the State, and thus plunging Church and nation alike into bitter controversy.

Eventually the bishops agreed on the declaration, asserting the inalienable right of the Church to formulate its faith in Our Lord and to arrange to express that faith in its worship. A year later the bishops, with the approval of the Lower Houses of Convocation, resolved that in the exercise of their administrative discretion they would in their several dioceses "be guided by the proposals set forth in the Book of 1928, and will endeavour to secure that the practices which are consistent neither with the Book of 1662 nor with the Book of 1928 shall cease." Again a year later the Assembly appointed a Commission to consider the present relations of Church and State. The decision of the bishops to take the rejected Book as the standard which they would use in their administration caused much controversy; not only was it disliked by the extremists of both sides, but many Churchmen and non-Churchmen felt that it was lacking in straightforwardness for the bishops to take for their guidance a Book which twice had been rejected by Parliament. This was stated strongly—perhaps too strongly—by Sir Lewis Dibdin, in saying the public "were greatly shocked at the spectacle of bishops disregarding—it is hardly fair to call it flouting—the decision of the House of Commons. It was remembered that that decision was given in accordance with the Enabling Act and within ten years of the Act having been discussed in Parliament, and notwithstanding the emphatic declarations of the bishops at that time, that the power of Parliament was intended to remain unaltered and absolute."[3] It is

[1] Iremonger, "William Temple," p. 358.
[2] Ibid., p. 359.
[3] "Establishment in England," p. 2.

extremely difficult to know what other line the bishops could have taken. They could not censure and discipline the clergy for rites and ceremonies which the Convocations and the Assembly had approved; it would have been folly to have attempted to enforce obedience to the Prayer Book of 1662 which was acknowledged to be too strait for the times; it would have been sheer silliness to have sent to Parliament a Measure containing all the uncontroversial matter, but omitting the very matters which had necessitated revision; and they would have been unfaithful to their duty if they had merely let things drift, throwing in their hands in despair. Looking back over twenty years I can see no other action we could have taken. Many of us were far from happy over this policy, we saw too clearly the criticisms which would be levelled at us. We regarded it, however, as only an interim policy "during the present emergency and until further order be taken." Personally I should have liked the bishops with the support of the Convocations and Assembly, to have sanctioned openly the use of the rejected Book but at the same time to have made it plain that the Church would not resist disestablishment if it was held by the State that the use of the Book was so inconsistent with the traditional relationship between Church and State that the tie between them should be broken. But this policy was never seriously discussed as it was felt it would be a direct challenge to the State. I have done my best, with most of the bishops, to use the Book as the latest authoritative expression of the mind of the Church on what it permits and forbids in public worship; I have given frequently both affirmative and negative rulings in accordance with it, but I have never concealed my conviction that the Church ought to accept disestablishment if the State demanded it as the price of this policy.

The Position To-day

Twenty years ago we spoke of "the present emergency," and it still continues. The rejected Book is widely used, with the exception of the second half of the Order of Holy Communion. Its prayers and services are used by clergy of very different schools of thought. The bishops have done their best to suppress practices inconsistent with the Books of 1662 and 1928, and with the exception of a few dioceses they have been largely successful. But the position still remains most unsatisfactory, for on a strict interpretation of the law all these permitted modifications and additions are equally illegal. The minister who in the statutory services prays for the missionary work of the Church, or who uses the new Orders of Baptism and of Marriage, is acting as wrongly, in the sight of the law, as the minister who changes the prayer of Consecration. The bishops who sanction these changes and additions are approving what a judicial decision has declared to be illegal. Meantime there has arisen the demand for further revision. Popular services are required for the occasions when a congregation unfamiliar with Mattins or Evensong is present; those of us who have been familiar from childhood with these services find it difficult to understand how perplexing and confusing they are to the non-churchgoer. Services simpler even than those provided in the 1928 Book are required for the non-churchgoers who bring their infants to be baptized and their dead to be buried. And with the growth of liturgical knowledge there is an increasing wish on the part of many Churchmen for an enriched and rearranged Order of the Holy Communion, and for a larger use of prayers and devotions drawn from the rich treasure houses of the East and the West. But the legality of every change made in public worship is doubtful, and might be condemned as contrary to the law if a case were taken to the courts. Very easily a crisis might be precipitated between obediance to the State and loyalty to the Church. At a time when the duty of order and obedience should be taught by the Church, it is open to the charge that its bishops and clergy are themselves breaking the law, and to this we can only plead guilty with extenuating circumstances. There is a really desperate anxiety on the part of Church people to be free from this reproach. With all our hearts most of us dislike and resent the position in which we are placed.

A Practical Proposal

There are some who still believe that the right policy would be to send to Parliament another Measure containing only those matters on which there is general agreement. There is far greater agreement than there was twenty years ago; in the presence of the menace of an atheistic secularism all have been drawn closer together; Churchmen of different views are much more ready to respect and understand one another. But on both sides there are the irreconcilables, who would do their utmost to wreck any settlement which did not coincide with their narrow views. They are few in number, but would again use all their influence to persuade Members of Parliament to support them by their vote. The old controversy would flare up to be fought out again in the Houses of Parliament, at the very time when national unity is so desirable. There is a growing conviction that it would be wrong ever again to invite an assembly many of whose members are neither Churchmen nor even theists to debate the manner in which Almighty God should be worshipped. We have no right to complain at the part which non-church members would take in such debates, or to expect them to be silent; they have a duty to their constituents. But there are large numbers of Churchmen who would definitely prefer disestablishment if the alternative is the discussion of worship and doctrine under conditions in which many who would take part in it by speech or vote have neither sympathy with, nor understanding of, the creed of a Churchman, and some of whom regard Christianity as an outworn superstition.

On the other hand it must be recognised that as long as there is an Established Church, the State has the right to be assured that proposed changes have the approval of the majority of the members of the Church, and that these changes are not such as would transform its nature. It is self-evident that it would be unreasonable for the State to continue its special relationship with a Church which, without its knowledge and consent, changed its faith and worship. The State has the right to require that any changes the Church makes are not inconsistent with its historic position. It is therefore necessary to find some method by which the Church revises its worship and the State gives its approval without a debate in Parliament. The Commission on Church and State makes a practical proposal. When a Measure has been passed by the Assembly dealing with the worship and doctrine of the Church, and the Archbishops of Canterbury and York, the Lord Chancellor, and the Speaker, certify that it relates substantially to the spiritual concerns of the Church of England, and when the Archbishops of Canterbury and York have certified that it has been approved by the Convocations, and twice approved by not less than three-quarters of the dioceses within the two

Provinces, that is before and after the revision of the Measure by the Assembly, and when the archbishops have further certified that the Measure is neither contrary to nor indicative of any departure from the fundamental doctrines of the Church of England, then, without being debated in Parliament, it shall be presented direct to His Majesty for the Royal Assent. The process thus proposed is long and cumbrous; it ought to be sufficient for the Measure to be presented only once to the dioceses, but even with this modification it would be impossible for any change in worship to be made without the fullest discussion and without the consent of an overwhelming majority of Churchmen; at the same time the proposed plan places upon the archbishops the responsibility of certifying that the suggested change is not contrary to the fundamental position of the Church. This plan would make it more necessary than ever for Churchmen themselves to reach an agreement before any Measure is sent forward. With these ample safeguards the State should be satisfied on the two essential matters, agreement in the Church and no departure from the fundamental doctrines and principles of the Church. For such a plan an Act of Parliament will be required. The first step will be for the Church to agree on this machinery, and to promote a bill asking Parliament to grant it. When the machinery is set up, the next step will be to reach agreement on the changes in public worship for which the Royal Assent is asked. In all probability Churchmen with the exception of small groups of irreconcilables, would reach sufficient agreement on a large number of the changes already in the 1928 Book so as to obtain the Royal Assent very quickly; other more controversial matters, such as the Order of Communion, would require delay until agreement is reached; stage by stage, and not all at once, the legalisation for the desired changes and additions would be carried through. This proposal has been before the Church for over fourteen years and no action has been taken to carry it out; delay has been partly due to the war and partly to the attempt to obtain agreement on the most controversial of the problems, instead of adopting the more statesmanlike policy of first reaching agreement on matters over which there is little difference, and then going on to those which are more difficult.

Lawful Authority

It will, however, take time before the necessary machinery is set up, and when set up it will take still more time before the Convocations, the Church Assembly, and three-quarters of the dioceses have expressed approval of the first group of changes required; meantime the need is urgent for some relief from a position which should be regarded as intolerable. Month by month large numbers of clergy promise that they "will use the form in the said Book prescribed, and none other, except so far as shall be ordered by lawful authority," but there is great doubt and confusion as to what is meant by "lawful authority." If asked the clergy would give very different replies; most would say "the bishop," or "the Convocations," but there are some whose definition of lawful authority would range from pre-Reformation books to the custom of the Western Church, to Parliament, or even to the authority of their own individual conscience. If a bishop is asked he would either confess he is uncertain or give a reply at variance with that given by the bishop of a neighbouring diocese. It is unsatisfactory that this uncertainty should exist over a declaration which has to be made by the clergy at some of the most solemn moments in their lives.

It seems clear that these words were intended to afford some relaxation from the stricter declaration in use before 1865. How strict this was is seen by an entry in the Greville Diary for June 17th, 1837, when William IV was dying: "An intimation came from Windsor that it was desired prayers should be offered up in the churches for him; so the Privy Council assembled to order this, but on assembling the Bishop of London objected to the form which had been used upon the last other occasion (an order made by the Lords to the Archbishop of Canterbury to prepare a form of prayer), asserting that *the Lords* had no power to make such an order, and it was even doubted by lawyers whether the king himself had power to order alterations in the Liturgy, or the use of particular prayers; and admitting that he had, it was in virtue of his prerogative, and as Head of the Church, but that the *Lords of the Council* had no power whatever of this kind. They admitted that he was correct in this view of the case, and consequently, instead of an order to the Archbishop, His Majesty's pleasure that prayers should be offered up was conveyed to the Council, and a communication to that effect was directed to be made to the Archbishop. The king's pleasure being thus conveyed, it is his duty to obey."[1] To meet similar difficulties an amended form of Declaration was passed nearly thirty years later, but unfortunately there was given no definition of the term "lawful authority." Certainly it does not, and cannot, mean that the man who takes the Declaration is the lawful authority; for he recognises that there is an authority above him which can order him. It as certainly refers to services not in the Prayer Book but ordered by the Privy Council or Royal Proclamation. Almost certainly it gives the bishop of the diocese *some* discriminating power. Archbishop Davidson held that while the insertion was intended to safeguard a clergyman using a service ordered by the Privy Council—and he gave as an instance the service, ordered at the time the Declaration was modified, in connection with the cattle plague—yet "the words as they stand now, part of the Act of Parliament, are capable of giving to the Episcopate some larger authority than existed before, seems to me hardly to admit of a doubt."[2] But to what extent have bishops this authority? A judgement, delivered three years after the new Declaration had been enacted, appears to regard the authority of a diocesan bishop as limited to allowing only some relaxation in the number of services to be performed. Out of sheer necessity, to escape from impossible rigidity, bishops have claimed that they have a *jus liturgicum* which enables them within limits to allow variations from, and additions to, the services in the Book of Common Prayer. But the question still arises, what are these limits? Until recently each bishop set for himself the limits to his discretion, with the result that services and practices are allowed in one diocese and strictly forbidden in another. Now, by the general agreement to take the 1928 Book as the standard by which a bishop both allows and forbids, there is greater uniformity in episcopal rulings; but there are bishops who do not feel bound by an agreement made before they reached the episcopate, and clergy who treat any rulings based upon this Book as self-condemned and as an incentive to disobedience.

In an important memorandum to the Report on Canon Law Mr. Justice Vaisey makes some interesting observations on "lawful authority"; precise definition of the term he regards

[1] Vol. I, p. 559. Edited by P. Whithwell Wilson.

[2] G. K. A. Bell, "Randall Davidson," Vol. I., p. 469.

as impossible—"It is true in a sense to say that nobody can be sure what the words mean, either to himself or to anybody else, and that their effect has been to convert an obligation which was impossible to perform into one which it is impossible to understand." Then he goes on to say: "Lawful authority is always (it is suggested) to be sought from the appropriate quarter—appropriate, that is to the particular occasion calling for its exercise. Acting under the order of lawful authority is the antithesis of acting according to one's own caprice or fancy. It excludes eccentricity, unrestraint, indiscipline, idiosyncrasy. It implies control, submission, regularity, orderliness. And when 'authority' is required it must be looked for with a measure of ordinary common sense, and not by any means always in the same place."[1] That is to say there can be more than one lawful authority. The proposed Canon XIII attempts to meet the difficulty by giving a clearer definition. If the canon is passed, "ordered by lawful authority" will mean (*a*) Public Service authorised by Royal Warrant or Proclamation with the approval of the two archbishops; (*b*) changes in the form prescribed by the Book of Common Prayer already authorised by previous legislation; (*c*) such additions, omissions, alternative use or otherwise as may be allowed by the two Convocations, provided they are not contrary to the doctrine of the Church of England; and (*d*) any form of service sanctioned by the Ordinary for special occasions when no provision has been made by the Book of Common Prayer, again provided it is not contrary to the doctrine of the Church of England. This recognises four lawful authorities—the Crown, Parliament, Convocation, and the Diocesan Bishop. A canon with this definition will require an Act of Parliament. If it is promulgated it will remove great perplexity, relieve the consciences of many, and give both authority and freedom in departing from the rigid observance of the Book of Common Prayer. Except for a special emergency, for instance a sudden call for public prayer, the bishops will seek for the authority of Convocation before they authorise changes and additions. The directions given by a diocesan will not be those of an autocratic prelate, but of a constitutional bishop who has behind him the authority of Convocation. It will be both advisable and necessary to consult the House of Laity before these deviations and additions are made, and no doubt the proposed canon will be amended to this

[1] "Canon Law in the Church of England," p. 221.

effect. The 1662 Prayer Book would remain the same as it is to-day, until changes are made in it by the Royal Assent after they have been approved by the Convocations, the Church Assembly, and the dioceses, in accordance with the plan recommended by the Church and State Commission. Until these changes are made there should be a period of authorised and orderly experiment in forms of worship which could be used at the option of the minister with the good will of his congregation.

There is general agreement on two principles; that the 1662 Book should be treated as the authoritative standard, next to the Bible, of the doctrine of the Church of England and of the whole Anglican Communion; and that new conditions since it was drawn up call for variations from and additions to the forms of service it provides. It must be remembered it is the Book not only of the Provinces of Canterbury and York, but also of the whole Anglican Communion, and, therefore, changes in it should be made with great caution and reserve. On the other hand both in England and overseas the old Prayer Book is no longer sufficient for the needs and outlook of an age so different from that in which it was drawn up, or for countries so different from that in which it had its origin. This was expressed by the resolution of the Lambeth Conference of 1920. "While maintaining the authority of the Book of Common Prayer as the Anglican standard of doctrine and practice, we consider that liturgical uniformity should not be regarded as a necessity throughout the Churches of the Anglican Communion." With complete loyalty to the structure and teaching of the Prayer Book, the various Churches of the Anglican Communion have adapted or added to it so as to meet the needs of the people to whom they minister; and they have done this as self-governing Churches. The Church at home requires freedom to bring its public worship more into relation with the thought and understanding of the people of to-day, to adapt it for evangelistic work, and to enrich it with the liturgical knowledge which was not open to those who drew up the present Book. But practical action should no longer be delayed. Forty years have passed since the Royal Commission on Ecclesiastical Discipline reported; twenty years since the Prayer Book was rejected; fourteen since the Commission on Church and State reported, and nothing yet has been done to set right a position regarded by all thoughtful Churchmen as profoundly unsatisfactory.

XI

THE REVISION OF CANON LAW

THE reform of our Canon Law has long been overdue. Alone among the Churches of the Anglican Communion, the Church of England is without a body of canons which has been revised and supplemented in modern times. Until the Canon Law has been authoritatively revised, it is unreasonable to expect the restoration of discipline and order in our Church. Order is impossible when those under obedience are uncertain as to the laws which they are expected to observe.

The Nature of Canon Law

There is such general ignorance of Canon Law that it is necessary to give some preliminary account of its nature. Canons are rules made by the Church for the direction and guidance of its own members, and especially of those who are its officers. The members of a Church are thus under a twofold system of law: as citizens, whether they are Churchmen or not, they are subject to the ordinary law of State, which they must obey unless it is contrary to the law of God. Some of the State law is ecclesiastical, and deals with the property and temporal affairs of the Church. In the case of an Established Church the amount of Statute law which concerns it is necessarily large. But in addition to State law the members of a Church are under another law, the law of the Church, which imposes upon them regulations from which other citizens are free. There is nothing unreasonable in this, for every society has its rules or bye-laws for the management of its own affairs: and a member of a political or social society agrees to obey its rules while he belongs to it. In the same way the oldest and largest of all societies, the Church, has its rules for its members. Those who dislike them can resign or withdraw from their membership; for in our day there is no longer compulsion for anyone either to join a Church or to remain within it; of their own free will they can transfer their membership to some other religious society, or if they so wish they can remain outside all Churches. The canons of the Church affect only its members, and chiefly those who hold office within it; they have been made for its spiritual welfare and for the sake of its good order.

The canons of the Church are spiritual in origin and in authority. They were not made by the State, but by the Church. They can be divided into two large groups. There are canons which are based on natural law or revelation; these are unchangeable and universally binding. The second group consists of the canons made by the Church at various times for practical purposes; these give guidance on specific problems. These canons can be augmented, amended, or rescinded by the Church as need arises. They often become inoperative through long disuse, and by the substitution of some contrary custom formally accepted, or tacitly assented to, by lawful authority. Canons are thus frequently changing, for they are the expression of the mind of a living society as it adapts itself to new conditions. There can be, therefore, no fixed and permanently closed body of canons. As the State, and every voluntary society within it, possesses the power of making and changing the rules which regulate the conduct of its business and the obligations of its members, so the greatest of all societies, the Church, possesses and exercises the same right. From its earliest days the Church made rules for the discipline of its members and for the conditions under which converts from paganism might be admitted. In the fourth century a series of Councils were held which made rules for the government of the various provinces and their dioceses; these rules were called canons, the word meaning a straight rod used for the purpose of measurement. The canon was the standard or measure by which the members of the Church were to judge themselves.

Pre-Reformation Canon Law

Gradually there grew up a vast and complicated system of canon law for the whole of Christendom. The canons of the first Councils formed the ground work of the law of the Church. They did not, however, sufficiently cover the whole field of Church life. There were frequent doubts about their application, and new problems arose to which the older canons gave no answer. The custom then arose of asking the Pope for advice; this he gave in the form of letters which were called decretals, and gradually these decretals, or decisions, outnumbered the canons. For convenience the canons and decretals were presently collected together, and with penitentials—handbooks of pastoral and moral theology which had their origin in Ireland—and the dooms or ecclesiastical laws enacted by the king, the bishops, and the chief nobles sitting in the primitive parliament of Anglo-Saxon days, they formed the law of the Anglo-Saxon Church. On the Continent from the end of the sixth to the middle of the eleventh century there was a further development in Canon Law by means of Forged Decretals. These were made by private individuals who brought together decretals and canons which seemed to give guidance on some pressing problem, and altered them to support the view the compiler advocated. To give them greater authority they ascribed them to some famous Pope or saint. The tendency of these Forged Decretals was to exalt the authority of the Pope as the supreme legislator and court of appeal. They "assert again and again that in the Pope, bishops have a person to whom they can appeal when they are molested and who will come to their help, using the power entrusted to him as the successor of St. Peter, granting them a fair trial if they are accused and quashing the proceedings of any provincial council which might attempt to depose them, on the ground that no provincial court could meet without the consent of the papacy or lawfully transact business without the Pope's approval."[1]

These theories of the Papacy as the source of ecclesiastical authority led to a great development in Canon Law. The papal chair was occupied in the twelfth and thirteenth centuries by lawyers who in the form of decretals replied to the questions addressed to them by prelates and ecclesiastical judges. "The register of Alexander III contains nearly four thousand decretals, and that of Innocent III over five thousand."[2] Three great Papal Codes, including a mass of previous canons and decretals, gave a comprehensive legal system to the Church during the later part of the Middle Ages. Throughout Western Christendom the Canon Law was accepted and applied; it was intricate

[1] "The Canon Law of the Church of England," p. 14. Throughout this section I have drawn freely from this Report.

[2] Ibid., p. 27.

and confusing, and a large body of ecclesiastical lawyers came into existence to interpret it, but then, as now, lawyers differed in their opinions, and innumerable appeals were made to the papacy for authoritative decisions. The medieval Papacy and the canon law thus became closely related; the canon law exalting the Pope as its source, its interpreter, and its protector.

At one time it was thought that the Church of England had been largely free of the Canon Law of Rome, which, though treated with great respect, was supposed to have no final authority in English ecclesiastical courts. In support of this it was argued that provincial synods had frequently promulged canons, and that the English Church had its own canonists, of whom Lyndwood was the most famous. But this view can no longer be held. It is now clear that the Church of England accepted the canons which bound the rest of Christendom. The canons of its local synods did not claim to over-rule the law of the rest of the Church; they were more of the nature of by-laws to meet local conditions, and had no validity if they contradicted the general Canon Law of the Church. The English canonists expounded and interpreted the universal canon law; the ecclesiastical courts applied it; and the secular courts accepted it, even when they disliked it. The appeals to the Pope from England were as frequent as from any Continental Church. Professor Z. N. Brooke sums up the position, "The English Church recognised the same law as the rest of the Church; it possessed and used the same collections of Church law that were employed in the rest of the Church. There is no shred of evidence to show that the English Church in the eleventh and twelfth centuries was governed by laws selected by itself."[1] When the English canonist Lyndwood collected various provincial constitutions, he assumed that they were the application of the common law of the Church to local circumstances; the only new legislation they contained was on matters which had not been dealt with in the papal code. It is now generally accepted that in the Middle Ages the Church of England never possessed a system of Canon Law, independent of, and apart from, that accepted by the rest of Western Christendom.

The extent and intricacy of Canon Law made it difficult to administer. The more comprehensive the law the harder it became to apply it to individual cases; there was always the

[1] "The English Church and the Papacy," p. 113.

danger it might be treated as the expression of an ideal too lofty to be observed; then by general disobedience to its directions it would be brought into contempt. To avoid this it became customary to grant dispensation from obedience to it in particular cases; in early days this power of dispensation was in the hands of the bishop, but as the Pope became the supreme legislator the claim was made and accepted that as he was the source and protector of law he alone could dispense from its observance. Thus a system of dispensations was created which had the advantage of affording individuals some relaxation from the law, of exalting the authority of the Pope, and of increasing papal revenues; at the same time it enabled legislation to be enacted without the fear that it "would have to be carried out; it became increasingly ideal, with diminishing relation to actual facts. The ingenuity of canonists was unfettered by any thought of the consequences of their conclusions, as it was thought comparatively easy to escape their consequences if desirable. . . . Men in the Middle Ages loved law, and could not have too much of it—on paper. Our ideas have changed in modern times, and we dislike to live under regulations which are not observed by the community."[1] Before the Reformation the strictness of the Canon Law was always tempered by the possibility of dispensation from it, and both Canon Law and dispensation rested on the authority of the Pope.

The Reformation

It was, thus, inevitable that with the repudiation of papal authority there should follow changes in the operation of medieval Canon Law in England. Its complete abolition was an impossibility; such a drastic step would have left the Church without any authoritative rules, and chaos would have been the result. It was expressly provided in Henry VIII's Act for the Submission of the Clergy "that such canons, constitutions, ordinances and synodals provincial being already made, which be not contrariant or repugnant to the laws, statutes, and customs of this realm, nor to the damage or hurt of the king's prerogative royal, shall still be used, and executed as they were afore the making of this Act" until a commission which was to be appointed had reviewed and revised the existing canons.

[1] Creighton, "The Church and the Nation," p. 197.

Part of the old Canon Law was at once abolished by the repudiation of papal authority and by the suppression of the monasteries; but much of it was to remain in operation until the commission had reported. Pre-Reformation canons were to continue as the law of the Church when they were not contrary to the laws of the land or the royal prerogative, "not because they were the work of the Pope, hitherto regarded as the Church's sovereign law-giver, but because they had been long observed in England and had acquired through this long observance the authority not of written but of customary law."[1] The king took precautions to see that the Convocations did not exercise freely their ancient right of making canons, for in the Act for the Submission of the Clergy it was laid down that Convocation should in the future only assemble when summoned by the Royal Writ and that no canons should be made "without the king's most royal assent and licence." On this a foreign envoy commented in a dispatch, "This is a strange thing; Churchmen will be of less account than shoemakers, who have the power of assembling and making their own statutes." But the commissioners appointed by the king did not produce a report; and when eleven years later another Act was passed giving the king again power to appoint thirty-two commissioners, this time with the power not only to revise existing canons, but to make new canons, no action appears to have been taken. In Edward VI's reign, another commission was appointed, and its work was nearing completion when it was brought to an end by the death of the king; but in 1571 the code which it had drawn up was revised by Archbishop Parker and published under the title of "Reformatio Legum," it had no authority and only is of interest as showing the canons which it was then thought to be of sufficient importance to enact. It was not until 1603 that work on a new code of canons was started; it was completed and passed by the Convocation of Canterbury and approved by the king in the following year; it was not, however, passed by York until 1605–6. The difference in the date of enactment by the two Convocations has led to the code being known as the Canons of 1603, the date when work commenced upon them. In the period between the Submission of the Clergy, 1534, and the new canons of 1603, the Church was under the old Canon Law, except when it was contrary to the laws and customs of the realm, as well as under the Statutes of

[1] "The Canon Law of the Church of England," p. 46.

Parliament dealing with ecclesiastical affairs and the various Injunctions and Advertisements issued by the sovereign or by the archbishops.

With the abolition of papal jurisdiction, papal dispensations were also forbidden. The medieval Canon Law and dispensations from its observance had both been closely associated with the Pope. In future the Archbishop of Canterbury was to have the power to grant dispensations not contrary to the Scriptures or the Laws of God "as heretofore hath been used and accustomed to be had and obtained . . . at the see of Rome." The Archbishop of York and other bishops were by the same Act authorised to "dispense in all cases in which they were wont to dispense by the common law or custom of this realm afore the making of this Act."[1] Under this Act the Archbishop of Canterbury still grants dispensations in the matter of pluralities, from various requirements concerning the calling of banns, the place in which a marriage is solemnized, and from what would be bars to ordination; while all diocesan bishops (including the two archbishops) may dispense their clergy from residence in their parishes; from the public reading of banns; and possibly both clergy and laity from fasting.

The Canons of 1603

The Canons of 1603 with a few later additions are the only canons which have post-Reformation authority for the Church of England. They were one hundred and forty-one in number and covered a limited field of matters on which there was urgent need of authoritative direction. They dealt with the Royal Supremacy; the nature of the Church of England as a true and apostolical Church; the worship, the ministers and lay officers of the Church; the furnishing of churches; the licensing of schoolmasters; the constitution of ecclesiastical courts and their officers. They have behind them the authority of the Convocations and the king; they are binding on the clergy, but not on the laity, as they were not passed by Parliament. In these canons there is little that is new; in the main they contain the old Canon Law, and some of the directions and regulations issued in previous reigns. "The purpose of the code promulgated in 1604 was the reduction of the existing

[1] 25 Henry VIII, c. 21 (1534).

chaos to an ordered and consistent body of regulations, duly authorised alike by Church and State. Hence it comes that the Canons of 1604 frequently repeat, generally with more or less important modifications, directions or prohibitions which had already been set forth in some of the earlier bodies of rules which they were meant to replace."[1] It is important to notice how they preserve and continue ancient customs and laws, some of which had their origin in Anglo-Saxon days. The new matter in them is chiefly concerned with the ecclesiastical courts, but most of the canons are based on pre-Reformation law and custom.

Since then various attempts have been made to revise or to add to them. In 1640 seventeen canons were passed by the Convocations under Royal Licence, and received the Royal Approval. These canons were popular with the High Churchmen of the time, especially Canon 7, which recommended that the Holy Table should be placed at the east end of the church, separated by a rail from the rest of the building, and also declared that it may be called an altar in the sense in which the early Church used the word. But as the Convocation which promulgated them had met at a time when Parliament was dissolved, it is doubtful if its proceedings were legal; its canons were condemned by the Long Parliament; and the Act of Charles II restoring the ecclesiastical courts expressly provided that nothing in it confirmed these canons.

With the suspension of sitting Convocations, it was impossible to enact canons. It was not until 1866 that an attempt at revision was made. A committee to prepare a report on the subject was then appointed by the Canterbury Convocation; after seven years it presented draft canons to the Convocation; the debate in the Upper House, according to the official report, could have barely taken two minutes. Subsequently the Archbishop of Canterbury suggested to the chairman of the committee that the canons should be sent for discussion in the rural deaneries of the Southern Province—a method of providing a decent funeral for an inconvenient report sometimes adopted in our own day. After six years the results of these discussions were reported to the Canterbury Lower House; the debate on this occasion seems to have lasted a quarter of an hour, and was closed by the Prolocutor saying that the House was hardly

[1] "Constitutions and Canons, 1604" (Oxford University Press Edition), 1923.

in a position to consider "the momentous questions raised by the report." Then the report, the result of thirteen years' hard work, passed completely out of sight for sixty-four years, until it was disinterred by a member of the recent Commission on Canon Law!

The Present Position

The position to-day is profoundly unsatisfactory. In addition to Parliamentary legislation and a few recent canons, the Church is under the 1603 canons and ancient Church law. There is no doubt that, except when they have been superseded, or become obsolete, or are contrary to the law of the land, ancient ecclesiastical law and custom are still operative, but there is often great doubt as to when they have survived these exceptions. The position of ancient Church law is made clear in a judgement by Lord Westbury in 1868 when he was discussing if it was necessary for a clergyman who had held preferment in another diocese to produce letters testimonial from its bishop before he was instituted. The judge said that the existence of such a rule had not been proved, and then went on: "If such a rule had been pleaded by the Bishop to have been the invariable usage of the Church from the earliest times down to the Reformation (which would be evidence of its being a law of the Church) and that it had been continued and uniformly recognised and acted upon by the bishops of the Anglican Church since the Reformation (which might have shown it to have been received and adopted as part of the law ecclesiastical recognised by the common law), the fitness of the rule ought not to be questioned."[1] The mere existence of a canon is not sufficient to show it is still enforceable. It need not be formally rescinded, for it becomes no longer operative if for forty years another custom, contrary to it, has taken its place, either with the tacit acquiescence or the formal approval of those in authority. Many canons have become obsolete in this way; not even the most august Synod can save them from this fate; the canon of the Council of Nicæa ordering all to stand for prayer has long been superseded in Western Christendom by the custom of kneeling. It is thus often very difficult to know when an ancient canon or custom is still binding. There are, for instance,

[1] Quoted in "The Canon Law of the Church of England," p. 64.

some who argue that the medieval canon enjoining the reservation of the Blessed Sacrament in every Parish Church is still operative and should be obeyed; there are others who hold that Reservation has been superseded, not for over forty years, but for over four hundred years, by the contrary custom enjoined by authority of the Private Celebration of Holy Communion in the sick person's house. This is only one instance out of many which might be given showing how difficult it is to know if the ancient law is still operative; but if obedience is to be expected, it is of vital importance that there should be no ambiguity about the law to be obeyed.

The 1603 Canons are quite inadequate for the present-day needs of the Church. This must be so, when it is remembered that for over three hundred years they have remained unaltered. During this time great changes have taken place in almost every direction, and within the Church numerous new problems have arisen. Statute law has been added to and amended, and year after year new Acts find their place on the Statute Book to meet new needs, but the Church has had no new canons to guide and direct its members on matters of difficulty. To all intents and purposes its canons remain unchanged.

Three main defects can be seen in the 1603 Canons:

(1) Many of them are obsolete. No longer is it necessary for a schoolmaster to obtain a licence from the bishop before he teaches in a public school or private house; no longer is he bound to teach in English or in Latin the Catechism or to bring the children to church on holy and festival days to hear sermons, and afterwards to examine them as to "what they have borne away of such sermons." No longer have the ecclesiastical courts jurisdiction over matrimonial cases and wills. No longer have ministers to present popish recusants every year, nor churchwardens to present "any faults committed in their Parishes and punishable by Ecclesiastical laws." No longer is it necessary to order proctors in the Courts of the Archbishops to refrain from "loud and confused cries and clamours." And it is hardly necessary to exhort ecclesiastical persons not "to wear any coife, or wrought nightcap, but only plain nightcaps of black silk, satin, or velvet."

(2) Many of the canons bear the marks of the controversies of the time in which they were promulgated. There is a fierceness in tone which is alien to our days, when we are ready to appreciate the lives and witness of those who are separated from our

Church. While it is true that the denunciations are mild compared to the anathemas attached to many medieval edicts, we are repelled by the repeated condemnation of " impugners " of the worship, doctrine, and ministry of the Church of England with the sentence, " let him be excommunicated *ipso facto*, not to be restored until he repent and publicly revoke such his wicked errors." And the canon merely excites derision which declares that " those who for obstinate refusing to frequent divine service established by public authority " shall every six months be denounced in the parish church and in the cathedral of the diocese and declared excommunicate " that others may be thereby both admonished to refrain their company and society."

(3) The greatest defect of the 1603 code is negative; it fails to give directions on matters where guidance is now most needed. To a large extent this was true when its canons were first promulgated, but since then new problems have arisen which could not have been foreseen in the seventeenth century. It is absurd to imagine that canons drawn up in an age so different from the twentieth century can meet present-day needs of the Church. The amendments and additions since 1603 have been comparatively unimportant; the canons dealing with the declaration of assent and subscription required by the clergy have been amended; the canon dealing with the time of day at which marriages may be solemnised has been changed so as to bring it into agreement with an Act of Parliament; canonical sanction has been given to a Clergy Discipline Act passed by Parliament; canons have been approved amending the constitution of the Lower Houses of Convocation, and in changing the Table of Prohibited Degrees. And this is all! The Code in substance remains the same as when it was promulged over three centuries ago. No attempt has been made to deal with the new problems. No wonder that little respect is paid to Canon Law in the Church of England; the laity hardly know it exists; most of the clergy disregard it; while ordinands are rarely taught it. No wonder that many of the clergy are a law to themselves through the absence of a clear and intelligible system of law which they can understand and obey. Everywhere else in the Anglican Communion the clergy and laity accept and honour the canons which have been made by the province or diocese to which they belong. They have been made by living Churches giving directions on practical problems. Through their canons the cohesion and good order of the

Churches are deepened and strengthened. But the Mother of them all, the Church of England, can only appeal to canons made three hundred years ago, or to vague and uncertain pre-Reformation laws and customs, the validity of which is often uncertain and frequently challenged.

Revision of the Canons

It became increasingly clear that without some drastic revision of the canons it was hopeless to expect the restoration of order in the Church. Formal expression to this conviction was given in a resolution of the Lower House of York in January, 1937, which asked the President "to take steps to introduce a measure into the Church Assembly facilitating the revision of the Canon Law of the Church of England by the Convocations." Two years later, after a debate on the legality of stone altars, the Lower House of the Canterbury Convocation asked for a Commission to consider the whole question of the revision and codification of the Canon Law. This request was supported in the same year by another resolution from the Lower House of York. As a result, later in the year the two archbishops, Dr. Lang and Dr. Temple, appointed a Commission to report on the present position of Canon Law in England and to prepare a revised body of canons. Though I had taken no part in the discussions on Canon Law and had no special knowledge of the subject, the archbishops invited me to become chairman. Archbishop Lang told me that it would be a long and trying ordeal, and that it was most unlikely that any agreement would be reached between the different schools of canonists ! I had, therefore, some considerable hesitation in accepting this invitation. When Bishop of Southwark I had had a brief experience of the complexity and interest of canon law. A small group of clergy were hesitating to obey some regulations I had issued on the ground that they were contrary to Canon Law. When I asked them for the Canon Law to which they made their appeal, they showed considerable perplexity, and I failed to obtain a concise reply. So, with the help of my then Chancellor, Mr.—afterwards Judge—Talbot, I found the canons to which the clergy had referred, and in addition a large number of other canons with equal if not greater authority, giving the bishop the right to regulate, and even to forbid, various ceremonies, processions, and prayers. When I next saw the spokesman of the little group, who were all ready to give loyal obedience to reasonable directions, I told him if they appealed to medieval Canon Law on one point, I should also have to enforce it on other matters. When I read to him some of the restrictive canons his comment was, "but these are intolerable," and the appeal to medieval Canon Law was dropped by mutual consent! This experience made me anxious to learn more about Canon Law, and as the commission had many experts whose knowledge more than balanced my ignorance, I accepted the chairmanship. I never regretted it. The meetings throughout were most interesting. Every member made some valuable contribution to the Report out of special knowledge. And, with the exception of a few secondary matters, a common mind was reached, and though the meetings had been postponed for a time by war conditions, the Report was finished and signed in May, 1946.

The Report was well received both by the clergy and the laity and by the secular and religious press. Some of the more advanced Anglo-Catholics regretted omissions; the Modernists feared new canons might restrict their liberty; while some of the Evangelicals felt that its recommendations were in the Romeward direction. But the great majority of Churchmen of all parties accepted the need for canon law reform, and while reserving full right to criticise in detail, were prepared to accept the draft canons as a basis of revision. There were of course a few diehards, and one of these advertised that the book containing the new canons would be destroyed outside his church, for "if these canons are not destroyed they will destroy the pure gospel in our Churches and in the nation." The book was duly burnt, in faithful imitation of the burning of Bibles by the pre-Reformation Church! But this was an individual outburst of silly fanaticism, and was not typical of the sympathetic care with which the representatives of the Evangelical as well as of other parties have discussed the draft canons in Convocation and elsewhere. There was no time during the meetings of the Commission when party issues were raised, the one aim of its members was to produce a code of canons which might be of help to the whole of our Church. All of us realised that the canons we proposed would be amended and often improved by the joint wisdom of the Convocations and of the laity whose advice and criticism would be invited.

In the Report there were two major recommendations. (1) The Commission was asked to report on the present status of canons in force before the Reformation, and the method which should be followed to determine which of these canons are now obsolete. Its reply was given both in the text of the Report and in draft Canon VIII, which states: "The Canon Law of the Church of England consists not only of this Code, meaning thereby these present canons as added to or varied from time to time, but also of the General Canon Law, meaning thereby such provisions of the Canon Law in force in England at the passing of the Act 25 Henry VIII c. 19 as are not expressly or by implication superseded by this Code, and by virtue of that Act still in force." It thus recognised that some of the ancient Canon Law not embodied in the proposed code would still be in force. It seemed rash and presumptuous to propose that it should be abrogated *in toto* by the new code. This would have followed the precedent set by the Church of Rome which abrogated in 1917 its old Canon Law in favour of its new Codex. But, to quote from the Report, "We do not think we have succeeded in achieving such substantial comprehensiveness of treatment as would justify us in recommending an abrogation of the ancient Canon Law *in toto*. That possibly might come later after our present code has been criticised and tested. It would indeed be presumptuous to suggest, before our work had been put on trial, that we have done it so well that the Church could safely and properly jettison the whole of its ancient law."[1] But the proposed canon goes on to state that the General Canon Law is superseded by the new code when they are in contradiction; and when any dispute or question arises as to the content or effect of the General Canon Law not superseded by the new code it shall be conclusively determined by the Archbishops of Canterbury and York "after taking expert advice." The Report thus recognises that some of the pre-Reformation law not included in the new code is still operative, but when there is doubt as to whether it is operative or not, or as to the extent of its operativeness, the issue is to be decided by the two archbishops. (2) The second major recommendation is found in the presentation of a draft code of canons, a hundred and thirty-four in number. No attempt was made to prepare a complete and comprehensive codification of the various kinds of law concerning the life of

[1] P. 84.

the Church, covering every department and detail of its activities. For various reasons it would have been both impractical and undesirable to have taken as our model the recently-revised Codex of the Church of Rome. It took thirteen years for the Papal Commission to prepare it, though much of it was already written law. But even if there had been time for this work and a sufficiently large secretariat for the necessary research, it would have been very unwise to have attempted to impose such a comprehensive code upon our Church. It would have been contrary to the spirit of English law which has always disliked and avoided the codification common on the Continent. If such a full code had been prepared, those who advocated its acceptance would have been accused of attempting to lay on men's shoulders "heavy burdens grievous to bear." "It has been a tradition of the Church of England since the Reformation that the law bearing on its life should be kept to a minimum. Code law keeps on multiplying so as to cover every conceivable exigency. In our opinion the majority of Church people would prefer their law in a form which allows many things to be settled by common sense, and the judges to expound and interpret the law when necessary."[1]

The 1603 Canons were, therefore, taken as the basis of the revision. Many of them were omitted as concerned with conditions which have long passed away. Many were re-written and re-arranged with the purpose of making them more intelligible. New canons have been drafted to regularise existing and accepted customs, and others to embody recent legislation, resolutions, and decisions of the Convocations and of the Church Assembly. In addition, there are new canons to give direction on problems which have arisen since 1603: among these are some making clear the authority of the minister of the church over the music and organ, the ringing of church bells, and laying down necessary restrictions on the performance of plays, the showing of films, and the giving of concerts in church.

The proposed code falls into eight sections: the nature, the doctrine, the worship, and the government of the Church of England; divine service and administration of the Sacraments; ministers, their ordination, function and charge; deaconesses; the lay officers of the Church; the furnishing and care of churches; ecclesiastical courts; the synods, assemblies and conferences of the Church of England. The draft canons thus

[1] Ibid., p. 82.

deal with a great variety of subjects : some of them of the first importance, such as lawful authority, the teaching of the Church on marriage, and the constitution of its ecclesiastical courts ; but others are concerned with small matters of detail such as the material of the Holy Table and the washing of fair linen. The great majority of them are entirely uncontroversial ; they re-state in modern language what has been for many years the law and custom of the Church. Of the few which are controversial, some could be postponed without serious injury to the code as a whole. If the code is substantially accepted by the Church it will give in broad outline an account of the external structure of the Church of England—its nature, its worship, its ordained ministers, its lay officers, the furniture of its churches, and the composition of its courts and assemblies. It forms the bones of a skeleton, the flesh and blood of which will be found elsewhere in the application and working out of the canons in the life of the diocese and the parish. If a stranger wants to know something of the general lay-out of the Church of England he will find an authoritative statement in these canons, and an ordinand will find in them the more important of the laws which he must obey after his ordination. The purpose and limitations of the proposed code are stated clearly in the Report on the Canon Law : " In drafting the new code we have tried to keep within the limitations set by the fact that canons are law, and to avoid the inclusion in them of anything which is not properly a law. In some cases we have had to take refuge in recommendations ; but as far as possible the canons are either commands, or prohibitions, or declarations of facts about the law of the Church of England. That, too, is why the canons contain no challenges, point to no grand ideals. Law, like good liturgy, should be restrained, impersonal, and contain as little as possible of the dreams and ideals peculiar to any one age."[1]

The Making of Canons

A long journey will have to be made before these or any other canons receive the Royal Assent. Canon by canon they must be discussed and approved by the four Houses of Convocation. When there are differences between the Southern

[1] Ibid., p. 88.

and Northern Convocations over the composition of a canon, they will have to be smoothed out by consultation, and possibly by joint conference in a National Synod. The canons will then be sent to the House of Laity for their opinion, and when they are returned this will mean further discussion and revision in the Convocations. Some of the canons will require a Measure in the Church Assembly; many of them (at least thirty), will require an Act of Parliament, as they affect previous legislation. Then at some point the Royal Licence will be required before the canons are cast into their final form, and eventually the Royal Assent must be obtained before they can be promulgated. The opportunities of obstruction by the pedant and the die-hard are almost unlimited. There is no chance of the canons being accepted within reasonable time unless the Church, both clergy and laity, is united in the determination to substitute for an obsolete code a system of ecclesiastical law which is coherent, intelligible and practical. It is the duty of the Church to make canons which are most appropriate for its work. There will, however, be times when it will be tempting to compromise and to be content with the second-rate rather than the best in the hope of avoiding a possible conflict with Parliament. The Convocations should not allow themselves to be influenced by the fear of the attitude Parliament might adopt when the canons are ready for submission. Such timidity would be unworthy of a spiritual society, and would meet with contempt from those it was intended to propitiate. The Convocations must decide on what they feel is best for the spiritual life of the Church, for its discipline and good order, without fear as to the possible action of Parliament. It will be time later on to consider any criticisms and suggestions which may come from the State. If reasonable, they will be welcomed and accepted by the Church. But the first duty of the Church is to frame canons which will be most helpful to its spiritual life. If Parliament should reject all or some of the canons, or even if the Royal Assent should be withheld on the advice of the ministers of the Crown, the draft canons would remain as an impressive record of what the Church regards as necessary for its good government, and they would have strong moral and spiritual authority over all its loyal members.

Dispensations

Canons and dispensations have been so closely connected that the acceptance of a new system of Canon Law may lead to the demand that some power of dispensing from its strict application in all cases should be provided. But since the Reformation the practice of granting dispensations has been looked upon with disfavour in the Church of England, and as the field covered by Canon Law has been greatly restricted, there is no longer the same necessity as in the Middle Ages for numerous dispensations from it. It is more in harmony with the spirit of our Church to have as few rules as possible, but to require that they should be observed faithfully by those they concern. There are occasions, however, when dispensation from the strict observance of an ecclesiastical law is most desirable—for instance, there will always be occasions when some departure from the strict following of the Book of Common Prayer is required. At present the incumbent usually gives himself the dispensation, without applying to any higher authority. Even when the Prayer Book services are revised, permission for deviation from it will sometimes be required. There are many other directions in which some relaxation from ecclesiastical law is occasionally required. The diocesan bishop should be the dispensing authority, but he should act not as an individual, but in accordance with agreements reached by the Upper Houses of Convocation in the two Provinces, after consultation with the clergy. The Commission on "Dispensation" appointed by Archbishop Lang states in its Report: "The Commission is convinced that no healthy extension of the practice of dispensation is to be looked for unless the Anglican Provinces will adopt the procedure which some of them have already adopted, namely, that in all matters where the right or advisability of giving dispensations is likely to be called in question, the bishops agree to follow in their own dispensations any rules or decisions which the Synod may adopt. In other words the Anglican Churches can only enjoy the benefits of the practice of dispensations if they recognise that the highest authority in the matter of dispensation is the bishops in their synods."[1] This does not mean that the Convocations would have to discuss individual cases; nor would it take

[1] P. 83.

away from the diocesan bishop existing rights of dispensation; but the bishops in Convocation would decide from which ecclesiastical law or custom they might legitimately grant dispensation in their own dioceses.

A Canon-making Church

When our Church once possesses an authoritative code of canons drawn up in relation to modern conditions, it can add to them from time to time as circumstances demand. Canons should not only be made on rare and special occasions, or to give ecclesiastical approval to laws already passed by Parliament, as in the case of changed hours for the solemnisation of marriage. They should be the normal and natural way in which the Church determines its own life and discipline. A code of canons should never be treated as closed and final; with changing conditions it should be revised and augmented. The Church of England can in this, as in many other ways, learn much from the practice of other Churches of the Anglican Communion which frequently legislate for themselves by the making of new canons. With the exception of Australia and India[1] the Canon Law in the overseas Churches "is the *corpus* of law enacted by their Synods since the middle of the nineteenth century."[2] We must hope that the State will assist the Church in this attempt at self-reform, and that the Royal Licence and Assent will be given to the Canons which are now being prepared.

[1] Both these churches make their own canons; but in the Church of Australia they must not contravene English Ecclesiastical Law; and in the Church of India, Burma and Ceylon the law of the Church of England is still operative, except when expressly abrogated or when contrary to the constitution, canons and rules of the Church of India, Burma and Ceylon.

[2] "The Mission of the Anglican Communion": G. Addleshaw on "Law and Constitution of the Church Overseas," p. 94.

XII

THE REFORM OF THE CHURCH COURTS

FOR the restoration of order in the Church of England it is essential that there should be both an authoritative statement of its law, and courts competent to enforce it. The revision of the Prayer Book and of the canons will go far to make plain the law of the Church, but this must be supplemented by courts in which the clergy and laity have complete trust. At present widespread dissatisfaction with the final court of appeal has undermined confidence in the whole system of Church courts; in the words of the Report of the Royal Commission of 1906: "The result has been unfortunate in many ways. Bishops and others have been naturally slow to appeal to a court the jurisdiction of which was so widely challenged; clergymen have claimed the liberty, and even asserted the duty, of disobedience to the decisions of a tribunal the authority of which they repudiate; and judgements of the judicial committee, though at least the reasoned statements of very eminent judges, are treated as valueless because they are Privy Council judgements. A court dealing with matters of conscience and religion must, above all others, rest on moral authority if its judgements are to be effective. As thousands of clergy, with strong lay support, refuse to recognise the jurisdiction of the Judical Committee, its judgements cannot practically be enforced." The good sense of the majority of the clergy and the spiritual authority of the bishops have prevented disorder developing into anarchy, but it is profoundly unsatisfactory that the system of Church courts should be generally regarded as ineffective and largely inoperative. A brief survey of the history of ecclesiastical courts in this country will show how this has come to pass.

The Medieval Courts

With the Conquest all ecclesiastical matters, with the exception of questions about advowsons, were withdrawn from the lay courts. There gradually sprang up a network of ecclesiastical courts. In the lowest range there were the courts of the archdeacon who, at one time, became a dangerous rival to the jurisdiction of the diocesan bishop. These were presided over by the archdeacon who was usually in deacon's orders, so that the priesthood should not be sullied by dealing with temporal matters. Above the archidiaconal courts were those of the diocesan bishop, the present consistory courts; over these, about the middle of the twelfth century, the bishop appointed officials to preside. The bishop retained his visitatorial rights, and on visitation heard complaints, redressed wrongs, and passed sentence on the guilty. Above the bishops' courts there were the provincial courts, the courts of the two archbishops. In addition there were the courts of the deans and chapters, with their jurisdiction over definite areas.

Ecclesiastical jurisdiction covered a very wide field. It was exercised over the laity as well as over the clergy; it was not confined to worship and Church property, but extended to morals and behaviour. Marriages, wills, legitimacy, intestacy, oaths and promises were dealt with in the Church courts. "The ecclesiastical jurisdiction claimed over the laity, *pro salute animæ*, was of the widest description and was exercised through a machinery of the most extensive character."[1] The bishop was assisted by an host of officials, from the archdeacon, "the bishop's eye," and the possibility of whose salvation the clergy debated with negative results, to the rural dean; and as a counsel of perfection the Statutes of Durham decreed in 1220 that there should be two or three inquisitors in each deanery to report misbehaviour to the bishop.[2] The penalties inflicted were various, and included public penance in a white shirt, holding a candle; pilgrimage to near or distant images and shrines; beatings; heavy fines sometimes in the form of an offering to a shrine; and behind these penalties there was always the dread threat of excommunication. Rich as well as poor came under the judgment of the Church—the Archbishop of Canterbury "ordered a wealthy layman, Sir Osbert Giffard, to be flogged three times round the church of the nunnery at Wilton, three times round the market place at Salisbury, and three times round Shaftesbury Church."[3]

A remarkable illustration of the working of the lower

[1] "Royal Commission on Ecclesiastical Courts," 1883, p. xxiii.
[2] J. R. Moorman, "Church Life in England in the Thirteenth Century," p. 209.
[3] Ibid., p. 207.

ecclesiastical courts is given by a medieval Act Book discovered in the York Diocesan Registry by the archivist, Dr. J. S. Purvis. This volume contains a record of charges over a period of eighty-nine years (1396–1485) against both clergy and laity within the Peculiar Jurisdiction of the Dean and Chapter of York. "The total number of charges entered is apparently 3,640; of these no less than 3,236 are for fornication, adultery, or similar moral offences." Against the clergy there were 1,381, and against the laity 1,855 charges of sexual offences. There were also charges of other offences, against the clergy for neglect of ministerial duties (the vicars choral "are so busied in fables and chattering" that the choir is scarcely heard), usury, assault and drunkenness; against the laity for slander and brawling. Half the charges were either unanswered or untried, while in many cases the accused cleared themselves by compurgation. Compurgation consisted in the sworn testimony as to the character of the accused by a specified number of his neighbours and acquaintances. Frequently, however, the defendant was of such unsatisfactory character that he failed to get the requisite number of compurgators. The punishments would seem to us both strange and humiliating: a vicar choral, besides suspension for a fortnight, is sentenced that "on the morrow between six o'clock and nine at dawn he should visit as a pilgrim the image of St. William in his chapel at Ouse Bridge, going barelegged and bare-footed, in his long tunic ungirt, and also on the next Tuesday the image of Our Lady in the church of the Hospital of St. Leonard in the same form, saying before each, kneeling five times the Lord's Prayer and the Angelic Salutation"; Richard Gylymer for assault in the churchyard of Wyghton is enjoined to "stand for three Sundays at the time of celebration of the greater Mass barefoot, clad only in his tunic, carrying in his hand a candle of the weight of half a pound of wax burning and that on the last day of his penance offer the same candle at the high altar."[1]

It is only through the study of the actual working of a court that it is possible for us to grasp the extent and intricacy of ecclesiastical discipline in the Middle Ages. The Church was a great school of morals, not limited to exhortation and warnings, but with the power to enforce its commands in almost every department of life. In one of its aspects it appeared as the stern schoolmaster reprimanding and punishing its children who

[1] For all the above see J. S. Purvis, "A Mediæval Act Book."

wandered from the ways of truth and virtue. This is indeed only one side of the work of the Church, but to the sinner it was always present. The bishop, the normal judicial authority in his own diocese, was to his clergy and laity the disciplinarian rather than the father-in-God. "The prevailing aspect of the bishop's paternity was its severity, and in the attitude of the pastor to his flock the spirit of correction was more prominent than that of compassion. In the language of the episcopal chancery the charge which he bore was the duty of moral reformation among the people and clergy subject to his jurisdiction, of planting virtues and plucking and rooting out vices with the hoe of his ordinary power of correction."[1] It was this spirit which pervaded the ecclesiastical courts during the greater part of the later Middle Ages.

The nature and jurisdiction of the courts led to their increasing unpopularity. They were disliked by the laity for their interference with their personal conduct. They were disliked by the judges and those responsible for good order, for the clergy and the laity were treated with a leniency which they would not receive in a secular court, and many a criminal by pleading the privilege of his orders was able to escape punishment. They were disliked by the king, because there was an appeal from them to the Pope. These appeals were costly, lengthy, and were made independently of the decisions of the Royal courts; often they were inconclusive, "not only might a matter of dispute be treated over and over again, delegacy succeeding delegacy, and appeal being interposed on every detail of proceeding one after another, but even after a definitive decision a question might be re-opened and the most solemn decision be reversed on fresh examination."[2] And clergy and laity alike resented the network of spies and informers connected with the working of the courts. Frequent attempts were made to restrain their jurisdiction and the appeals from them to Rome. They were never allowed to deal with disputes over advowsons, and on numerous occasions injunctions were issued withdrawing matters from their cognisance. A series of Statutes was passed against appeals to Rome, though their efficacy was destroyed by collusion between the king and the Pope.

[1] A. Hamilton Thompson, "The English Clergy and Their Organisation in the Later Middle Ages," p. 40.

[2] Stubbs, "An Account of the Courts which have exercised Ecclesiastical Jurisdiction in England up to the Year 1832": Historical Appendix to Royal Commission of 1883, p. 30.

The Courts after the Reformation

Early in the English Reformation an attack was made upon the courts in the Petition of the Commons presented to the king in 1532. This really was prompted by the king, for among the State papers there have been found four drafts of it, the corrections being usually in the handwriting of Thomas Cromwell.[1] The protest contains a general attack upon the clergy for appointing infants to benefices, and for the observation of an excessive number of holy days which took people from work; but the main accusations are against the courts for inflicting penalties upon the laity, for their delays, for trivial charges brought in them against the poor, for excessive fees, and for the imprisonment of innocent people. But unpopular as the courts were, Henry VIII's legislation did comparatively little to change their character. All through the Reformation reigns they continued their work without apparent interruption. They heard cases, issued faculties, and gave directions in the same form as in the past. A study of the registers and records of the ecclesiastical courts from Henry VIII to James I would give no indication of the extent of the religious and social changes then taking place, though for a short time during the reign of Edward VI the Royal Arms appeared on the seals of the courts.

Three changes of permanent importance were made by Henry VIII. First, appeals to the Pope were finally and absolutely forbidden. Since then, with the possible exception of the reign of Mary, no appeals have been made which had any legal sanction. From the courts of the Roman Catholic bishops in this country appeals still are made to Rome on marriage and other disputes, but the Papal decision carries no legal authority in Great Britain, and has no effect on what has been decided or may be decided by the courts of the land. Decrees of nullity granted by Rome bind only the members of that Church, and are void of all legality. Secondly, it was provided that in the future there should be an appeal from the ecclesiastical courts to the king in Chancery; these appeals should be heard by such persons as should be named by the king, and their decision should be final. This was an important alteration from the Statute of Appeals passed earlier in the reign, by which the

[1] Gee and Hardy, "Documents," p. 145.

archbishop's court was the final court of appeal, except when it concerned the king, and then the case was to be heard in the Upper House of Convocation. From this new Statute there came the Court of Delegates which until 1832 was the final court of appeal on ecclesiastical matters. Thirdly, a Statute was passed that married doctors of civil law might exercise ecclesiastical jurisdiction; previously all who had had such jurisdiction had been in some kind of orders—Canon Law had insisted upon this. These were the three changes of permanent importance. Statutes and Proclamations make plain the Royal Supremacy as the source of judicial authority; the king assumes that he may exercise this authority himself, and that his claim is in accordance with the ancient customs of the realm.

When Elizabeth ascended the throne two great groups of ancient Church courts were in existence—the diocesan which received authority from the bishop, and the provincial which had the authority of the archbishop. Appeals were made from the diocesan to the provincial court; appeals to the Pope were again abolished, and the Court of Delegates became the Crown court of final appeal. In addition there was created the Court of High Commission which presently brought upon both the Church and Crown great odium. Henry VIII had acted through temporary commissions, and this precedent was at first followed by Elizabeth, but before the itinerant commissioners had finished their work the permanent High Commission had been set up. Its judges, both clerical and lay, were appointed by the Crown; its powers were extensive and were for "the visitation of the ecclesiastical state and persons, and for reformation, order, and correction of the same, and of all manner of errors, heresies, schisms, abuses, offences, contempts and enormities." At one time it did good and useful work[1], but under Archbishop Laud it became very unpopular. The court inquired into charges of heresy and schism; of criticism against or attacks upon the Prayer Book and any ministers or officers of the Church; and it could deal with sexual offences and misdemeanours committed by any clergyman. From its decisions there was no appeal.

[1] "Its jurisdiction, more equitable at many points than that of the Common Law Courts, was in demand among suitors, and it remained a popular Court except in regard to its penal jurisdiction": D. Lindsay Keir, "The Constitutional History of Modern Britain," p. 168.

Only five per cent. of the cases it heard were due to its own action; the rest were the result of complaints by informers and private persons, often with a grudge against some individual. "The majority of cases that came before it were, in numerical order, suits for alimony and divorce, then adultery and other moral offences, and thirdly simony, drunkenness, and other sins of the clergy."[1] Its proceedings were secret, and it made its own rules of procedure. Most offensive of all was the "ex-officio oath" by which the accused was compelled to bear witness against himself. The court was abolished in 1641, and was only revived for a short period by James II who proposed to use it as an instrument for the destruction of the Church. "By it he was enabled to make effective his powers as Head of the English Church, a position which as a Catholic he ought to have repudiated as an encroachment on the rights of the Pope. These powers . . . he determined to use for the subversion of the English Church and for the advantage of the Church of Rome."[2] It was an Erastian court, the creation of the Crown, and it is much to be regretted that archbishops and bishops took an active part in its proceedings.

The Court of Delegates had a longer and somewhat more reputable history. It was the final court of appeal to the Crown from the diocesan and provincial courts. Its powers were full, and it dealt with all manner of appeals. But evidence before the Commission of 1884 shows that only seven appeals which came before it were even remotely connected with questions of doctrine; the delegates consisted of bishops, judges, and civilians, though from 1751 to 1838, when the last case was heard by it, no bishops were included among the delegates. The court was criticised mainly on three grounds: (1) Insufficient care was taken over the choice of the delegates; they were selected casually without any special reference to their qualifications. It was, so far as the civilian element went, frequently composed of junior and inexperienced doctors; in fact judges preferred to appear before it as advocates than to sit on it as judges. (2) Its proceedings were undignified, especially the custom of payment of a guinea a day to each judge by the successful party at the end of the case. (3) The judgement was announced without giving the reason on which it was passed, though this was not altogether a disadvantage, for as Bishop Stubbs com-

[1] G. Davies, "The Early Stuarts, 1603–1660," p. 77.
[2] F. C. Turner, "James II," p. 317.

mented, " The silence of the delegates as to the grounds of their decisions had at all events the effect of saving the country from the infliction of an authoritative exposition of law from the mouth of inexperienced judges." The popular criticism of the Court was that it was both expensive and slow. Dickens mocks at it in " David Copperfield " as a " rotten old ecclesiastical cheese." " You brought a divorce case, or a restitution case into the Consistory. Very good. You tried it in the Consistory. You made a quiet little round game of it, among a family group, and you played it out at leisure. Suppose you were not satisfied with the Consistory, what did you do then? Why, you went into the Arches. What was the Arches? The same court, in the same room, with the same bar, and the same practitioners, but another judge; for there the Consistory judge could plead any court day as an advocate. Well, you played your round game out again. Still you were not satisfied. Very good. What did you do then? Why, you went to the Delegates. Who were the Delegates? Why, the Ecclesiastical Delegates were the advocates without any business, who had looked on at the round game when it was playing in both courts, and had seen the cards shuffled, and cut, and played, and had talked to all the players about it, and now came fresh, as judges, to settle the matter to the satisfaction of everybody." While the Commission of 1832 found that no charge of injustice or excess of power could be proved against the Court of Delegates, it recommended that it should be abolished and that the Privy Council should be substituted as the final court of appeal for ecclesiastical cases. It was thought that more experienced judges would thus be available. After a short period the judicial committee of the Privy Council was created the final court of appeal.

The Work of Church Courts To-day

The main structure of the ecclesiastical courts continues the same—the diocesan courts, the consistory presided over by the bishop or his chancellor; the provincial courts of the archbishops, the Court of the Arches in Canterbury and the Court of Chancery in York; and above them the final court of appeal, the judicial committee of the Privy Council.

During the nineteenth century the jurisdiction of the church courts was greatly reduced. Testamentary and matrimonial causes were removed to other tribunals. Suits for defamation, and charges against laymen for brawling, no longer came before them, and their business was further reduced by the abolition of Church rates and Church tithes. The chief business of the church courts to-day is to deal with faculties and with proceedings against the clergy for either moral or ecclesiastical offences. According to the 1884 Commission " disputed applications for faculties have been more numerous, and the number of proceedings, both civil and criminal, in which questions of doctrine and ritual have been raised has, during the last thirty or thirty-five years, been out of all proportion to that in previous periods."[1] This would no longer be true of the last thirty years; for though applications for faculties and disputes over them are more frequent than ever, questions directly concerinng doctrine and ritual have not come before the courts for several years. Some attempt must now be given to account for this remarkable change.

(1) The law concerning faculties for alterations in churches and the introduction of new ornaments and furniture is with general good will observed more strictly than in the past. Our churches suffered greatly at one time through the uninstructed enthusiasm of incumbents, churchwardens and the congregation. In the desire to make the church either more beautiful or comfortable, irreparable damage was often done to the actual fabric; ancient chapels, and sometimes the chancel itself, were blocked by cumbrous organ cases; Jacobean pulpits were replaced by ostentatious marble rostrums; heavy over-ornamented reredoses were erected at the east end of the church; the old Norman font of stone standing solidly on the ground was removed to the churchyard or the vicarage garden, and in its place was substituted a modern font of stone, richly decorated and set on a pedestal with a flight of narrow steps dangerous both to the minister and to the infant he held; ancient pillars were hacked and mutilated to make room for iron stoves and pipes; medieval paintings on the walls were white-washed; brass ornaments of every kind were introduced and glittered incongruously in medieval or Georgian churches, while no church was regarded as completely furnished unless the entrance to the choir was guarded by a fantastic bird of aggressive brass. Occasionally the damage was more serious. Small churches built by our Anglo-Saxon or Norman ancestors were ruthlessly swept away

[1] P. 6.

by their later-day descendants, so that they might build a Victorian Gothic church according to the prevalent fashion. Far more harm of a permanent character was done to our churches in the first enthusiasm of the Oxford Movement than by the iconoclasm of the Reformers and Puritans; these stripped the church of its ornaments and defaced its images, but the Tractarians pulled down whole churches for the greater glory of God. The harm done by the introduction of a few controversial and unsuitable Roman images, candlesticks and ornaments, was nothing compared with the thoughtless damage due either to incumbents and churchwardens accepting unsuitable gifts and memorials, lest by refusal they should offend some wealthy donor, or by parishioners without artistic knowledge attempting to make the church they loved more beautiful or homely regardless of its history and structure. The damage done was so serious that at one time the suggestion was made that all ancient churches should be placed under State control. To avoid this Archbishop Davidson promised that the Church would deal with the problem. As a result of this pledge advisory committees have been set up in every diocese which give preliminary consideration to all proposals for memorials and ornaments or for alterations in parish churches, and advise the chancellor whether a faculty should be granted. The decision remains with the chancellor; he is not bound by the advice the committee gives him. These committees are carefully chosen: their members have architectural and artistic knowledge; they have saved our churches from many unsuitable ornaments and harmful changes, and have given expert advice about windows and church furniture, thus helping donors to make the best use of their money. As a rule these advisory committees have prepared the ground so successfully that the chancellor is able to grant the faculty without difficulty. But this insistence on greater care over the fabric and furnishing of our churches has necessarily led to a large increase in the number of applications for faculties.

(2) Some mention must be made here about the disciplinary work of the courts in connection with the morals of the clergy. Compared both with the Middle Ages and with the centuries immediately after the Reformation, there has been a most welcome and remarkable decrease in the number of cases which come before them dealing with the morals of the clergy. A study of the records of any medieval ecclesiastical court shows

how frequently it had to deal with charges of immorality against the clergy; these, however, included many who were in minor orders, and who claimed privilege to escape the greater sternness of the Royal Courts. The standard of priestly life and conduct is probably higher to-day than it has been in any previous century. In the Middle Ages the condemnation of a priest for fornication would have had no news value; to-day it is announced in the press with head-lines! There are still grave cases of moral delinquency which are dealt with by these courts; after the secular court has pronounced against a priest sentence of imprisonment with hard labour, or when he has been divorced for adultery, the bishop in his consistory court automatically, without further trial, deprives him of his benefice; or, in rare cases when there seems no hope of reform, he can unfrock him. But in cases of immorality which have not come before the secular courts, and the offence is sinful rather than criminal, the priest will usually show his penitence by accepting judgement from the bishop without any public trial, and thus save further scandal in his parish. In recent days the bishops usually hesitate to use their courts, and prefer either to withdraw their licence from the offender or to forbid him to exercise his ministry for a period of years. Though some minor forms of procedure are desirable, there is no serious objection to these courts. They work well and smoothly when they have to deal with moral offences. From them there is an appeal to the provincial court, and from that there can always be an appeal to the Crown.

During the last few years a new method has been authorised to deal with clergy who, either through age or infirmity, are unable to perform their duties, or who have shown themselves unfit for the work of the parishes of which they are incumbents. A committee is elected by the clergy of the diocese, and when the bishop has come to the conclusion that some action should be taken, he refers the matter to it; the incumbent concerned is allowed to state his case before it personally or through counsel; the recommendations of the committee are forwarded to the bishop, and he is able to declare the benefice vacant if this is the advice given to him, and he is of opinion that this is necessary. But proceedings taken in this way are quite distinct from those taken in the ecclesiastical courts; and no shadow of discredit rests upon the incumbent. Another and more complicated procedure, which seems unlikely to be much used, enables a bishop to remove from a parish an incumbent when he has been proved negligent or unsuitable.

(3) Most significant of all is the change from 1884 when the Commission stated that "the numbers of proceedings, both civil and criminal, in which questions of doctrine and ritual have been raised, during the last thirty or thirty-five years, has been out of all proportion to that in previous periods." During the last thirty years the number of cases brought before the ecclesiastical courts on questions of doctrine and ritual has been negligible. The chief reason for this was stated by the Royal Commission on Discipline in 1906, which found that one of the chief causes "of the failure to secure obedience has been the constitution of the Court of Final Appeal." Whether their attitude is justified or not, the great majority of the clergy and a considerable number of the laity, are united in unbending opposition to the recognition of the judicial committee as the final court of appeal on questions of ceremonial and doctrine. This is an undeniable fact. The opposition to the judicial committee has also weakened the authority of the admittedly spiritual courts, both diocesan and provincial. Their judgements are suspect because they are bound to follow those which have already been given by the judicial committee; and even if litigants are ready to accept the jurisdiction of the lower courts they know that there is an appeal from them to the judicial committee. Objection to the Court by Churchmen is due to the conscientious conviction that matters of worship and doctrine should be decided by the Church and not by a court set up by the State.

The Judicial Committee of the Privy Council

When the judicial committee became the legatee of the Court of Delegates there does not seem to have been any intention of making it a court of appeal on matters of worship and doctrine. The Court of Delegates was the substitution of the Crown for the Pope in appeals from the ecclesiastical courts, but it is doubtful if appeals were ever made from the English ecclesiastical courts to the Pope on questions of ceremonial and doctrine. The Court of Delegates as far as is known had only seven appeals remotely connected with doctrine, though this may be partly due to the fact that at one time it was overshadowed by the High Commission. It was thus a considerable and unexpected innovation when the judicial committee which succeeded it had to adjudicate on a number of questions concerning both doctrine and worship. The committee was never intended for this purpose; Lord Brougham, some thirty years after the judicial committee had been made responsible for the hearing of ecclesiastical appeals, stated in the Lords that it "had been framed without the expectation of questions like that, which produced the present measure, being brought before it. It was created for the consideration of a totally different class of cases." Dr. Stubbs, afterwards Bishop of Oxford, in a memorandum on the historical and legal position of the judicial committee as a court of final appeal presented to the Commission of 1883 expressed the opinion that "by no conscious act of the legislative, and by no conscious acquiescence of the Church, but rather by a series of overlookings and takings for granted, by the assumption of successive generations of lawyers and the laches and want of foresight on the part of the clergy, the present condition of things has been brought to pass."[1]

The first doctrinal case of importance which came before the committee was on the subject of baptismal regeneration when the Bishop of Exeter refused to institute the Reverend C. G. Gorham to a parish in his diocese. The case eventually reached the judicial committee. The greatest interest was taken in the judgement: on March 9, 1850, Greville enters in his diary: "Yesterday judgement was given to Gorham's case at the Council Office. The crowd was enormous, the crush and squeeze awful. I accommodated my friends with seats in the Court, and there were Wiseman and Bunsen sitting cheek by jowl." The judgement purported to declare the doctrine of the Church on baptismal regeneration.[2] Fourteen years later the subjects of "inspiration" and "eternal punishment" were dealt with by the committee. When the controversy over ceremonial was at its height, the committee had to give its judgement on matters so varied as the cross and candles on the Holy Table, on the eastward position, the mixed chalice, wafer-bread and incense. Some, but not all, of these judgements were adverse to these practices, and the clergy concerned refused to obey

[1] Report, Appendix I.

[2] "The Gorham case showed how the appellate jurisdiction of the Privy Council could be employed to encroach on ecclesiastical independence even in strictly ecclesiastical cases": D. Lindsay Keir, "Constitutional History," p. 433.

them; with the result that on action being taken by the Church Association some of them, devout and hard-working men, were imprisoned for contempt of court. Their imprisonment caused great scandal, and many of those who disliked their practices were moved with deep indignation at this form of persecution. Since then the bishops have used their right to veto prosecution of the clergy for alleged ceremonial offences, and have felt it wrong either to allow or to set in motion prosecutions which might eventually bring their clergy before a court which they refuse conscientiously to accept, and which might possibly result in their imprisonment.

In the Middle Ages it was the laity who were the most bitter critics and the clergy the strongest supporters of the ecclesiastical courts. To-day the opposite is true; most of the laity are ready to accept them, while the clergy strongly object to the state court whose decisions overrule those of the lower spiritual courts. The argument of the laity is simple and intelligible—the judicial committee is famed throughout the world for its wisdom and impartiality—it consists of judges both learned and experienced; it represents the Crown to which every subject has the right of appeal. Further they would say, the court does not make or lay down the doctrine of the Church; it declares it, deciding between opposing interpretations. Judges accustomed to consider cases impartially, without being moved by fear and prejudice, are more likely to give the right interpretation of Church documents—their rubrics, canons, and articles—than clergy and laity without judicial experience and influenced by the party controversies of their time. According to the Report on Ecclesiastical Courts, 1884, "the function of such lay judges as may be appointed by the Crown to determine appeals is not in any cause to determine what is the doctrine or ritual of the Church, but to decide whether the impugned opinions or practices are in conflict with the authoritative formularies of the Church in such a sense as to require correction or punishment."[1] The defender of the present system would argue that if there must be an appeal to the Crown, no more responsible and capable court could be devised than that of the judicial committee.

Those who object to the judicial committee as the final court of appeal in ecclesiastical questions would do so on the grounds both of principle and of actual practice. In principle they would say it is wrong for a secular court, however excellent it may

[1] P. liii.

be, to declare the law on doctrine or worship. The Church alone, under the guidance of the Holy Spirit, has the right to formulate its doctrine and worship. It has been the tradition of the Church from the Apostolic Ages that the bishops should act for the Church. After consulting the clergy and receiving the assent of the laity, the bishops—and they alone—have the right to declare the doctrine of the Church. The judicial committee is a secular and not a spiritual court; its origin is parliamentary and not spiritual. It was created by the State; it is responsible to the State, and its power depends upon the State. Its judges need be neither churchmen nor even believers. That such a court so constituted should be the final arbitrator on Church doctrine is contrary to the whole conception of the Church as a spiritual self-governing fellowship, inspired and guided into all truth by the Holy Spirit.

The objections to it are practical as well as on the grounds of principle. It is contended that the judges do not merely declare the doctrine of the Church, but by their decisions and by the reasons they give in pronouncing them they set the seal of authority on one of the views over which there is controversy. And in future cases the arguments used by the judges as well as their actual decisions may impose upon the Church some doctrine which its bishops and Convocations have never accepted. "The point which is now clearly seen and strongly felt is that the decisions of a law court are often not merely automatic and declaratory. A personal element enters into all interpretations and when a judge applies a law to cases not contemplated by the legislator, he does more than interpret the law, he carries the principles expressed in the relevant legislation to points which the legislator did not contemplate. . . . A judgement, therefore, is often more and sometimes is much more than a mere declaration, and in so far as it is more it is a legislative act. A series of such legislative acts made in the name of a religious society by an external authority may easily misrepresent its mind, and in the case of a society which has no remedy in speedy legislative action the results may easily by accumulation become serious."[1]

Whatever weight may be attached to these opposing arguments, the hard fact remains that there are a large number of clergy and a considerable body of laity who for over half a

[1] H. J. Bardsley. Article "Courts" in the Prayer Book Dictionary (Revised Edition).

century have been determined that on conscientious grounds they must refuse to accept as binding and must disobey, even at the risk of imprisonment, decisions reached by the judicial committee. The grounds for their opposition were stated clearly and authoritatively by Bishop Blomfield nearly a century ago, before ritual cases had been heard by the judicial committee, when in the House of Lords in 1850 he stated: "There can hardly be a more satisfactory tribunal of ultimate appeal, in all cases but those which involve a question of purely spiritual discipline than the judicial committee of the Privy Council as at present constituted. In all matters requiring judicial acuteness and calmness, impartiality and firmness, for the discovery of the truth of facts, and for the explanation and application of the law, nothing more is to be desired. It is only when questions of doctrine arise, and points of faith are to be determined, that I object to that tribunal as incompetent; it is competent to decide all questions of ecclesiastical law, but not matters purely spiritual, involving questions of divine truth; for this office it is not properly qualified with reference either to the Church's original constitution, or to the personal qualification of the judges." This is the position taken by large numbers of Church people to-day. They admire the wisdom and impartiality of the judicial committee; it is a great State tribunal surpassed by none other in the world; but on principle they feel bound to assert that only a spiritual court has the right to define and declare the doctrine and worship of the Church.

The impossibility of restoring order until some changes have been made in the final court of appeal has been widely recognised for many years. A series of proposals have been put forward in this century. The Commission on Ecclesiastical Courts in 1883 made a number of valuable recommendations, but nothing was done to carry them into action. The Report on Ecclesiastical Discipline of 1906 declared that "the machinery for discipline has broken down. The means of enforcing the law in the Ecclesiastical Courts, even in matters which touch the Church's faith and teaching are defective and in some cases unsuitable." The Report with one modification accepted the recommendations of the Committee of 1883; but again nothing was done to carry them out. In the Upper House of Canterbury in 1920 a resolution was carried unanimously "that the reform of Ecclesiastical Courts urgently demands attention, and trusts that the National Assembly will find an early opportunity of considering the question with a view to action being taken either under the Enabling Act or in other ways to amend existing procedure that discipline may be restored and maintained with the general good will of the Church." Archbishop Davidson supported the resolution and ended by saying that if the Assembly went forward with the preparation of a Bill, it would find that a great deal of the ground had already beeen won "and it was for us to occupy what was almost ready for occupation." The Church Assembly in 1923 appointed a Commission on Ecclesiastical Courts which reported in 1926; again a number of useful recommendations were made, but nothing was done! In 1935 the Commission on Church and State made some further recommendations, accepting in the main with some modifications the proposals of the earlier Commissions. Sixty-six years now have passed and nothing has been done! Recently the Commission on Canon Law has produced some new proposals, and at the moment of writing their fate is very uncertain. It stressed in the closing sentence of the Report the importance of the reform of the courts. "Authoritative Commissions have, after elaborate investigations, recommended the reform of the ecclesiastical courts not less than four times in the last sixty years—namely in 1883, 1906, 1926, and 1935—but no serious attempt to give effect to any of their recommendations has ever been made. If the policy of postponing the reform of the Ecclesiastical Law and the ecclesiastical courts is allowed to continue, it will result in grave hindrance to the work of the Church."[1]

It is unnecessary to give in detail the recommendations made by these commissions. It is sufficient to say that the 1926 commission recommended that the court "should be a permanent body of lay judges, appointed by the Crown, and that each member should sign a declaration that he is a member of the Church as by law established. That when an appeal before the Court concerns the doctrine, discipline, or use of the Church of England this should be referred to an assembly of the archbishops and bishops of both provinces, and that the opinion of the majority should be binding on the Court." The Commission on Church and State regarded this as rather cumbrous, and proposed that the final court should be appointed by the Crown from a list or panel of persons of high judicial experience, and others especially qualified, nominated by the Archbishops of Canterbury and York with the

[1] P. 98.

approval of the Convocations. In both these proposals the rights of the Crown as the final court of appeal in ecclesiastical matters are preserved, while at the same time the right of the Church to be the final authority for its doctrine is safeguarded. The proposal of the Canon Law Commission is different from the two earlier Commissions—" There shall be an appeal from a Provincial Court to a Final Court consisting of the Archbishop of the Province and four other members ; of whom two shall be members of the Upper House of Convocation of the Province, chosen in turn according to seniority in point of membership of that House from a panel of eight appointed by that House at the beginning of each Convocation ; and two shall be communicant members of the Church of England who hold, or have held, high judicial office, nominated from time to time by the Lord Chancellor." While the other suggested courts would be appointed by the Crown and be lay in their composition, this court, though not directly appointed by the Crown, would have on it a majority of bishops. But the bishops and the judges were originally appointed by the Crown, and another section of the draft canon makes it clear that any of His Majesty's subjects who feels aggrieved for lack of justice or abuse of process in any proceedings in an ecclesiastical court has the right to apply at any stage in these proceedings to His Majesty's High Court of Justice. These proposed courts could not be set up without an Act of Parliament, and they would require to have behind them the spiritual sanction and approval of the Convocations and of the Church Assembly.

It is not likely that any of these proposed courts would be accepted without considerable hesitation by the State. They would meet with criticism both from some of the judges and those who are disinclined to see the slightest modification in the Royal Prerogative. But the Church should make up its mind as to the composition of the court it regards as most suitable, and then enter into discussion with the State authorities. It is essential that the Church of England should possess the right to determine its doctrine and worship. This has long been the right of almost all the other Churches in the Anglican Communion. In asking for a new court of final appeal, the Church recognises fully the impartiality and ability of the present court, only harm is done by ill-considered denunciations of it ; the demand is based on principle, and on the impossibility of securing order under the present system.

An Interim Proposal

Notwithstanding the optimism of the Archbishop of Canterbury twenty-nine years ago there is little hope of an immediate solution of this problem, and meantime there will arise occasional disputes as to the validity of directions given by the bishop of a diocese on questions both of doctrine and worship. For reasons already given it is doubtful if the clergy concerned will accept the verdict of the courts, both consistorial and provincial, which are admittedly spiritual; for they will always be afraid that the judges of these courts may feel bound by previous decisions of the judicial committee. It is the practice that the lower courts should act on the decisions of the courts above them. Only the judicial committee can review and reverse its previous decisions. It is also very doubtful if the proposed pastoral tribunals suggested by the Church and State Committee will meet with general approval. So far no attempt has been made to set them up. While bishops are appointed as at present neither the complainant nor the defendant would feel complete confidence in them. The tribunal would be useless unless both parties beforehand bound themselves to accept its decisions. The Commission is right in saying that " questions of doctrine, ritual and ceremonial should be normally dealt with administratively "; but the difficulty has been that there will always be some who will refuse to accept any decision unless it gives them all they desire. Bishops have usually spoken in these matters " the language of the father-in-God rather than that of the judge, paying regard above all else to the circumstances of the particular case." But these methods often fail, for the incumbent suspects that the bishop is giving utterance to his own personal opinions, and is swayed by his own prejudices, rather than expressing impartially the doctrine and law of the Church.

There is, however, a procedure which, if generally adopted, would do something to remove these misgivings. When I became Bishop of Southwark I was at once confronted with a number of problems connected with public worship on which definite rulings were required. I felt convinced that the clergy would wish to obey the directions of their bishop, provided they saw they were not autocratic orders issued without consideration of the arguments of those opposed to them. I decided therefore to call a synod of all the clergy, to tell them what I had in mind, and to ask their views on certain highly controversial questions. I told them that if I was disobeyed I would not appeal to the courts, but I would bring the matter before the synod, and would ask the clergy if they approved or disapproved before I placed the priest concerned under discipline; on the other hand I should be equally willing to allow any aggrieved priest who felt I had been unfair to him to ask me to summon a synod so that he could put his case before it, and if the synodical council (to be elected by the full synod) felt this was right, I would hold a special synod for this purpose. Perhaps I may quote from one of my addresses to the synod: "Often it is insufficient for the bishop to rely on his own arguments; he must show that he is acting in accordance with the mind of the Church. He can do this sometimes by showing that he is in agreement with decisions reached by the bishops, or by the Convocations of the Province. Or if such decisions have not been given, he can ask for the counsel of his clergy in synod and discover if they interpret the law and custom of the Church in the same way as he has done. It will not be necessary for him in every case of dispute to call a meeting of the synod especially if it has already expressed its opinion on the issue. But he should be able to show that the regulation he has laid down or the ruling he has given is not the arbitrary command of an individual, but it is in accordance with the wishes and intention of the Church as interpreted and expressed by the bishops or Convocations or by his diocesan synod." If after I had admonished or censured in synod a disobedient priest, he still continued obdurate there was little I could have done beyond inhibiting him from preaching in any parish but his own, and refusing to license curates to him. But the collective conscience of the diocese would have condemned him; he would be defying not the bishop alone, but the bishop and the clergy. I believe the moral and spiritual support which a bishop would have behind him would be almost irresistible; if one individual remained obstinate and disobedient, there would be many more who would surrender their personal wishes and practices in deference to regulations issued by the bishop with the assent of his clergy. I never had to use fully this synodical method; but again and again in my early days in Southwark, when I was asking or directing some of the clergy to give up some practice they valued, it was the greatest help both to me—and I think to them—to be able to say, "the regulation

I am asking you to obey has been approved by the clergy in synod," or "if you feel I am unfair, you shall be given full opportunity of stating your case at the next synod." It is vital that there should be complete freedom of discussion at the synod, that special care should be taken to see that a minority is given every opportunity of expressing its views, and that the voting should be by ballot so that no suspicion should arise that the eye of the bishop or his archdeacons had influenced the timid. I am sure there is much to be said for this as a method of securing order in a diocese with the full co-operation of the clergy themselves. It creates a conscience on the side of order. There would be, of course, always the possibility that the synod might by a majority refuse to support the bishop; then if he is wise he will think twice or thrice before he continues on the course he had taken. Probably he will find that the clergy were right, and that either he was mistaken in his decision or had failed to make clear his reasons for it.

Trial of Bishops

It is felt strongly by many that it is inconsistent to provide for increased discipline of the clergy, and to make no provision for the trial of bishops. As long ago as 1883 the Report on the Courts contained the statement: "We are of opinion that it is desirable that any scheme of ecclesiastical courts and discipline should make provision for the trial of offences alleged to have been committed by bishops or archbishops." At present there is some doubt as to the court before which a bishop could be arraigned; for though Archbishop Benson tried Bishop King of Lincoln and the judicial committee declared he had jurisdiction to issue a citation, the bishop—supported by a large number of clergy and laity—protested against the court, arguing that a bishop could only be tried by the bishops of the Province assembled in Convocation. But whatever might be the result of such a trial, it would be extremely difficult for either archbishop or the bishops in Convocation to enforce their decision. When in 1695 the Bishop of St. David's was tried for simony before Archbishop Tenison, it was ten years before his deprivation was made effective, and then only because of a strict party vote in the Lords that his application to appeal was refused![1]

[1] A full account of the long and complicated proceedings before the bishop was finally deprived can be found in Phillimore's "Ecclesiastical Law," Vol. I, pp. 67–71, and in E. Carpenter's "Thomas Tenison," pp. 205–229.

There are, however, many who have felt that it is so unlikely that a bishop would commit a grave offence against Church order, that it is hardly necessary to set up a special court against such a remote possibility. But Popes have caused scandal by immorality, and bishops by false doctrine. The harm done to the whole Church by a bishop who retained his see after he had abandoned the faith he had promised to hold and teach, would be very great. The scandal would be the greater if a bishop, by some strange aberration of conscience, claimed his right to enjoy the dignity, privileges, and emoluments of his position while speaking and writing against the doctrines "which he had given his word to uphold: at his consecration he must have promised 'to banish and drive away all erroneous and strange doctrine contrary to God's word'." If the Church acquiesced in this it would demand a lower standard of honour from its chief ministers than that customary among professional and business men. To avoid such a danger it is necessary that a court should be set up competent to receive accusations against, and to censure, suspend or deprive, archbishops and bishops. Such a court would consist of bishops of the Province, with its archbishop as President; but no sentence of deprivation would have effect unless confirmed by His Majesty in Council.

Summary

There are a number of reforms in procedure which are required in the diocesan and provincial Courts, and have been recommended by successive committees; but it is generally admitted that the courts are working well, with occasional jolts in their machinery through lack of use. I have, therefore, deliberately in this chapter concentrated on the reform of greatest urgency, namely, the setting up of a final court of appeal to which ready obedience will be rendered by the clergy. Until such a court is created it will be very difficult to secure obedience to the laws of the Church.

XIII

THE REFORM OF THE PAROCHIAL SYSTEM

THE reform of the parochial system may seem to be more the concern of the Church than of the State. But Church and State have been for centuries so closely linked together in the parishes that any serious departure from their traditional organisation would be a matter of importance to the State. Under the pressure of modern conditions some such departure is unavoidable, and the good will of the State should be invited by a frank statement of the difficulties. Some of the proposed changes will require legislation; and the co-operation of the Crown as the patron of many benefices will be essential if the re-arrangement of parochial work is to be carried through smoothly and efficiently.

Historical

The division of England into numerous parishes each with its incumbent, church, and parsonage house is so familiar that it is not always realised that many centuries passed after the coming of St. Augustine before the parochial system was established as we now know it, and that subsequently it was modified in various ways.

At one time it was generally believed that Archbishop Theodore was responsible in the seventh century for dividing the country into ecclesiastical parishes. This theory has now been abandoned, for he was the organiser of dioceses rather than of parishes. The creation of the parochial system came later, and was a gradual process. England was first evangelised by itinerant missionaries coming from the south and the north. The bishop was the centre both of evangelistic and pastoral work, sending out priests from his church and home into the near and distant parts of the area for which he was spiritually responsible. As the number of converts grew, there had to be some decentralisation, and groups of priests settled by large churches they had built—" minsters " as they came to be called—and ministered to those who were far away from the cathedral church. But this again was only one stage in meeting the spiritual needs of the nation. Something was required nearer the homes and fields of the people, so the great landowners obtained priests who would minister to their households and their tenants. It was natural for them to do this as probably when pagan they had their own priests and controlled their temples. The lord of the manor appointed the priest, built a church, and set aside sufficient land for his livelihood. The estate became the parish, though sometimes the parish might include more than one estate, and the church and property attached to it belonged to the landowner. The produce of the glebe land, originally given to the church, was increased subsequently by the offerings and fees of the people, and by the payment of tithe. The founder of a church was inspired by motives of gain as well as of piety. " Through the old English period the founder of such a church regarded it as his property, which would yield an income to him and his heirs. The origin of lay patronage in England lies in the custom which allowed the founder of a church to appoint its priest."[1] The priest often had to make an agreement with his patron that he would pay to him a certain proportion, sometimes a considerable proportion, of the income of the church. The bishops attempted to check the authority the landowner exercised by requiring the parish priest to be instituted before he commenced his work, and so to come under episcopal control. But for long the benefice was treated as the private property of the patron, and as such all disputes concerning it came before the civil and not the ecclesiastical courts. Only gradually was the right of the patron over the church and its property narrowed down to presentation on a vacancy and to transferring to another the church and its revenues in perpetuity. It became customary for patrons to give all their rights to a neighbouring monastery, and thus they gratified their pious instincts without personal cost. The monastery appropriated the church and its property, and after making provision for a priest to take the duty in the parish, retained the rest of the income for its own purposes. This system of appropriation was naturally very popular with the monks; they encouraged it as it gave them additional

[1] Stenton, " Anglo-Saxon England," p. 149.

revenue and often saved them from financial ruin; but frequently it was only used to improve the food and table comforts of the monastery. The parishes for whom the revenue had been intended were the sufferers; originally tithe had been divided into three portions—for the priest, the poor, and the repair of the church. The churches were neglected and allowed to fall into ruin, and the monks regarded themselves as the poor. Langland, in "Piers Plowman," complains bitterly that the monks are regardless of the rain on the parish altars, and have "no pity on the poor or pretence of charity."[1] They wholly appropriated two-thirds of the tithes for themselves, and used only part of the remaining third to pay some unattached priest to take the duty in the church; for it was quite exceptional in England for the monks to do this themselves, as it would have interfered too seriously with the life in the cloisters. The evils of the system were apparent to some of the great diocesan bishops of the thirteenth century who attempted "first to assert the necessity of episcopal permission for appropriation; next to uphold the right of the bishop to full jurisdiction in spiritualities; and finally to insist that the vicar should have tenure for life and an income fully adequate for his maintenance."[2]

In 1215 a Lateran Council denounced the practice by which patrons of parish churches claimed the profits for themselves and left the priest they deputed to serve with a fraction sometimes as small as one-sixteenth of the tithe, and directed that where possible the rector was to live and officiate in his parish, but if he lived elsewhere he "should take care to have a *perpetual* vicar canonically instituted" who should have a fair share of the profits of the Church. This, writes Dr. Hartridge in his authoritative book on "Vicarages in the Middle Ages," "may be termed the Magna Carta of the parish priest."[3] Often ignored, often over-ridden, often misinterpreted, it stood firm throughout the Middle Ages, as the bedrock of the vicarage system. The *perpetual* vicar, to whom it refers—that is the vicar who was instituted by the bishop—could only be removed by judicial procedure and must be given a minimum payment. He had both a freehold and a secure stipend.

The rector—whether a corporation or an individual, a layman

[1] "Passus," X, line 328. (Edited by H. W. Wells.)

[2] Knowles, "The Monastic Order in England," p. 600.

[3] P. 21.

or in orders—received the greater tithes and the larger part of the revenues of the church; the vicar received the smaller amount, on an average one-third of what the rector appropriated; but he was in a far more satisfactory position than the priest engaged by the year who had neither security of tenure nor of payment. The Council of Oxford in 1222 declared that the minimum stipend for a perpetual vicar should be five marks a year, with the exception of those parts of Wales where the poverty was very great. But out of them the vicar had to meet various charges; for though the appropriating body had to pay his fees to the bishop and archdeacon, he was left to provide for the chaplain, the parish clerk, and the boy, who made up the staff of a church. On this apportionment Dr. Hartridge remarks that the "monasteries displayed inordinate greed," and "it was grossly unfair for a monastery to take two-thirds of the tithes, and leave the vicar the other third plus most of the burdens."[1] After the Lateran Council the establishment of vicarages became general. They were the result of dissatisfaction with the system by which the rector, often non-resident, took the revenues of a parish and allowed the work to be performed by some miserably underpaid and ill-educated hedge priest. The vicar was not always paid a fixed sum, occasionally when the monastery was near the parish some of his stipend was paid in the form of clothing, food, or a meal in the precincts. The vicar of Bishopthorpe, the parish in which the Archbishop of York has had his home for seven centuries, was to be given each Sunday his dinner with the servants of the nuns of Clementhorpe, to whom the parish had been appropriated, and if he grumbled at his food he must wait until he was ready to receive it without complaint.[2] The bishops had a long struggle to see that the vicars were protected in their rights against the encroachments of the rectors, whether they were monasteries or individuals. The two keystones of their position were the right of freehold and a minimum income: the first prevented the rector or patron arbitrarily dismissing them from their parish, and the second—small though it was—gave some kind of security from penury: five marks were equivalent in the thirteenth century to £3 6s. 8d., but, according to Dr. Coulton, this should be multiplied by forty to discover its value in 1934.

The two great abuses throughout the Middle Ages were

[1] Ibid., p. 43.

[2] Moorman, "Church Life in England in the XIII Century," p. 46.

pluralities and absenteeism. Pluralities, by which a rector or vicar held more than one benefice, were due to greed or poverty. Greed was often the motive, for the pluralist increased the income from the benefice he originally held by adding to it as many other benefices as he could secure, and using only a small proportion of their incomes on the parishes to which they rightly belonged. There were scandalous cases in which courtiers became rich through the acquisition of benefices they never visited, and for which they did no work. But poverty as well as greed was a motive for pluralism, for many benefices were so poor that it was necessary for the incumbent to augment the income they brought him. Plurality inevitably led to absenteeism, for even a hardworking and conscientious rector could not be in more than one place at the same time, and when he was responsible for three or four parishes it was impossible for him to reside in all of them. Popes denounced these evils, but they granted dispensation easily for both, and by the system of provisions (the right to provide for the next vacancy) they encouraged both pluralities and absenteeism by appointing foreign priests to parishes in England which often they had no intention of visiting.

Besides the rectors and vicars there were a large number of assistant clergy with no security and poorly paid. These were the parish priests, chaplains, or curates. They assisted the incumbent when he was present, and when absent they took his place, celebrating and hearing confessions for him. "The term parish priest was used exclusively of this type of chaplain."[1] They were also attached to the chapels which had been built in more remote parts of scattered parishes.

In the Middle Ages the parishes were usually separated by dense forests and bogs; roads were few and very rough; tracks and pathways were frequent, but unsafe. Robbers and outlaws added to the danger of a journey. Most of the villagers remained all their lives in the parish in which they were born and knew little of their neighbours a few miles away. Local feuds between village and village increased the isolation—the echoes of these are heard to-day when a parish vigorously resists proposals for a union of benefices on the ground that the people of the other parish are "a bad lot." The parochialism which so often stands in the way of diocesan unity is a legacy from the Middle Ages.

[1] Hamilton Thompson, "The English Clergy," p. 122.

Until the industrial revolution England was a rural country. In the thirteenth century town parishes were few in number, some four to five hundred in all, against nine thousand country parishes.[1] But the average population of the rural parish was about three hundred; in the town it was only two hundred. The parish church was the natural centre for the worship and fellowship of poor and hard-working villagers, who had few interests except those of religion and labour. The church was their theatre, their cinema, their concert hall, their school, their art gallery, as well as their place of worship. Often close to it were the parsonage house and the village hall. We must not think of the parsonage house of the Middle Ages as the substantial building to which we are accustomed. We must picture it rather as a one-storeyed building of wood, with two rooms, and possibly a loft. It was not occupied by the incumbent alone; sometimes there lived with him three or four men in Orders, and the "priest's boy" who acted as a kind of page. The furniture was as simple as the house. In 1303 an inventory of the vicar of Bradford's property showed that he owned a brass pot, a water pot, some plates, a tripod and andiron, and in the brewery one leaden vat and a large tub with brewing apparatus. If there was any bedding or household furniture it probably belonged to the house and was not the property of the incumbent.[2] Round the house there were various farm buildings—a barn, to which the parishioners brought their tithe, sheds for cattle, and pigsties. The priest spent most of the week working, as the rest of his parishioners, on his fields and looking after his animals. The payments he received were insufficient to live upon, so it was necessary for him to work on week days with those who on Sunday formed his congregation. The endowments and revenues of the Church were not large enough to pay adequately the vast number of ordained men. It has been estimated that there were at least forty thousand secular clergy in the country in addition to nearly seventeen thousand monks and friars[3], and this for a population of about three million.

The Reformation did little to improve the lot of the parish priest, but it brought to an end further appropriations, and lay

[1] Moorman, "Church Life in England in the XIII Century," p. 5.

[2] Ibid., p. 60.

[3] Ibid., p. 52. Some authorities would reduce this estimate by 10,000! No one really knows!

patronage was largely increased by the transfer of monastic property to the Crown and great landowners. The marriage of the priest led rapidly to a change in the nature of the parsonage house. But the parish as a whole remained unchanged throughout the Reformation period; it remained an ecclesiastical unit: tithes were paid as in the past: the clergy for the greater part retained their benefices, for most of them did not feel that the changes in Church order were so serious as to call for their resignation. The twin evils of pluralities and absenteeism continued unchecked; in the seventeenth and eighteenth centuries there was still a gulf between the well-paid pluralist and the curate who did his work. Probably Shuffle, the humorous but disreputable curate in "Roderick Random," expressed what many really thought of pluralist incumbents: "There the old rascal goes, and the d——l go with him. You see how the world wags, gentlemen. By Gad, this rogue of a vicar does not deserve to live, and yet he has two livings worth £400 per annum, while poor I am fain to do all his drudgery, and ride twenty miles every Sunday to preach—for what? Why truly for £20 a year." It was not until 1838 that the holding of more than two benefices with a cure of souls was prohibited.

The Nineteenth Century Parish

Until the second half of the nineteenth century the parish boundaries and village life were not greatly changed. The clergy through the rise in the value of tithe had gained, the peasants through the enclosure of common fields had lost. The movement from country to town was still taking place, but until 1843 a new parish could only be created by Act of Parliament, so very few had been made except in some of the cities. By an Act of 1843, supplemented later by other Acts, new ecclesiastical parishes could be formed by Order in Council on the recommendation of the Ecclesiastical Commissioners. In town and country alike new parishes were created, and during the last half of the nineteenth century the rural parishes began to be affected by the coming changes. A Rip Van Winkle of the Middle Ages would have found himself at home in the seventeenth century parish, but he would have been lost in the same parish in the last years of the nineteenth century. In many parts of the country he would find great changes in cultivation. There would be large farms with their enclosed fields, instead of strips of land and common pasture open to all. Instead of the simple timbered parsonage house of the thirteenth century, he would often see a large mansion such as Mr. Crawford, in Jane Austen's "Mansfield Park," admired so greatly—" a solid, roomy, mansion-like looking house, such as one might suppose a respectable old country family had lived in from generation to generation, through two centuries at least, and were now spending from two to three thousand a year in" ; and it would be occupied not by a group of celibates, but by a married man probably the father of a large family. He would find the incumbent frequently a man of some means, no longer labouring on his glebe, but occupied with his ministerial duties, taking the Sunday services regularly, visiting his parishioners, especially the sick, and also on terms of equality with the squire. Usually he would be kind and charitable with a high standard of conduct, though occasionally there would be repeated Miss Crawford's[1] criticism made earlier in the century: " A clergyman has nothing to do but be slovenly and selfish; read the newspaper, watch the weather and quarrel with his wife. His curate does all the work, and the business of his own life is to dine." Pluralism and absenteeism would be rare, and grave clerical misconduct so exceptional that it would have " news value." Our awakened Rip Van Winkle would be surprised to find that besides the Church, Roman Catholics and various denominations had their chapels and held their worship without fear of either the law or the mob. He would, however, find that beneath these outward changes, and they were great, the spirit of the village remained very much as he had known it.

I can look back on the Victorian village as it appeared to a child some seventy years ago. My father was vicar of Tongham, a small village of some four hundred people about a mile and a half from Aldershot and three miles or so from Farnham. The parish itself was much larger than Tongham, for two miles away there was the equally large village of Badshot Lea, as well as several hamlets and farms. Only a few years before Tongham had been cut off from Seale, the mother church a mile away, but separated from it by the chalk ridge of the Hog's Back. The church was modern, but the village itself was old—the name is an indication of an Anglo-Saxon origin—and

[1] Also in Jane Austen's "Mansfield Park."

irreverent outsiders infuriated the villagers when they said it was only an abbreviation of tongue and ham. Though Aldershot was spreading, Tongham was still a village with an independent life of its own. Most of its inhabitants were employed on its three farms, and at the hop-picking season women and children all went out to help and to earn some additional shillings. Agriculture was still primitive and picturesque; there were no machines, the corn was reaped with the sickle, the last corner of the field preserved for the "old man," who made out of straw was hung in one of the farm-houses to bring good luck; in the field there could be seen the gleaners gathering what had not been bound in the sheaves; as soon as the corn was dry it was taken in great loads by horse-drawn carts to the farm, where the ricks were built up and carefully thatched over. Later in the season there was the threshing with a flail of the corn spread on the floor of a barn. Wages were miserably low, and though many of the cottages were attractive from without, within they were dark, damp, insanitary and overcrowded. Outbreaks of diphtheria and typhus were common. The village had its butcher, its grocer, its carpenter, its cobbler, its saddler, its blacksmith, as well as its post office, part of a small general shop and the centre of all the latest news. Three times a week the baker drove round with his bread. There were three public houses, the largest of which overlooked the small village green which once a year was the meeting place of huntsmen and hounds. Just off the main street were the school, the church, and the vicarage. The school was very small, its playground was of gravel, and was only separated from the churchyard by a low wooden fence. Within and without it would offend all modern standards of education, but at any rate the children learnt how to read, write and count, and the Scripture lesson was always given with great care. The parents had to pay some small sum for their children, not more than a penny or two weekly, and the annual deficit, usually rather large, was made up by local subscriptions. No doubt the limitations of the school were great, but I think of it as friendly and noisy, with a crowd of happy children. The church next door was a simple modern building with an apse. It was the parish church to all the people, for even the few Nonconformists who had a small chapel on the outskirts of the village, wished their children to be baptized at its font, to be married at its altar, and their dead to be buried in its churchyard. Most of the people, with the exception of the men in charge of the cattle, came to church once a Sunday, and on the Harvest Festival the whole village. The churchyard itself was kept as carefully as any garden. The vicarage was a minute or two further up the road, and was not too large for a family of five children. It was not only a perfect home to us, but it was also a real centre to the village. Here the people came with their troubles and worries, for advice, comfort, charity and relief. It is easy to-day to pour scorn on charity, but in those days the aged and the sick would have gone without many necessary comforts, the poor would have been worse clad, and sometimes near starvation if it had not been for the assistance provided by the church: it is true there was the Poor Law, but even as a child I sensed the horror with which the villager spoke of the "house," and of the hard terms on which out-of-door relief was granted. It was the Church also which organised the simple recreation which brought some relief from the monotony of the long winter nights. In the village everyone counted for something, for good or for evil; we all knew about one another. We had our black sheep; "he is a radical" had no political significance, but was the description of the rowdy and insubordinate. We had our poachers, some of the best among the labourers, and they were sentenced severely when caught. There were the thriftless, always in debt and begging. There was plenty of heavy drinking among the men, and as children we knew of this through the drunken men we occasionally saw on our walks; it was their quickest road of escape from a hard and tedious existence. The knowledge that the public houses were then associated with drunkenness made the clergy under-rate the warmth and friendliness which they provided for many who were hardly ever the worse for drink. One side of country life was concealed from us, the immorality and illegitimacy found in most villages. But these country folk were good, kindly, and hard working. Most of the adults were uneducated; some had never been to a large town or to the seaside. I have no wish that we should return to what many now call "the good old days." I only wish with all my heart that these kindly village friends of my childhood could have had the education, the good houses, the higher wages, the holidays and, above all the security against want in old age that their children and grandchildren now enjoy. And yet sometimes I ask myself—"Would they have been more happy"?

I have spoken here of Tongham, not because it was an

exceptional or ideal village, but because it was typical of thousands of self-sufficing country parishes, where the village life was strictly parochial, where there was a definitely communal spirit with its standard of right and wrong, and where the parish priest was still the "parson" of the parish, its representative on all public occasions, and usually the inspirer and organiser of its education, charity and recreation, as well as its religious leader. It is this experience of childhood which makes me regret most profoundly the necessity of any re-arrangement of ecclesiastical organisation which will make it impossible for every parish to have its own clergyman. But the days I have described have gone beyond recall, and no amount of nostalgia for the past and of wishful thinking for the future will ever restore them.

Changed Conditions of the Twentieth Century

There are three reasons which make necessary a reform of the parochial system.

First, there are not sufficient clergy to staff adequately all our parishes. In 1930 a Commission on the Staffing of Parishes reported that at that time there were 16,745 clergy engaged in parochial work in the two Provinces; if, however, the Church was to be staffed so that its clergy were sufficient in number to visit and care for the general body of parishioners, another 1,583 clergy were required as a minimum. Taking the very moderate average standard of one clergyman to 3,000 parishioners, another 333 ordinands would have been required to meet the growth of population in the ten years from 1930; in addition 438 would be required each year to meet the loss due to death, resignation or removal. The Commission reached the conclusion that by 1940 the Church should have an ordained ministry of 18,661, and that therefore during those ten years there should be ordained annually 630. Five years of war destroyed these hopes. It is estimated that there are now only 15,000 clergy at work, instead of the 18,600 regarded as the target for 1940, and this is a heavy drop compared with the 20,000 of 1914. In 1938 there were 4,554 assistant curates; in 1948 they had fallen to 2,189. The average number ordained in the two immediate pre-war years was 590; in the two years post-war it was 183.[1] It is true in the next few years there will be a considerable increase in ordinands, as the men leave the

[1] G. F. Townley, "The Supply and Distribution of Assistant Clergy," in "Theology," December, 1948.

theological colleges, but they will not do much more than replace the normal annual loss, and will do little, if anything, to make up the existing deficiency in numbers. It is doubtful, moreover, if the numbers of expected ordinands will be maintained when the Government grants to service candidates come to an end; few of the candidates will be able to pay for their own training, and the Church will find it very difficult to raise the large sums of money required. I therefore see no possibility of the Church obtaining in the next fifty years the 18,000 ordained men who twenty years ago appeared necessary for the adequate staffing of the parishes.

The results of under-staffing are very serious. In the large towns hundred of incumbents are working single-handed in parishes which used to have two or three assistant curates. Most of their time is engaged in conducting services, in visiting the sick and special cases. The over-worked vicar suffers both in body and mind, and becomes physically and mentally exhausted. Overstrain frequently leads to a complete breakdown in health. Anything like regular parochial visiting, the chief evangelistic and pastoral method of the Church of England, has to be abandoned. The incumbent, through lack of time to do otherwise, is compelled to concentrate all his attention on the regular members of his congregation who need his help. It is almost impossible to exaggerate the greatness of the loss when there is no regular pastoral visitation. The Church of England is becoming congregational instead of parochial. In Liverpool, Manchester, Southwark and London there is only one priest to over 5,000 people; in two cities of the diocese of York, Hull has one clergyman to 7,600 people, and Middlesbrough one to 6,331. Bishops under these circumstances are compelled to watch some of their best men grappling with a task beyond their capacity, and breaking down in health. Urgent appeals for help are made by incumbents and churchwardens, but the bishop can only reply that "there are no men available." In many country districts an incumbent finds himself in charge of two or three parishes, each expecting its own service on Sunday however small the congregation may be; with the help of a curate there would be no serious difficulty in working these parishes, and when they were originally united it was assumed that there always would be an assistant curate.

In yet another way the ill-effects of understaffing are felt. It is very difficult to make quick and suitable appointments to vacant parishes. Some parishes have to remain vacant for months or even for years before an appointment is made. When it is made, both bishop and patron only too often know that the appointment is far from ideal, but it was the best that could be made from a very limited field of choice. Young men with insufficient experience are taken prematurely from their curacies and given posts of responsibility for which they have not had sufficient training.

The poverty of the clergy will also compel a change from the traditional parish, each with its own incumbent. There is nothing new about the poverty of the clergy; it has been a recurrent problem. It was partly solved for a time through rise in the value of tithe or of glebe, or through the efforts of the Ecclesiastical Commission and the dioceses; but unforeseen difficulties have arisen—the cost of living has gone up, the sources of clerical income have dwindled, and the clergy find themselves with a house and buildings which can only be maintained by a larger income than that which they possess. We are passing through one of those periods when the clergy have a desperately hard struggle to make both ends meet, and when the funds of the Church are insufficient for the demands made upon them. If the Church had to-morrow the 18,000 clergy it requires, it is very doubtful if the money could be obtained to pay them adequately. Just at the time when the need for grants is greatest, the income of the Church is smaller than it was a few years ago. The Tithe Act reduced every £100 of clerical income from tithe by at least 20 per cent. The Coal Act may cost the Church £150,000 annually. The nationalisation of the railways will lose the Church over £100,000 a year. The redemption of Local Loans is affecting the income of over 4,000 benefices. The clergy, like everyone else, have to pay increased income tax, higher rates, and find that the purchasing power of the pound is far less than it used to be. The small margin of solvency which most of them possessed has been rapidly vanishing; holidays, books, and minor luxuries have had to be given up to avoid debt. But while the teacher in the school, the workers on the railways, in the mines and in the factories, have had their stipends and wages adjusted to meet the higher cost of living, there has been no such proportionate rise in the incomes of most of the clergy. Their difficulties are increased by the large houses in which most of them live. They cannot afford to pay for domestic or garden help, and frequently even if they could pay for it, they would not be able to obtain it. The vicar and his wife must do as best they can in the house, and this means that the vicar has to devote to domestic chores time which should be given to the parish; while the vicarage garden, once such an attractive feature of England, is left to go to rack and ruin, until it is hard even to discern the drive through the overhanging trees and the weeds growing over what once was gravel. Lack of food, fuel, and staff makes it no longer possible for the vicarage to be the centre of hospitality, for the vicar and his family are now often compelled to make the kitchen their drawing-room and dining-room, and most of the house is closed.

There is another factor which makes the re-organisation of the parishes necessary. Originally they were cut off from one another by forests and marsh; to-day they are not only connected by road and railway, but by bicycle and car it is possible to move quickly and easily from one village to another. In the middle of the last century the clergy either drove, walked or rode round their parishes. The wealthier clergy, like Archdeacon Grantly, had their carriage and horses; "he had kept a separate pair of horses for the exclusive use of his wife since the day of his marriage," and was not unnaturally annoyed when Mrs. Proudie on his first visit to the palace had mentioned five times within a few minutes "the bishop's horses"; on the other hand, Mr. Crawley of Hogglestock proposed to walk fifteen miles each way on the occasion of his famous visit to the palace at Barchester when he crushed Mrs. Proudie with the words, "Peace, woman," sustaining himself by the thought "that he would go before the bishop with dirty boots—with boots necessarily dirty—with rusty pantaloons, that he would be hot and mud-stained with his walk." All the incumbents either walked, drove, or rode in the 'seventies and 'eighties, and I can just remember the horse which had to be given up when my second brother was born, and then—though my father was well over sixty—he visited his parish on foot, except on Sundays in winter when he hired the local "fly" to drive him to the other village. None of the clergy at that time would have contemplated riding bicycles, even if they had been available. Now very few villages, except in a severe winter, are completely isolated; they are usually connected either by train or by a good bus service. The clergy all have their bicycles or cars and a visit which may take now barely an hour, seventy years ago would have taken the whole afternoon. It is thus possible, in a way it was not in the past, for the parish priest to carry out his duties over a much larger area. But the new facilities have also done much to break down village life. The younger among the villagers, when their work is over, spend the evening in a neighbouring town. The school has lost its position through the children over eleven being taken to a central school in some other parish, and the village no longer means to them what it did to their parents. On the Sunday, excursions, the coming and going of visitors, all tend to destroy regular habits of worship. Many of the arguments which once could have been fairly used against the union of parishes have now lost their weight; for the conditions no longer exist which once made it necessary for every parish to have its own vicar. And in the towns parochialism has been superseded by congregationalism; often the townsman is as ignorant of the name of his vicar as he is of his representative on the borough council. Probably with the prevalent understaffing he has never been visited by the parish clergy, and if he goes to church it will be to one with which is connected by past associations, or because he prefers its manner of worship.

The old parochial system as it existed for nearly a thousand years has broken down. Once again the Church must be prepared to adapt it to entirely new conditions. Already steps have been taken to do this. The plurality system, detested by reformers, has to be revived; under the Act of 1838 the holding of more than two benefices with a cure of souls was prohibited, and for more than one a dispensation from the Archbishop of Canterbury was necessary. By an Act of 1930 the distance between the two churches must not exceed four miles, and the annual value of one of the benefices must not be above £400; but under certain conditions more than two benefices may be held without limits of distance or annual value. Now it is proposed that simpler methods should be employed for the effecting of a plurality, without a dispensation from the Archbishop of Canterbury. The advantage of proceeding by plurality is that it allows an experiment to be made which on proving unsuccessful can be terminated at the death or resignation of the incumbent of the two benefices. The Suspension Measure is another step on the same lines; by it an appointment can be suspended for three to seven years after certain permissions have been obtained, without the patron losing by lapse the right to appoint. The Reorganisation Areas Measure, 1944, has set up machinery to enable the Church to re-organise parishes in areas which were war damaged, or are affected by planning schemes or movements of population. Under the Union of Benefices Measures a number of benefices either have been actually united or orders for union have been directed; in all, 1,222.[1] In 563 cases the parishes as well as the benefices have been united, leaving one church only as the parish church, though in a number of these the other church is still used for worship. Considerable progress has therefore already been made in parochial reorganisation; but more clearly defined aims, greater vigour, and possibly further legislation will be required before the parochial system is brought more into relation with modern conditions. In five directions reforms are necessary.

Five Reforms

(1) The union of parishes should be vigorously pressed. The Church has neither the men nor the money to staff the old parochial system; nor does there seem any prospect in the future of a supply of ordinands large enough to give the Church anything like all the incumbents and curates it requires. This does not mean that all small country parishes will have to be combined with others. There will always be some which should be kept as they are now, either because of their isolation or because they are very scattered with many distant farms and hamlets. There are other parishes which for different reasons should always be worked as single parishes either for the sake of clergy who through health or age would be unable to minister to several churches, or for the scholar-priest who requires time and quiet for reading and writing. We should never forget the number of writers and scholars who have had country parishes: Gilbert White of Selborne, John Keble of Hursley, Charles Kingsley of Eversley, Richard Dixon of Warkworth, and Mandell Creighton of Embleton (the last two the authors of standard books on the Reformation and the Papacy) are representatives of the many who have written their books in rural parsonages. To my own knowledge there are many to-day who are continuing the same honourable tradition. We should also remember the children of the parsonage who have become famous

[1] To November 30th, 1948.

through their books, the names of Jane Austen and the Brontës instantly rise in our minds. When every allowance has been made for the delicate, the aged and the student there would still remain a large number of parishes with a population of under five hundred which should be worked with others. Something, however, is needed more than the mere union of adjacent parishes. Whole groups of parishes should be worked from a common centre; this would be a partial return to the old plan of a minster church with its clergy going forth from it to take the services and visit the people in a wide area. There are many market towns to which the inhabitants of the neighbouring parishes gravitate for business and shopping. A small staff or community of clergy living together under the direction of the vicar of the mother church might well minister to several of the small parishes within a radius of a few miles. They would be able by car or motor-cycle to be in and out of these parishes every day of the week, and the younger men on the staff would have a good training for country incumbencies of their own. In the large towns a halt should be called to the policy of creating parishes with populations of 5,000–6,000. Where possible past mistakes in this way should be undone, and especially in the new towns and housing estates a policy of subdivision should be avoided. For the whole of a large district containing anything up to a population of 40,000 there should be one parish with a central church and two or three district churches. If unmarried the clergy would live in a central clergy house, or if married in a house in the district to which they were especially attached. Fewer clergy would be required than would have been the case if four or five separate parishes had been created, each with its own incumbent and assistant curate. There would be one incumbent instead of several, and the cost and work of a number of small organisations would be avoided. One strong parish with a crowded congregation will have greater influence and more attractive power than a number of weak parishes with small congregations struggling to keep their heads above financial disaster.

From this amalgamation of parishes two advantages will follow: it will save man-power, for it will not be necessary to find incumbents for hundreds of small parishes; and it will also help to solve financial problems. Where a small parish with a small income gives its incumbent neither enough to live on or to do, when united to a neighbouring parish it offers both a living wage and sufficient work, and any balance can be used to increase the income of a third parish. When two small parishes with incomes of £350 and £400 are united, an income of £600 is provided for the incumbent of the united benefice, while the balance of £150, plus the proceeds from the sale of the superfluous parsonage house, can be used to augment the income of one or more parishes below the diocesan minimum. £500 gross should be secured as a minimum for every incumbent. Often, after a time, young and active men find there is not enough to do in a small country parish; the better men become restless and oppressed with a sense of frustration, the weaker men rust away. But when by union they are given charge of two or three villages they find plenty of scope for pastoral work.

Proposals for a policy of extensive union will be vehemently opposed by many. That they are necessary is deeply to be regretted—the beauty of the old English parish with its resident vicar, as described for instance in the "Vicar of Wakefield," is great. The parish priest in every parish has been a great influence for good. We hear of the failures and misfits, and we forget the great multitude of unknown parish priests both in town and country who have been true ambassadors of Christ and sympathetic friends of their people. But those who deplore the further union of parishes must honestly face the two hard facts which govern the present position—there are insufficient clergy to staff the parishes, and there is insufficient money to pay them. The laity already are giving large sums for the support of their clergy, the diocesan budget cannot bear many more burdens, and the Church Commissioners are using to the full their funds. It is wrong to demand a vicar for every parish if it means he will be underpaid, and either overworked or underworked. The opponents of the union of benefices would carry more weight if they would show how their clergy are to be paid. Successful opposition to a comprehensive scheme for uniting and grouping parishes would doom many of their incumbents to prolonged poverty, and the parish—when vacant—to long delay before it was filled. It is not possible either to provide the men or the money for the maintenance of the traditional parochial system. No amount of sentimental rhetoric can escape from this unpleasant fact. The choice is between helplessly and incompetently drifting to disaster or carrying through a far-reaching policy of reform. It is folly to laud the glories of the past and to ignore the problems of the present.

(2) The union of parishes is very closely bound up with the re-distribution of man-power. It is vital that the best use should be made of the limited number of clergy now possessed by the Church. They should go to the parishes both in town and country where they are most required, and to those strategic points where evangelisation is most urgently needed, or where the pastoral work must be strengthened. The Commission on the Staffing of Parishes reported in 1930: "It is plain that the grave problem of the shortage in the total number of clergy is greatly increased by this unsystematic and unreasonable distribution of man-power. It is in those parishes which are most exceptionally difficult and exhausting, and where the need for missionary work is the greatest, that the scarcity of clergy is most acutely felt." The Archdeacon of York in the article from which I have already quoted, shows there is a striking difference between the numbers of people to each priest in rural dioceses and the much larger number in urban dioceses like London and Liverpool. There is one priest to every 920 persons in the diocese of Bath and Wells, and one to every 970 in Salisbury; while in the dioceses of London and Liverpool the proportion in the one case is a priest to every 5,030, and Liverpool to even 5,411. The contrast between the staffing of the south and the north is also very striking; in the Southern Province there are only three dioceses which on an average have only one priest for a population of over 3,000; in the much smaller Province of the North there are no less than nine dioceses with one priest to over 3,000. To put it another way—37.03 per cent. of the population of England is in the Province of York, but it has only 26.54 per cent. of the parochial clergy. Figures also show that five of the northern dioceses have only 33 per cent. of their pre-war curate strength, while most southern dioceses average 60 per cent. Various reasons can account for this—some for reasons of health prefer the warmer climate of the south; some think the educational facilities are better; some have been encouraged to stay in the south by the Principal of their theological college, probably situated in a southern diocese; and others are attracted by the higher stipends usually paid to curates in the south. But whatever the reason may be, the result is the same; the seaside resorts and country parishes of the south have an undue proportion of the number of clergy available.

It is difficult to know how to remedy this. Anything like

compulsion would be resented. But the theological colleges could do more than they do at present in encouraging their students to seek a title in the north. The best of our ordinands will be ready at the beginning of their ministry to go where the need for help is greatest, but they require authoritative guidance. The problem is more difficult with senior men who have already served their title. The most practical suggestion was made by the Staffing Commission which recommended that the diocesan bishops might make some arrangement among themselves about the number of curates they would accept in their respective dioceses: "No attempt should be made to enforce a hard and fast rule, but the bishop who found that the number of his assistant curates was in excess of what was allotted to his diocese should not ordinarily fill vacancies caused by their departures by accepting men from outside the diocese, until his numbers had fallen to the proposed standard." All such arrangements both for ordinands and priests would have to be voluntary and could not be enforced, but the present position is clearly wrong when one part of the country is staffed at the cost of the great industrial cities of the north.

(3) Less important from the practical results which would follow is the necessity of removing some of the more glaring inequalities in the payments of the parochial clergy. Only some five per cent. of the parishes have an income which might be described as excessive, the surplus from these would only be a small contribution towards increasing the incomes of the underpaid clergy. But the moral effect would be considerable. The criticism of the large incomes a few of the clergy receive, contrasted with the poverty of the many, has been heard for years. The prejudice this creates is out of all proportion to the number of parishes affected. Ninety years ago Anthony Trollope contrasted the lot of the vicar of Framley, an attractive parish and £900 a year, with the vicar of Hogglestock, a parish with full work for two men and a stipend of £130, and commented: "In other trades, professions and lines of life men are paid according to their work. Let it be so with the Church. Such will sooner or later be the edict of a utilitarian, reforming, matter-of-fact House of Parliament." There are some parishes where the conditions of work are such that a higher income than the average is necessary; there are others where it is usual for the incumbent to set aside a considerable portion of his income for some parochial purpose—the income of the parish

of Portsea was £1,000 a year, but unmarried vicars paid the larger part of this direct into the curate fund. But it is impossible to justify an incumbent with a small parish receiving a large income, while within a mile or two his neighbour with a huge population has barely £400 a year. It is not only the laity who feel there is something wrong about this, but most of the clergy feel it with equal strength. Whatever may have been the historical reasons for these arrangements, they can no longer be defended, and the sooner they are brought to an end the better; this will be for the good name of the Church. The recent Pastoral Reorganisation Measure, while preserving the rights of existing incumbents, enables the excess income of a benefice to be paid, under certain conditions, into the stipends fund of the diocese, and thus to be available for the poor Hogglestocks. The amount of relief that this will give will be small, but it will save the Church from the charge of tolerating indefensible inequalities in the payment of those engaged in the same spiritual work.

(4) Much more serious and far-reaching is the problem of the parsonage house. In the past the house had to be provided by the rector, and then the incumbent was responsible for keeping it in good order. Dilapidations on ecclesiastical property were the cause of endless disputes. From the thirteenth century at least efforts were made by the central authority to see that the parsonage house was kept in good repair during the lifetime of the incumbent. When this was not done the new incumbent was entitled to repair it and could demand payment from his predecessor or his executors. Dr. Purvis gives an interesting case, which incidentally throws light on the hours of labour, in connection with the rectory of Kirby Misperton in Yorkshire, where in 1581 the executors disputed an estimate for £96 6s. 8d. for repairs—they make a strong point in arguing that labour and material were both cheaper at Kirby than at York, where those who drew up the estimate lived—"that by the custome of the Cittie of York bricklayers and carpenters have not usuallie wrought dayelite worke anie longer than from VI of the clocke in the morninge until VI at night. Or from V in the morninge until VII at night at the furthest. But bricklayers and carpenters of the countrye usuallie have wrought and worke from sonne rysinge till sonne sittinge there dayelite worke and sometymes longer."[1] But these disputes

[1] "Dilapidations in Parsonage Property," p. 20.

were brought to an end by the present law of dilapidations by which the incumbent pays an annual instalment on a quinquennial assessment. Though this change in the law is a great improvement on the old system, it does not relieve the incumbent of the burden which is placed upon him by the possession of a large official house of residence, nor does the amount he pays annually for dilapidations always cover the actual cost.

In the spacious years of the eighteenth and nineteenth centuries it was the custom to build large parsonage houses. Usually the rector had private means and a large family. There was no income tax, the rate of tithe was high, and domestic servants were easy to obtain and their wages were small. As the rector was expected to entertain, a large dining-room, a good cellar, and an adequate staff were regarded as necessary. Parson Woodforde in his diary shows how large were the meals and lavish the hospitality in the parsonage of the eighteenth century. Readers of Anthony Trollope will recall Archdeacon Grantly's visit to St. Ewold's parsonage and his indignation over its limitations—the cellar excited his wrath: "This cellar is perfectly abominable. It would be folly to put a bottle of wine into it till it has been roofed, walled and floored." Even greater was his scorn of the dining-room: "Look here, it is just sixteen feet by fifteen." My father's vicarage was not large, it had a hall, three reception rooms, a parish room also used as our play room, with kitchen, scullery, store room and pantry; on the first floor were five bedrooms, a nursery, and two dressing-rooms (bathrooms were at that time unknown), and a large and a small attic at the top of the house. Most of the neighbouring rectories were much larger. All had well-kept gardens—the paths free of weeds, the lawns beautifully mown, the flower beds and herbaceous borders were rich with the colour and scent of old-fashioned plants; by the drive were many lilacs, laburnums, and guelder roses, and the walls of the house were usually covered by climbing roses, which tried to make their way through the windows. Though my father's income was small—£300 a year, and a pension as chaplain in the old East India Company—we had a nurse and nursemaid, a cook and kitchen maid, and a maid of all work; and for the garden a whole-time man and his boy. But to-day vicarages even smaller than the one at Tongham are difficult to run.[1] Fuel cannot be obtained

[1] Country vicarages seventy years ago were without the labour-saving devices of to-day. At Tongham we had neither gas nor electricity and the water had to be pumped up daily.

for warmth ; it is hard to carry out necessary repairs ; and the high wages of servants make it impossible to obtain a domestic staff, or even occasional help. The vicarages are now often dilapidated within and without, while most of the gardens have become wildernesses. The strain on the incumbents and their wives in maintaining these large buildings is almost intolerable. The reasons which made them necessary have gone : the families of the clergy are smaller than used to be the case ; no longer is special prestige attached to the man who lives in a house larger than his neighbours ; and entertaining on a large scale is not possible. No greater relief could be given to most of our clergy than a move to a smaller house, fitted with labour-saving devices.

As soon as conditions allow, the Church Commissioners, the diocesan authorities, and the parishes, must combine in a carefully planned effort to relieve the clergy of the anxiety caused by their over-large houses. The clergy have to give up time from their proper work to assist their wives in their household duties ; the wives are breaking down under the strain ; and the huge parsonage may bring discredit on the Church as the worst-kept house in the parish. It has been proposed that the Church Commissioners should take over all the parsonage houses and be responsible for their upkeep ; but this would lay a great burden of work on the central authority, and would take from the incumbent and the parish an incentive for local responsibility. Usually repairs can be carried through more quickly and economically by the men on the spot than by direction from London. Short of this drastic change of ownership, central and diocesan authorities should help in three ways—by selling the over-large vicarages and building in their place small labour-saving houses ; by modernising existing houses so that part can be let out to a tenant, and the rest occupied by the incumbent ; and where they cannot be divided, superfluous outhouses and wings should be demolished, and the houses thus reduced to a reasonable size. In carrying out these changes it is, however, necessary to remember that some large vicarages will always be required. Frequently I have had parishes refused because the house is too small for the family, and occasionally of late years vicarages have had to be enlarged. It would be deplorable if all the parsonage houses were such that no man with a large family could ever accept a parish, and the impression was given that the Church encouraged its clergy to limit their families to two children.

There are other means of supplementing the usual accommodation provided for the clergy. Houses in which the clergy can live together in community should be encouraged. For twenty years I lived, first as assistant curate and then as their vicar with sixteen other clergy. Our life was simple, but healthy; the food plain and good; the hours of work long but regular. In the happiness of work and fellowship we were not conscious of any hardships—I remember how astonished I was when a visiting bishop spoke of "roughing it in the clergy house"; none of us had the slightest idea that we were roughing it! The days of large clergy houses like Portsea are over, but not only many of our urban parishes would gain by a small body of curates living together, but sometimes a whole rural deanery would benefit by a clergy house in its midst where the curates of different parishes lived together with a senior man at their head.

I am, however, convinced that a much more drastic step is required. In the industrial parishes, and especially in the new towns, some of the incumbents should be encouraged to live in the ordinary working-class houses of the district. Instead of a vicarage being built at considerable cost, a house should be bought or built of the same character as the ordinary houses in any street of the parish. The incumbent by living in it would lose much that is attractive in the traditional vicarage; he would miss the quiet and the garden, but he would be living among his people as one of them; this would not only save cost, but it would do something much greater—it would remove the prejudice created by the vicar living in different and more comfortable surroundings. I am not advocating that this policy should be universally adopted (the traditional parsonage house would still continue to exist); but I should like many of our young and keen clergy to live among the people in working-class houses. This has already been done on a small scale; there are some scores of parish priests living in this way; but not scores—hundreds are wanted. Later the men who have spent the earlier part of their ministry in these houses could look forward to a different type of vicarage and parish.

(5) It is generally agreed that the systems of patronage and of freehold both require some modification. The earlier part of this chapter showed how they came into existence—patronage through the landowner regarding the church as his property—the freehold through the bishop protecting the incumbent against the patron.

Patronage has changed hands on a very large scale since the Anglo-Saxon days. From landlords it passed to the monasteries, the bishops and the Crown. At the Reformation, with the destruction of the monasteries, there was a large increase in the patronage both of the Crown and the laity. To-day patronage is exercised by the Crown, the bishops, corporate bodies such as deans and chapters and colleges, by incumbents, chiefly of mother parishes, by party trusts, and by laymen. The whole system of patronage is illogical and haphazard. It does not, however, work badly in actual practice, and it is impossible to devise any form of patronage which would ensure that every clergyman received preferment in strict accord with his merits. The most serious weaknesses in the present system are two. By trust patronage a certain type of Churchmanship is imposed on a parish from which it has no escape ; and when the trust is narrow its field of choice is correspondingly limited, and men are appointed who may have little to commend them except their skill in repeating the correct shibboleth. The larger trusts take great care in making appointments, and are very liberal in the interpretation of their trust deeds ; most bishops would, I am sure, acknowledge gratefully the care with which appointments are made by the larger trusts. But some of the smaller trusts are driven to make appointments from which the parishes suffer without hope of relief. Lay patronage is also open to considerable criticism ; when the layman lives in the parish or takes an interest in it, he will usually spare no trouble over the choice of an incumbent, taking fully into consideration all the peculiarities of the parish. Addison's Sir Roger " that he might encourage the young fellows of the parish to make themselves perfect in the Church Service promised upon the death of the present incumbent, who is very old, to bestow it according to merit " ; but when the lay patron no longer lives in the parish, or has no connection with it, he may regard the appointment as a nuisance, and will accept the first man who applies for it. It is very difficult to see how the present methods of appointment can be changed. A recent committee on the subject has made four practical suggestions. First, that the Church Council should be allowed to suggest definite names instead of making a general statement of the needs of the parish. Secondly that no lay person shall be entitled to exercise the right of presentation unless he is a member of the Church of England and qualified as a parochial elector. Thirdly, that before the actual appointment is made and announced, the bishop should be notified so that he might have the opportunity of discussing it with the patron, and possibly saving the parish from an unsuitable appointment. Fourthly, that the diocesan Board of Patronage should be strengthened and patrons encouraged to transfer their advowsons to it.

The freehold is an even more difficult problem than patronage. It was created to safeguard the incumbent against the unreasonable demands of, or unjustifiable dismissal by, the patron. It has given the clergy independence against bishop, patron and parishioners which otherwise could not have been obtained. It is a valued defence for freedom, and should not be destroyed lightly; an incumbent cannot be turned out of his benefice because of his unpopular opinions, either ecclesiastical or political. His parishioners may storm, and the bishop remonstrate, but the incumbent knows that his feet are on firm ground. But the freehold may be abused; it may protect a lazy, incompetent and quarrelsome parson who is useless in his parish. The people may protest, but year after year passes and nothing is done. The bishop, who is powerless, is criticised, and the neighbouring clergy share in the discredit of the offender. There are comparatively few such cases, but the scandal they cause is very great. The various measures which so far have been passed are not likely to be effective. It is possible to deprive a priest for a grave moral offence, and to declare the benefice vacant when it has been proved that—for physical or mental reasons—he is incapable of doing his work; it is, however, under the present law, almost impossible to remove an incumbent who performs the statutory duties, but who is notoriously lazy or who repeatedly quarrels with most of his parishioners. The clergy themselves must look for a remedy; they are fearful lest the bishops or the laity may destroy a highly valued privilege, for security of tenure is important to a profession with a low scale of pay and is some compensation for it; but before the laity promise to give more generously to the support of their clergy, they will require to be satisfied that there is some method by which a priest who has shown himself totally unsuitable for his parish can be removed. For the satisfactory working of any method the good will of the clergy is essential: in their Convocations they have the responsibility of devising some plan by which their freehold is preserved, but its abuse is avoided.

XIV

THE CHURCHMAN AS CITIZEN

IN the previous chapters the relationship of the Church to the State has been discussed. It is necessary now to consider the duty of the individual Churchman as a citizen. For he is a member of the State as well as of the Church, and therefore has a twofold loyalty. However faithfully he may fulfil his duties to the Church, the State also has a claim upon him. The good Churchman must also be a good citizen.

There are some Churchmen who would interpret very narrowly the meaning of good citizenship. They obey the laws of the land, pay regularly their taxes and rates, make an honest return of their income, and encourage the frequent singing of the National Anthem in the churches they attend. But they are strongly opposed to the Church interfering with politics, and resent Church assemblies, or the clergy—and especially the bishops—expressing in public any views on political, social, or economic problems. In the early days of the Christian Church "certain lewd fellows of the baser sort" accused St. Paul of interfering in politics. It was then a dangerous charge and might have had fatal results. To-day the charge is not so dangerous, and it is made usually not by the enemies of the Church, but by those who are among its most faithful members. They believe that those who are called to be citizens of a heavenly city should avoid the controversies of the market place. They are afraid that religion may suffer injury. "Let the Church mind the things of God, and the politician the things of Cæsar." "Let the Church care for the souls of men and the State for their bodies" express their convictions on the right relationship between Churchmanship and citizenship.

No thoughtful Christian can accept this position. The suggestion that the Church should look after men's souls while the State concerns itself with their bodies is comparable to the Victorian philosopher's famous proposal for a concordat between science and religion by which the former would have the known and the latter the unknowable as their respective provinces of work. Christianity cannot be limited in this way; it is the religion of the Incarnation and is therefore concerned with the whole of man and not only with his spirit. Body and soul are so closely connected that it is futile to attempt to deal with one and to ignore the other. Environment, which the State can change or modify, may have a profound influence on man's life and character for good or for evil. The Church must not be indifferent to the cry of under-nourished children, to the unhappiness and discomfort of the multitudes who have no decent homes, to the stunted lives of those who are below the poverty line, and to the sense of frustration which comes to all who suffer from prolonged unemployment. While the Church has already done much by personal service and charity, the State alone has the resources to deal adequately with large-scale social evils. The Christian should use his political influence to encourage and support legislation which would remove social injustice and give greater opportunities to all to make the best use of life.

But the State may be a terrible power for evil. Instead of encouraging the good life and protecting the Church, it may become a modern anti-Christ, for it has at its disposal unprecedented powers. Through compulsory education, a controlled press and wireless, through the cinema, through conscription, and through a network of police and spies, it can mould the minds and control the actions of its citizens from the cradle to the grave. The totalitarian State, both Nazi and Communistic, has used ruthlessly these means of obtaining control over its citizens. In Germany a whole generation was perverted by the group of cruel and unscrupulous men who ruled the country. To-day communism is destroying nations which once were proud of their freedom. If the Christian takes no part in politics, he is handing the State over to the secularist and atheist. The rise of the Nazis to power in Germany would not have been so rapid if the Lutheran Church, at an earlier stage, had resisted instead of accepting passively their rule. When the State discovers that the Church has abdicated all responsibility for its politics, it will become aggressively secular, ignoring the claims of the Christian, and confident that it will meet no opposition. The refusal of a Church to take part in politics is both the betrayal of a responsibility, and the surrender of a great opportunity.

It is from a recognition of the good and evil that can come

through State action that many Churchmen have advocated the formation of a Church party, independent of and separate from all other political parties. This is a revival in a modified form of the medieval theory that the Church should control the State. Churchmen have been haunted from time to time by the vision of a theocracy which would establish the Kingdom of God on earth; and though few to-day have any belief in the rule of the saints, there are many who would like to see the Church organising its political power both to protect its own interests and to promote Christian legislation. At the beginning of the century Nonconformity was a great political force in this country, and at times dominated the Liberal Party. To-day on the Continent the Roman Church has in the Christian Democrats a powerful political weapon against an atheistic communism.

But the Church loses spiritual influence when it either commits itself to one of the existing parties or forms a party of its own. In winning political victories it may lose the Kingdom of God. At the height of its political power, it may be at the lowest ebb in spiritual influence. Political work is very engrossing, and calls for time and care if it is to be effective. The time spent on perfecting the political machine may be secured at the cost of other and far more important duties. In England there is suspicion of the parson who preaches political sermons and appears on party platforms; it is felt that he is deserting his real work—the care of souls. It is also easy to overrate the material advantages won by political success. Baron von Hugel was once told by an enthusiastic owner of a factory of the steps he was taking to make it more Christian; he had described the welfare system, the dining-room, the dental clinic and the swimming pool, when the old Baron interrupted him with the indignant exclamation, "You haven't begun to understand what Christianity is; Christianity is not refreshment bars and swimming pools—it is a soul in the presence of God."[1] Advocacy of social reform must not be allowed to hide the real purpose of the Church, which is the extension of the Kingdom of God. Political action leads to strange alliances, and in the determination to gain victory at the polls truth and principle may be sacrificed.

Another danger follows from a Church party in politics. Those who are actively opposed to it and its programme,

[1] A. Zimmern, "Spiritual Values and World Affairs," p. 23.

associate the faith of the Church with its politics, and reject both together. A Church may easily be so closely associated with one party that though it benefits by its success, it suffers with it by its defeat. The more vigorous its political advocacy, the more enemies the Church will create, and they—when their hour comes—will treat the Church as a political enemy to be weakened and injured. "Anti-clericalism is the enemy" was Gambetta's cry after the French Church had intervened in foreign politics, and afterwards successive French Governments treated the Church as an enemy. The bitterness so often found on the Continent against the Roman Catholic Church is due more to its political activities than to its faith and worship.

Official and Unofficial Action of the Church

There is an intermediate course for the Church between withdrawal from an active participation in the world of politics. This is well stated by a resolution of the Lambeth Conference of 1920: "The Church cannot in its corporate capacity be an advocate or partisan, 'a judge or a divider' in political or class disputes where moral issues are not at stake; nevertheless even in matters of economic and political controversy the Church is bound to give its positive and active corporate witness to the Christian principles of justice, brotherhood, and the equal and infinite value of every human personality." The report on which the resolution is based interprets it by stating "that while individual members of, or special groups within, the Church may rightly advocate some specific programme or policy, the Church should never, as a Body, concern itself with a political issue unless it involved a clear moral issue, and then only in the interest of morals and righteousness, and not in the interests of parties." It is of great importance that this distinction should be drawn between the political action of the Church in its official and corporate capacity, and that of groups and individuals belonging to it. Failure to make this distinction has often led to misunderstanding. The utterances of individual churchmen must not be treated as necessarily the expression of the mind of the Church on some political or economic problem.

Political action on the part of the official Church should be strictly limited. Neither the bishops nor the members of the Convocations and the Church Assembly are chosen because of their knowledge of politics or economics. Most of them have not the technical experience to enable them to speak or advise authoritatively on the more complicated problems they often present. If they do so the best intentions may not save them from harmful blunders. Professor Zimmern states what is too often forgotten, that "there is a technique of politics. Cæsar has a business of his own, which requires knowledge, training, skill, a special quality of judgement. Politics—and more especially international politics—require more than good will and fine aspirations. It has its own expertise—like medicine (which it perhaps most closely resembles in its methods—the body politic is a very helpful analogy) or engineering or accountancy or any other whole-time occupation. When we say that a man is a good doctor or a good engineer we mean, first and foremost, that he is good at his own job."[1] Professor Zimmern goes on to give some examples of the way in which distinguished ecclesiastics by intervening with imperfect knowledge in foreign affairs have nearly sabotaged the cause they had at heart. Good will and rhetoric are no substitutes for knowledge and sound judgement. Nothing is more irritating to responsible statesmen trying to carry through a practical policy of reform than to find that they are criticised and hindered by the ill-informed advocates of an alternative policy, which would neither be acceptable to the nation nor workable if it should be accepted. Ecclesiastical gatherings should be slow in passing resolutions and making pronouncements on great subjects on which they have inadequate knowledge. Resolutions are often quickly passed at the instigation of a few enthusiasts, but unless there is behind them real knowledge they carry no weight with responsible persons. Such resolutions light-heartedly carried are pigeon-holed by those to whom they are sent; they have no influence on practical policy, and seriously prejudice the likelihood of the Church obtaining a hearing when it is compelled to make a deliberate and public appeal to the conscience of the nation.

The official Church in its corporate capacity, groups within the Church, and individual members of the Church, have their respective functions in applying the Christian faith to political and social problems.

[1] Ibid., p. 7.

The Prophetic Duty of the Church

The official Church has a prophetic duty. It has to proclaim the true end of man—which William Temple described as "the glory of God in the welfare of His people." In the anxiety to plan, the planner often forgets to ask what is the end and purpose of planning. The secularist State plans for this world alone, and treats man as a being whose life is ended by death. The Christian has a wider horizon, and plans in the faith that what is done here will have results for good or evil which are eternal. There is something very depressing in the knowledge that many civilisations have vanished, that very many more are likely to rise and fall before the earth becomes too cold for human life, and that the age in which we live and which seems to be so important is only an almost infinitesimal portion of the time during which man is likely to inhabit the earth.[1] Confronted with this spectacle of vast and almost unlimited expanse of time it seems that so little can be done which will endure, and that the results of human effort will soon be engulfed in oblivion. But the Christian, on the other hand, sees each generation of men and women carrying into eternity the good and the evil they have acquired during their brief sojourn on earth. Life is seen then as of infinite value, and all that is done here has results which may be permanent. The Christian is convinced that what is done to improve and develop the characters of men and women is of profound importance. He judges, therefore, all political proposals by the way in which they would help or hinder the education of souls called to eternal life. While the secular politician speaks of prosperity, comfort, happiness, as the supreme end of legislation, the Christian, while not denying their value, looks beyond immediate results and judges life by a different and higher standard. With John Keats he views this world as "a vale of soul making," but it is the making of souls for eternity.

The Church, therefore, must call men to the vision of God as the living Sovereign and Judge of the whole universe Whose laws of righteousness individuals and nations must obey; and as the Father Who cares equally for all, whatever their colour or race. And from these fundamental truths there follow

[1] *Vide* A. J. Toynbee, "Civilisation on Trial."

certain great principles which the Christian Church must both declare and apply. Because God is the Lord above all, no nation must claim to be a law to itself; it must live in obedience to the law of righteousness, respecting the rights of other nations, and, however great its own power, refrain from obtaining its ends by violence. Again, because God is the Father and calls to sonship the men and women He has created, they are all of value in His sight. Man must not be treated as a mere tool for the State to use as it thinks best or as a cog in a vast industrial machine to be scrapped at will, but he has rights which belong to him as man. The Christian Church must insist that all men whatever their colour have rights which should be universally respected. The Lambeth Conference of 1948 declared "that among such rights are security of life and person: the right to work, to bring up a family, and to possess personal property; the right to freedom of speech, of discussion and association, and to accurate information; and to full freedom of religious life and practice, and that these rights belong to all men irrespective of race or colour." The Church must show it is the champion of the rights of man, for it believes that he is made in the image of God and called to be a child of God. This is the fundamental difference between the Christian and the Marxian Communist view of man. The one treats man as an end in himself with rights given to him by God; the other as a means to an end with no rights except those which it may please the State to allow him. "The good of civilisation is also the good of the human person, the recognition of his rights and of his dignity, based ultimately on the fact that he is the image of God. Let no one deceive himself; the cause of religion and the cause of the human person are closely linked."[1]

These convictions of the Sovereignty and Fatherhood of God, of the value of man, of the laws of righteousness, mercy and truth, must be shown to be relevant to the practical problems of the day. Ideals are gladly accepted and applauded as long as they are confined to cloud cuckoo land, but they are regarded and attacked as impractical, dangerous and revolutionary if an attempt is made to express them in legislation or administration. The ineffectiveness of the social witness of the Church has been often due to its enunciation of sound standards and high ideals without making a serious attempt to apply

[1] J. Maritain, "Redeeming the Time," p. 122.

them to existing conditions. When the Hebrew prophets proclaimed that the righteous God demanded justice and mercy from His people, they went on at once to show how this demand should affect the workaday lives of the people of Judæa and Galilee. They condemned social injustice, the intrigues of statesmen, the greed of the powerful in accumulating wealth, the callousness of the rich who ground the faces of the poor, the unscrupulousness of the landlord who added field to field, and the luxury of the great in drink and food at the banquet. The unpopularity of the prophets was not due to their speaking of the Majesty and Holiness of God, but to their criticism of contemporary politics—both domestic and foreign—and their exposure of current immorality and selfishness. So the Church of to-day must apply the Christian standards to existing conditions. When it teaches that God is the righteous Sovereign of the nations, it must also renounce power politics, and require the substitution of law for violence in international affairs. When it speaks of the nations as members of the family of God, it must demand the removal of injustices which cause them to hate and fear their neighbours, and must support treaties and unions which may draw them closer to one another. When it speaks of the Fatherhood of God and His care for individuals, it must condemn oppression and cruelty, the exploitation of the weak, and must call for justice and help for the poor, the aged, and the unhappy refugees. When it speaks of the value of man, it must condemn unemployment and conditions of work which deprive him of the opportunities of using the special gifts he possesses, and must demand for him both political and economic freedom. No one to-day pays much attention to the vague statement of abstract principles, but both interest and opposition are aroused when their application to daily life is made plain.

The Political Action of Groups within the Church

But while the official Church—to use again a cumbrous term—should both proclaim the principles of Christian morality and show their application to society and the individual, it should not attempt to work out detailed schemes of international or domestic reform. Bishops and members of Assemblies, chosen for special qualification in ecclesiastical and religious affairs, are acting rashly if they attempt to produce programmes of political and social reform. The Church in its corporate capacity should not attempt to do this, but the necessity for this restraint does not apply to groups and individuals. Within the Church there should be men and women who have studied carefully the urgent problems of the day, and are able to speak with authority on them. Not even an archbishop need be silent either in the House of Lords or elsewhere if he can make some contribution to the discussion of a subject to which he has given thought and study, and of which he may have had personal experience! Many of the clergy have closer and more intimate knowledge of the social problems of town and country than most professional politicians or economists. Groups of clergy and laity should specialise in international or social questions so as to give informed guidance to their Church and the nation. By making public the convictions they have reached and by pressing them upon the electorate, they are not committing the whole Church, but they are educating it as well as helping to awaken the conscience of the whole community. Fifty years ago I belonged to one of these groups now long defunct, the Christian Social Union. Its members were comparatively few; it had no popular programme; it was theoretical rather than practical, with the exception of its white list of Oxford tailors, which contained the names of those who paid their workmen fair wages; but it encouraged its members to study and to discuss social and political problems from the standpoint of the Christian. Bishop Westcott, Charles Gore and Canon Scott Holland were among the strongest supporters of this Union. I joined it while I was at Oxford, and at my ordination I intended resigning from it when Randall Davidson, then Bishop of Winchester, with unexpected vigour almost directed me to remain a member saying that he considered it essential that some of the clergy should study as well as speak on social reform. Some of us who belong to an older generation owe much to this little Union. There are to-day several societies in which clergy and laity make a specialised study of different problems, and through which they promote international or social policy on Christian principles.

The Duty of Individuals

Most important of all is the influence which the individual Churchman should exercise as a member of a political party. Instead of joining a Church party he should carry into his own party his religious convictions. The days have long passed when it could be assumed that a Churchman would also be a Conservative; to-day large numbers belong to the Conservative and Labour parties, though comparatively few would call themselves Liberal. The Churchman should attend regularly the meetings of his party, not because he wishes to obtain some special advantage for his Church, but that he may carry into the field of politics Christian ideals and standards. The more genuine interest he shows in the concerns of his party, the more likely he will be to gain a sympathetic hearing when matters are raised which specifically concern the Church. He may find it sometimes difficult to agree with all the proposals of the party to which he belongs, and for the sake of what he feels to be of greater importance he may have to acquiesce in minor matters which he dislikes; only conscientious convictions on major issues should lead him to resign. William Temple gives good advice to the Christian who does not feel altogether happy with his party ties—"The Christian citizen who is a member or officer of any association must work loyally with the association. He is not at liberty to think out for himself what is on Christian grounds the best course of action, and then take that course. He may commend it to his fellow members; and if he persuades them he and they will follow it together. But he is bound to act with the association or withdraw from it. On the other hand he may be able to do much, while remaining in it and co-operating in actions which seem to him other than the best, to bring it nearer to a Christian standard than it would be without his effort."[1] But whether the Churchman belongs to a party or not, it is his duty to use his vote. Many are too slack to go to the poll. No elector has the right to complain of the mismanagement of public or local affairs if he does not take the trouble to record his vote. The exercise of the franchise should be looked upon as the fulfilment of a responsibility to God and to man.

[1] "Citizen and Churchman," p. 97.

The individual Churchman, if suitable, should be ready to stand for election to Parliament and to local Councils. It has been said with truth that the Free Churches are more largely represented on the Borough Councils than the Church. This is not due to any hostility to members of the Church of England, but simply to the fact that so few of them are ready to stand for election even when invited to do so. Local authorities have such extensive powers that they are now able to do much for the education, the health and recreation of the people. It is therefore necessary for the good of the community that among those who administer these vast powers there should be some convinced Christians. In many cases Churchmen would be able to stand for election in co-operation with Nonconformists, for no one would wish to revive the days when elections were fought on denominational lines. From various sides the criticism is heard that the personnel on our public bodies is weak, and that the difficulty is great in getting men of independence and experience to stand for them. Among their members there should be men and women disinterested in business contracts, sitting loosely to party politics, but standing firmly on Christian convictions. There are many Church laymen who are well qualified to render valuable service both to Church and State in Parliament or on some local Council.

Personal Service

But apart from the exercise of their votes and by serving on some public body, there are other ways in which church people can contribute to the well-being of the State. In recent years it has taken over much welfare and social work which once was the responsibility of the Church, and has a great army of paid workers in the place of those who once were voluntary and unpaid. It is able to provide community centres, clubs for youth, and organisations for welfare on a scale quite impracticable for any voluntary society. But buildings are not enough, the man or woman in charge of the centre is far more important; technical training, important as it is, does not necessarily provide the firm and sympathetic character able to secure obedience and win confidence. With the pressure of work in the post-war world there is sometimes the danger that many of these plans for welfare may fail through the inability of the

State to obtain the right kind of helper. Under wrong management a club for young people may do more harm than good. Already many members of the Church are rendering good service under the State in the schools, in various community and welfare centres, and in youth organisations. But there are more who should find in educational and welfare work a field for the use of the gifts God has bestowed upon them. It was this that inspired one of the resolutions of the Lambeth Conference, 1948. " Since the State, industry, and community services are offering an increasing number of posts which may be made spheres of Christian influence, the Conference calls upon Church members to bring to such posts not only professional training and a sense of vocation but also a sound knowledge of the Christian doctrine of God and man." Church people who take such posts should fulfil their duties in them as unto God as well as unto man, as vocations as well as professions.

There is, however, a vast field unoccupied by the State for which voluntary workers are always required. Lord Beveridge in his Report on Voluntary Action shows that notwithstanding the extension of the State there is still the need of voluntary action both in the giving of money for welfare schemes for which the State has made no provision and still more in the giving of voluntary personal service. There is a danger lest it should be assumed that an omnipotent State can provide everything. Personal sympathetic service cannot be bought with money. " The State is or can be master of money, but in a free society it is master of very little else. The making of a good society depends not on the State but on the citizens, acting individually or in free association with one another, acting on motives of various kinds—some selfish, others unselfish, some narrow and material, others inspired by love of man and love of God. The happiness or unhappiness of the society in which we live depends upon ourselves as citizens, not only the instruments of political power which we call the State."[1] The Church should be a reservoir from which there flows a wide and unending stream of men and women who will give voluntary work where it is most needed for the love both of God and of man. Where they can give useful service they should be prepared to take the least important place at the committee table, and to do the most tedious work. They should be ready to work with all people of good will whatever their

[1] Lord Beveridge, " Voluntary Action," p. 320.

religious views may be. "The Church is most likely to preserve its integrity by penetrating at every possible point the secular community and encouraging its membership to co-operate with others in the life of a nation without fear or favour."[1] In no nobler or more effective way will the historic connection between Church and State be continued than by the readiness of Churchmen and Churchwomen to give paid or voluntary service to social work under the control of the State, and by joining with all men of good will for the protection and help of the young, the weak, and the old, for whose happiness and comfort the State has not yet made sufficient provision.

[1] Lambeth Conference Committee Report on "The Church and the Modern World," p. 19.

EPILOGUE

XV

FOR WHAT PURPOSE?

CHURCH reform is not an end in itself; by itself it will not make the Church either more holy or more zealous; it is a means to an end, and that end must be of sufficient importance to justify an attempt at this time of world crisis to change the traditional relationship between Church and State in England. The attempt will mean tension, controversy will be stirred up, and it is possible that the issue of disestablishment may be raised. The old criticism will be heard that the Church is discussing constitutional and administrative reform when it ought to be concentrating all its efforts on the extension of the Kingdom of God. "*Cui bono?*" "What good will these reforms serve?" is the challenge which will be given. The answer is fivefold. A readjustment of the present relationship between Church and State will help the Church—in its work of evangelisation; in its witness to the nation in the cause of truth and righteousness; in the defence of man's freedom; in the removal of an obstacle in the way of Christian reunion; and in making the Church of to-day more after the likeness of the primitive and apostolic Church.

The Conversion of England

The greatest of all duties laid by its Master upon the Church is that of evangelisation. A century ago it was generally assumed England was a Christian country, and that the duty of the Church at home was to strengthen and edify its members in the faith, while its missionary work was concerned only with the heathen in distant lands. At home the work of the Church was primarily pastoral, overseas it was evangelistic. This outlook was always unduly optimistic; even when the churches were crowded there were many of the worshippers whose knowledge of the Christian faith was very slight, and whose church-going was due to convention rather than to conviction; in the densely crowded cities there were great masses to whom Christ was only a name, and the church a building they never thought of entering. But to-day the position is far worse; the habit of church-going has been largely abandoned by all classes; Sunday is now a day of amusement rather than of worship and rest; churches once crowded are now half empty; and there is widespread ignorance of the elementary facts and beliefs of Christianity. To most the Church is irrelevant to their lives except for baptisms, marriages, and burials. In the past the preacher speaking to a crowd in the open air could assume that most of his hearers believed in God and in a life to come; now this is no longer the case; the background to which he could once have appealed has vanished. Religion has lost the place it once had in the life of the nation. Lord Beveridge in his Report on "Voluntary Action" points out that no less than eight of Charles Booth's eighteen volumes of his London Survey (1886–1903) were devoted to "Religious Influences," and adds: "It is difficult to believe that any present-day survey of social conditions in Britain would give proportionate space to the Churches and their influence."[1] At one time it was thought that the Christian faith could be abandoned without any loss of the Christian moral standard. But 52,000 divorces in 1948, and the increase in crime are grim reminders of the close connection between faith and morals. The Church Assembly Report on evangelism published in 1945 under the title "Towards the Conversion of England" was a clear and valuable statement of the position, though if anything it under-estimated the difficulties in the way of an evangelism in a mental atmosphere in which religious terms and spiritual values have lost their meaning, and in an age when a mechanical and technical world is the only real world known to most of the younger generation. The chief duty of the Church is to preach Christ and His Gospel both in our own country and overseas, and to commend by its own life its supernatural and spiritual mission.

This work of evangelisation is hindered by the difficulty the Church finds in adjusting its organisation and its worship to the modern situation. The traditional parochial system was intended for pastoral work, but when the ministry was well

[1] P. 224.

staffed and the population settled it also was used for evangelisation through house-to-house visitation by the clergy. Now, when the clergy are fewer in number, the population larger and always on the move, new methods are necessary. Both men and money should be diverted from the parochial system to more direct methods of evangelism. Colleges of missioners carefully trained in preaching should be established at various centres. Picked men should be set aside for work among those who, on account of the nature of their employment, cannot be reached in the parishes. In the new universities there should be hostels for clergy whose work would be among the students, and who would be capable of meeting on intellectual terms the teaching staff. For purposes such as these the Church will require more extensive powers to enable it to make the best use of its existing resources. Already Parliament has given the Church much discretion in the union of parishes and the redistribution of their endowments; and if experience shows that still further powers are necessary, there is reason to hope that the State will be ready to confer them. The parochial system will still remain vital to the work of the Church, but it must be supplemented by special methods.

For evangelistic purposes some revision of the Church services is also required. The beauty and dignity of the Prayer Book appeal to those who have been brought up from childhood as members of the Church. But to those who are unaccustomed to its worship the arrangement of the services is confusing, and their phraseology often incomprehensible. On special occasions, when many are likely to attend church who do not usually do so, the clergy are compelled either to adapt the statutory service, or to compose some other form for use. The results of these amateur efforts are sometimes more popular than edifying; and at the best these changes in the services are, by a strict interpretation of the law, illegal, for judicial decisions have made it plain that no departure from the Prayer Book is allowed except in the very modified forms permitted by the Shorter Services Act. The Church should be given the power to revise its worship and thus bring it more into relation with modern needs, and more especially in connection with its evangelistic work.

National Witness

Only second to its duty of evangelisation is the duty of the Church to witness to the nation of social righteousness in obedience to the law of God. If the Church is to do this faithfully, it must be ready to incur unpopularity by condemning many of the opinions and customs of the world. Sometimes it has been silent when it should have spoken, blind to flagrant injustice, and deaf to the cry of the poor and destitute. It must not, however, be forgotten that laymen of the Church led the attack on slavery, and on the worst conditions of work in factory and mine. Every generation has its special social sins. The chief social sins of the first half of the last century were the honour paid to riches and the cruel callousness with which the poor were treated; later in the same century, self-complacency and luxury were the great sins. To-day we have been aroused to the evils of poverty, malnutrition, unfair conditions of work, bad housing, and to the existence of two nations—the rich and the poor—within the same community. The social sins of our time are the deterioration in sexual morality, and the widespread departure from the old standards of truthfulness and honesty. On the sinfulness of fornication, adultery, falsehood, and dishonesty, the Church is speaking plainly. It is more difficult, and often unpopular, to speak with equal boldness on the duty of hard and honest work in return for just wages, and the strict observance on both sides of agreements between the employer and the employed.

The Church must also demand that the Christian standards of truth, justice and mercy should be followed in the relationships between nations. It must, therefore, support all that makes for international peace, and rebuke the national pride and arrogance which so often lead to war. But, great as are the blessings of peace, the Church must always remind the nation that righteousness is even greater. Peace secured at the cost of injustice is built on shifting sands. The Church knows and must declare to the nation the cause of so much of the misery and unhappiness in the world, and of the repeated failures of the noblest plans for the regeneration of mankind. There has been no scarcity of plans for the promotion of international peace during the last fifty years. If one quarter of them had succeeded, the world would be a far happier and more peaceful place than it is to-day. Their failure has created a widespread sense of frustration and bitter disappointment. The Church knows that sin is the root cause of these failures and that as long as man disobeys God disappointment and disillusionment will ever dog his steps. It is the duty of the Church to call the nations as well as individuals to repentance for their sins.

But the Church will fail in its witness to national and international righteousness unless in its own life it shows the holiness of God. If it is worldly, using temporal weapons to further ecclesiastical interests, its appeal for national righteousness will fall on deaf ears, or will be met with the retort "Physician, heal thyself." Its claim to rebuke the nation will be challenged unless the Church stands sufficiently apart from the world to judge it. It can only do so if in its own life there are clearly recognisable marks of its spiritual origin and authority. By its holiness it must show that it is indeed the Body of Christ, the visible society which its Lord is using. In organisation and administration it must be free from all taint of injustice and unfairness. We can most thankfully claim that the Church for centuries has shown the authentic marks of holiness through the lives of a multitude whom no man can number. It has the heritage of the saints of all ages, and since the last name was entered upon its Calendar there has never been a generation of Churchmen which has not had its saints, both known and unknown. The succession of saintship has continued unbroken, and for those who have eyes to see there are still among us saints of God showing forth His holiness and love. But this holiness is not so unmistakably seen in the actual organisation of the Church. Holiness means separation—to be in the world and yet not of the world. The critic who gladly recognises the holiness of individual members of the Church, questions if this quality can also be seen in its external organisation, for the Church seems to be so closely associated with the world that it is hard to distinguish the two. The Churchman may reply that within the earthen vessel there is a heavenly treasure, but the opaqueness of the vessel conceals from the outsider the value of what it contains. To many the Church seems to lack that spiritual distinctiveness from the world which should be found in the body of Christ. The supernatural character is not shining through it as clearly as it does through many of its members; and the enquirer, hesitating on the threshold of the Church, wonders if it is indeed the supernatural Body of Christ.

In all organisation and administration there must be something of the world, the wheat and the tares cannot be separated in this life. But its over-close association with the State tends to conceal the spiritual authority of the Church, and the spiritual freedom which is inherent to its life.

The Defence of Freedom

The Church at the present time should be in the forefront of the battle for human freedom, for it teaches that all men are of value in the sight of God, and that it is His Will that they should have freedom to live as His sons and daughters, and to make the best use of the gifts and opportunities life offers them. On the Continent in recent years both the Roman Catholic and Protestant Churches have resisted, even unto death, the attacks made by the totalitarian State on freedom. For on a gigantic and unprecedented scale an assault is now being made on man's freedom. The dark shadow of an aggressive communism has already blotted it out in many parts of Europe and Asia. Against this deadly menace the Church must stand firm in defence of the rights of man, and must be in the vanguard of the fight for freedom. The struggle for freedom is for the possession of the human soul. Without freedom man has no responsibility, and becomes a mere instrument in the hands of industry or of the State. Christianity knows both the source and the true justification of freedom; it is God's gift to man so that he may do His Will. Any attack on freedom, whether it comes from the capitalist or the communist State, is an attack on the Christian doctrine of man.

There is little danger in our own country of a deliberate and open attack on personal freedom such as is taking place elsewhere. Here the attack will be less conspicuous and more subtle; the State by multiplication of controls and over-centralisation may destroy initiative and responsibility; and by using the press, the wireless and the cinema set standards of thought and conduct which discourage individuality. By bringing all education under Whitehall the predominant party in the State will have the power to mould the minds of the children into the pattern most serviceable to its interests. The Church must always be on the watch against insidious, as well as open, attacks on freedom, though it must accept the fact that some planning and controls are necessary if economic selfishness is not to be rampant.

If, however, the Church is to bear effectively its witness for freedom, it must itself be secure from the danger of undue State interference. It has for practical purposes great freedom; the State does not interfere with its day-to-day work; but the legal position is such that the State could progressively deprive the Church of liberty; it could appoint to bishoprics, deaneries and several hundreds of parishes only those who supported the party in power; it could refuse to allow the Church either to make changes in its Prayer Book, or new canons to improve its discipline; it could veto all Bills and Measures for ecclesiastical reform. It may be said that all this is extremely unlikely; but much that a few years ago seemed most improbable has happened both on the Continent and here. It is folly to refuse to recognise the dangerous possibilities of the present position, and it is wrong for the Church to allow year after year to pass without attempting to obtain greater protection for the freedom which is vital to its witness.

Re-Union

It is very doubtful if the Free Churches would ever enter into union with the Church of England while its present relationship with the State remains unaltered. Large numbers of Nonconformists are opposed on principle to an Established Church. A statement of this point of view was made by Mr. Bernard Lord Manning in his evidence before the Church and State Commission—"any control of the 'gathered Church' by any person or body outside is an infringement of the 'Crown Rights' of the Head of the Church. . . . The Church, and the Church alone, through its own councils (which it regulates for itself) is the arbiter of forms of worship, the interpreter of doctrinal statements and standards, the guardian of the Faith once delivered to the saints, the ground and pillar of truth." Establishment by itself need not be a barrier between ourselves and the Free Churches; their relationship with the Established Presbyterian Church of Scotland is very close; but it is difficult to believe that the Church of England and the Free Churches could enter into anything like organic union, unless and until the Church of England has obtained a far larger measure of freedom from State control than it possesses at present.

The Central Argument

But the fundamental and decisive argument for a change in the relationship between Church and State is scriptural and spiritual. There are differences of opinion over the nature of the ministry in the first century of Church history; but there is agreement on the main outlines of the picture given of the Church in the New Testament and other apostolic writings. We see a self-governing fellowship of men and women who have been baptized and who are regular at "the breaking of the bread" on the first day of the week; they are united in the faith that Jesus Who was crucified and rose again from the dead was the long-promised Christ, and was now their Living Lord and Saviour. It was a visible society with its apostles, presbyters, deacons, prophets, evangelists, each with their special function, but all united in the one Body by the same Spirit. We see the apostolic Church under the direction of the one Spirit choosing its ministers, and regulating its own discipline. We see its members witnessing freely to the presence of the Spirit by changed lives. To those who belonged to it, the Church was the temple of the Lord, the body of Christ, the home of the manifold wisdom of God, the household of faith. Its members were united in love, speaking truth in love, growing "up in all things unto him which is the head even Christ; from whom all the body fitly framed and knit together through that which every joint supplieth, according to the due measure of each several part, maketh the increase of the body unto the building up of itself in love." We are given a vision of a fellowship governed and controlled by the Christ Who both dwells within it and is its Head, and which is able to respond freely to His Holy Spirit as He leads it into all truth; it is this vision of a living spiritual society free from all external constraint which is so difficult to reconcile with a Church whose chief pastors are nominated by a Prime Minister who need not belong to it; whose corporate worship cannot be enriched or changed without the approval of an assembly whose members need not be Christian; whose rules for the better government of its affairs cannot be made without the licence of the Crown; and whose doctrine and worship are interpreted in cases of dispute by a State Court. When every citizen was a Churchman, or even when most of them were Churchmen, when the Parliament and the judges were lay members of the Church, then it was possible to defend this position. But under the totally changed conditions of our time, it is impossible to justify by any appeal to the Scriptures the arrangement by which a Christian society can be to such a large extent controlled and governed by those who do not belong to it, who may be uninterested and ignorant of its worship and teaching, and who may even be bitterly hostile to it.

It is for these reasons that the Church should ask the State to agree to some alteration from the present position. It should not ask for disestablishment; most church people do not want it; if it comes it should be on the initiative of the State; disestablishment at this time would be generally interpreted as the national repudiation of Christianity and its effects would be felt far beyond the borders of the Church; disendowment would cripple and hinder the Church in its spiritual work for the nation, for it would reduce drastically financial resources already far too small for its work. Only in the last resort, if the State refused all reform and actively interfered with the Church, would the Church be right in asking for disestablishment. This may prove to be unavoidable, but until this is clear we must appeal to the State to give the Church the larger measure of freedom required for its spiritual work.

I have been an ordained minister of the Church of England for fifty years, and for thirty of them I have been one of its diocesan bishops. I know, therefore, from within both the weakness and strength of the Church. It has often failed to use the great opportunities given to it, and lukewarmness, indecision, and lack of vision have frequently hindered its work. But I also know that it has brought to millions the knowledge of the love of God and the hope and comfort that come from the preaching of the Gospel; that in thousands of parishes for many centuries there have been multitudes of men and women loyal and faithful members of the Church, the shining lights and lamps of their several generations, living in close communion with their Master, and by their teaching and example helping to form the character and ideals of the English people. It was the Church which gave help to the destitute, food to the hungry, and comfort to the despairing when the State was indifferent to their cry. To-day, in town and village alike, without break or intermission, the work of the Church continues, keeping the light of faith burning where otherwise there might be darkness. No longer is the Church of England an island Church, but the mother of a world-wide communion which has spread to the farthest parts of the earth, and whose vigour and strength were revealed in the recent Lambeth Conference. Most thankfully I see what great things God has done through our Church in the past and is doing in the present, but I am profoundly convinced that He is calling it to sterner ordeals and to greater service in the years to come. If it is to respond unreservedly to the call of its Master, it must have greater freedom than it has at present, so that without external restraint or hindrance it may be able to obey His guidance in making more perfect its faith, worship, discipline and evangelism.

INDEX

INDEX

INDEX